A VOICE OF HIS TIME

Also by Jerry Shinn

A Great, Public Compassion:
The Story of Charlotte Memorial Hospital and Carolinas Medical Center

Loonis! Celebrating a Lyrical Life

Dixie Autumn

— • —

with Hunter Gorley
Servant Leader: The Life of William F. Mulliss

A VOICE OF HIS TIME

A BIOGRAPHY OF
CHARLES HARVEY CRUTCHFIELD

Jerry Shinn

LORIMER PRESS

WITH SUPPORT FROM THE LYNNWOOD FOUNDATION

DAVIDSON, NC 2016

Published by Lorimer Press, with support from
The Lynnwood Foundation

Printed in China

ISBN 978-0-9961884-2-5
Library of Congress Control Number: 2016957959

ADDITIONAL ACKNOWLEDGMENTS & PERMISSIONS:
Photos are courtesy of the Crutchfield family archives with these exceptions: Pages 42, 59: Briarhoppers photos, courtesy of Jim Scancarelli and btmemories.com; Page 191: Doug Mayes and page 213: Alan Newcomb, courtesy of Reno Bailey and btmemories.com. Author photo on jacket by Donna Dicks.

For Jack Claiborne

A Personal Introduction

SOME OF MY MOST pleasant childhood memories center on that magical box called a radio. At that time, the 1940s, we considered the very idea of television as something out of science fiction, although most of us would have a set within a decade. Radio itself was still an infant medium, but its pioneers had developed programs to arouse a youthful imagination. We transformed the voices, the music, and the sound effects into moving pictures in our minds. In the afternoons after school I listened to 30-minute adventure shows: *The Sea Hound*, with Captain Silver and Jerry; *Don Winslow of the Navy*; *The Lone Ranger*; and others. At night, after homework, there were mystery shows: *Casey, Crime Photographer*; *Inner Sanctum*; *Sam Spade*; *Mr. Keen, Tracer of Lost Persons* (the theme song of which, I learned years later, was a former popular tune called "Someday I'll Find You").

It was during those same childhood years that I first heard the gutted-muffler voice of Charles Crutchfield, and that voice is forever linked to two very different bits of music. One is the *William Tell Overture*. With its galloping rhythms and soaring, dramatic release, it was the perfect theme music for *The Lone Ranger* radio show. (A significant benefit of early radio dramas – and of early movies, too – was that some of them used existing serious, or classical, compositions as theme and background music. This exposed thousands of Americans who would never buy symphony tickets or classical recordings to important fragments of Western culture.) The Rossini music and Crutchfield's voice are part of the same boyhood memory because I was a regular listener to *The Lone Ranger*, which aired in the late afternoons on WBT radio adjacent to a live, local music program featuring a band called the Briarhoppers. That now legendary program was created by Crutchfield and featured a country music band assembled by Crutchfield, with Crutchfield as the announcer. He began the show with the rhetorical question, "Do y'all know what time it is?" One or more members of the band responded, "Hit's Briarhopper Time!" That triggered the Briarhoppers' theme song, a high-energy rendition of "Wait 'til the Sun Shines, Nellie," and the show was off and running.

I was never truly a Briarhoppers fan, but for some period of time in the 1940s I heard them often, because I wanted to make sure I had the radio tuned to the right station, and with my ears nearby, when *The Lone Ranger* came on. I also enjoyed hearing Crutchfield poke fun at his sponsor's products – mostly high-proof cure-all tonics and hair dye. Thus the unlikely musical pairing of the *William Tell* Overture and the Briarhoppers' rendition of "Wait 'til the Sun Shines, Nellie" are connected in my mind, part of the same aural memory as the voice of Charles Crutchfield.

A few years later, as a young adult living and working in Charlotte, I realized that the Charles Crutchfield who headed Jefferson-Pilot Broadcasting, which included radio station WBT and television station WBTV, was the same man I used to hear announcing the Briarhoppers. He still had a very public image, but of a very different type. He was no longer the comical radio announcer exchanging gags with a gang of hillbilly musicians and pitching patent medicines with irreverent ad lib commercials. He was now an executive of a major corporate enterprise, a nationally prominent pioneer and leader in the broadcasting industry, active in local and state civic affairs – and a man known for his outspoken political views, which were well to the right of my own.

I never got to know him well personally, but whatever negative impressions I had regarding his political opinions were more than offset by the opinions of two of my good friends who worked with him. One was Larry Harding, who handled public relations for WBT and WBTV and wrote many of the editorials aired on those stations. Larry started out as a newspaper sports writer, as I did, and he and I served together in the Army Reserves. We sometimes argued, over long lunches, about the content of his editorials, but I had great respect for him, and he often expressed his admiration and affection for his boss, Charles Crutchfield.

The other friend was Loonis McGlohon, the musician and composer whose day job involved radio and television production and community relations for WBT and WBTV. Loonis was one of the greatest people I have ever known, and he thought Charles Crutchfield was one of the greatest people he had ever known, which for me was a more than sufficient endorsement. I would have loved to interview Larry and Loonis for this book, and I would have loved for them to read it. Sadly, they are no longer here.

And so, as another announcer invited us on those long-ago radio days, over the exciting rhythms of Rossini's overture: "Return with us now to those thrilling days of yesteryear, when out of the past...."

Charles Crutchfield and Joseph Bryan

PROLOGUE

JOSEPH M. BRYAN would later become known as one of the towering philanthropists in the history of his adopted state of North Carolina. In earlier years, he was known as an intimidating figure in the Greeensboro headquarters of the Jefferson Standard Life Insurance Company. For one thing, he was the boss's son-in-law, which made his colleagues a bit wary of him. But he was no passive beneficiary of Julian Price's nepotism. Maybe that had put him on the executive ladder, but his ambition, intelligence, and persona were what propelled him up the rungs.

He was a vigorous, muscular man, an active sportsman who radiated vitality, and tall enough to look down on most of his contemporaries. His thick hair, swept back and beginning to turn silver at the temples, framed a handsome face with a strong nose and piercing eyes. Sometimes he wore a bristling mustache, which gave him the appearance of British aristocracy. He had little patience with banality and foolishness and generally held himself aloof from internal corporate politics. Admiring acquaintances variously described him as "charismatic," "regal," and "cutting a striking pose everywhere he went...."

Subordinates were known to tiptoe past his office for fear of disturbing him, and to check with others to see if he was in a good mood before approaching him about anything. A native northerner in a Southern environment of at least superficial gentility, he was sometimes perceived as gruff and rude. His Yankee Irish accent had a harsh, cutting edge among his Carolina colleagues' flattened vowels, slurred diphthongs, and dropped g's.

Corporate subordinates weren't the only people intimidated by Joe Bryan's presence and manner. Former University of North Carolina President William Friday, one of the state's most respected and revered citizens, once described him as "a great big bear of a man" who "could scare the daylights out of you."

One December day, near the mid-point of the 20th century, Bryan, head of Jefferson Standard's new broadcasting subsidiary, was sitting in his office, in a swivel chair, flanked by a few associates, and across the desk from him was Charles Crutchfield, vice president of the broadcasting subsidiary and general manager of radio station WBT in Charlotte. Crutchfield was there to present his proposed annual budget for Bryan's approval.

In backgrounds, the two men had more in common than they probably realized. More obvious at that moment were the differences. Bryan had started his career on Wall Street before marrying the daughter of a wealthy and powerful North Carolinian and moving South. Crutchfield had begun as a teenage announcer at small Southern radio stations and gone on to hawk patent medicines and hair dye as an announcer for a hillbilly band on WBT. Bryan was in his fifties; Crutchfield was in his thirties. As were most men of his generation, Crutchfield was physically less imposing than Bryan, and he was at least a bit less authoritarian. More important, he depended on Bryan for his job. But "Crutch," as many of his friends called him, was not so easily intimidated.

On this occasion, Bryan was nitpicking Crutchfield's budget, and Crutchfield was losing patience. It wasn't the first time he had suffered through this exercise. Ever since Jefferson Standard bought the Charlotte radio station in 1945, Crutchfield had made the 90-mile pilgrimage to Greensboro each December. Bryan would look at the budget figures and begin to nickel and dime Crutchfield's plans. Now he was questioning the proposed raises for WBT employees, which Crutchfield considered quite modest and hardly worth Bryan's attention. Finally, Crutchfield snapped.

He tossed his budget papers across the desk and stood up. His exact words to Bryan have never been reported in print, for fear that some readers would find them offensive. But, to use a venerable Southern euphemism, Crutch suggested that Bryan take his radio station and put it where the sun don't shine. Then he walked out of Bryan's office.

Several of the men in the meeting followed Crutchfield down the hall, urging him to go back and apologize, but he refused to turn back. He drove to Charlotte, went to his office and gathered some things out of his desk, and then went home to await word that he was fired.

Later that day, the doorbell rang and Crutchfield opened the door to find Joe Bryan standing outside. *Aha*, he thought, *Bryan drove all the way from Greensboro for the pleasure of firing me in person.* But Bryan didn't fire him. Instead he said to Crutchfield, you were right, I was wrong.

It was a turning point in the life of Charles Crutchfield. And it was a small but significant moment in the history of American broadcasting. Instead of being fired and drifting on to another job, from that day on Crutchfield was able to exercise his considerable talents and his usually bullseye instincts without worrying about micromanagement and second-guessing from corporate headquarters in Greensboro. With Bryan's support and encouragement, Crutchfield maintained and strengthened the dominant radio station in the Piedmont Carolinas, with a signal that reached the entire east coast, from Canada to Cuba; established the first television station in the Carolinas and assembled a nationally respected staff of on-air and on-camera talent; and was a catalyst for the establishment of public television in North Carolina. He became a nationally recognized visionary and leader in the telecommunications industry and an important civic leader in his community and state. He served his nation on overseas missions and was a friend and confidante of some of the most influential and powerful people in America.

When Charles Crutchfield retired in 1977, Joe Bryan wrote:

Once in a great while a man comes along with a special quality about him. You can discern it in the way he walks, the look in his eye, the way he carries himself.... It is a personal force, but more than that. It defies definition, but you will always find it in the authentic leader.

I spotted this quality in you early on.... Some people credit me for "discovering" you.... But I really deserve credit for only two things: (1) the wisdom to see the enormous potential in you and (2) the good sense to let you alone to do your thing....

...your retirement marks the passing of an era – an era in which it sometimes seemed that madness had possessed the world and that the planet was doomed...the bomb, Korea, the Kennedy and King assassinations, the Vietnam War, Watergate.... But men of sanity and capacity – men such as you – prevailed, and we have endured....

PART
1

CHOCK

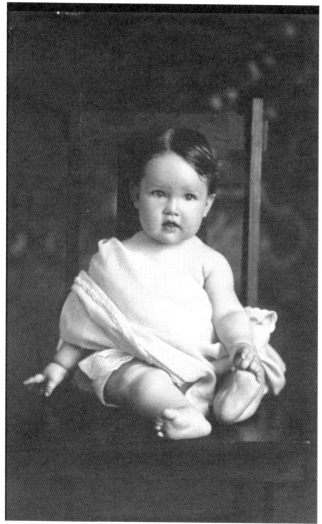

Charles Harvey Crutchfield, Jr.
circa 1913

CHAPTER ONE
The Wild West

ROOTS ARE IMPORTANT, but in this case, the significance of the roots is overwhelmed by the astonishing reach of Charles Crutchfield's particular branch on the family tree. He would grow up to take a firm grip on the controls of the two most transforming technologies of the first half of the 20th century: radio and television. It is not surprising that among his direct forefathers were people of good reputation, adventurous spirit, and respected accomplishment. There were promising genes in the bloodline. His ancestors came from England, but his American roots were on the frontier, most importantly in Texas, which was still part of the Wild West when Thomas Ferguson Crutchfield arrived there with his wife, Frances, and their six children, in 1847.

Thomas Crutchfield was of a line of pioneers who had been moving westward into new and often dangerous territories from the earliest years of the Republic. His grandfather, James Crutchfield, had been killed by tribesmen in the Tennessee wilderness in 1783. James Crutchfield's first son, John, had moved west from Virginia into Kentucky, where he married Nancy Ann West in 1796. They had three children there. The youngest was Thomas, who married an orphaned heiress, Frances Maria Lampton, in 1824. Thomas established a store in Franklin, Kentucky, where he built the first brick home in the community. Later he had a store in Louisville. Perhaps it was an inherited restlessness that prompted him to continue the family tradition of pushing on to the next frontier. Whatever the reason, in 1847 he gave up his well-established career as a Kentucky merchant and took his family, some fine horses, and several Negro slaves and moved southwest, across Arkansas into Texas, which had been part of the United States for only two years.

He obtained a land grant from the state of Texas for 640 acres along Five Mile Creek, southwest of a settlement called Dallas, founded seven years prior, but not yet incorporated. He settled his family on the property, where he raised livestock, corn, and hay and sold butter, honey, and beeswax. He also became the Dallas postmaster and held that position for many years. But it was as an innkeeper that he became prominent in the history of the community and the state. In 1852, with logs hauled on wagons from the banks of the Red River north of Dallas, he built the Crutchfield House, offering rooms and board, at a crossroads that soon would become the courthouse square. Although rustic inside and out, it quickly became known as the finest hostelry, offering the best food, in that frontier region of north Texas. Crutchfield had a reputation as a hunter, his wife was a good cook, and the inn employed a French chef who also was a good hunter and fisherman. A large bell that hung from a post in the yard was used to summon guests to meals. (A tradition that ended when the bell caught the attention of a drunken gunman, who shot it down.) The dining room's offerings of fish, quail, and wild game also attracted a good number of non-guests from across the region. One account of the bill of fare included "venison, wild fowl or catfish stuffed with cove oysters."

The dining room helped make the Crutchfield House a small outpost of civilization in an area that was still largely uncivilized. There were stockades around most of the few homes in Dallas, to protect against tribal attacks, and the inn itself was not immune to the hazards of frontier life. On one occasion in the 1850s, during a term of court, several prominent lawyers were dining there when someone burst in, shouting that Indians were coming. Some of the guests were armed, and they rushed out to do battle, killing and wounding several of the attackers before the rest retreated. It was reported to have been the last fight between Native Americans and settlers in or around Dallas.

Through much of the second half of the 19th century, the Crutchfield House served as a center of social and civic life in the growing Dallas community and the surrounding region. Among its guests were prominent political, military, and business leaders, including Sam Houston, Confederate Gen. Jubal Early, and the railroad entrepreneurs whose visions would connect Dallas, and Thomas Crutchfield's descendents, east into Arkansas.

By 1860 there were some fifteen commercial buildings in the town, and all of them, including the Crutchfield House, were burned to the ground that year. A group of vigilantes believed the fire was set by Thomas Crutchfield's slaves, and they demanded that he turn them over to their accusers to be beaten. Crutchfield refused. He promptly made plans to rebuild his hotel, this time with two stories, using brick as well as wood. But both brick and wood had to come from Houston by ox cart, which took six months. That inability to transport goods, either bought or sold, was a serious commercial handicap for Dallas and a major impetus for establishing rail connections there.

Texas seceded from the Union and joined the Confederate States of America in 1861. The rebuilt Crutchfield House continued to thrive through the Civil War, and in 1870 Texas was readmitted to the Union. By the mid-1870s Dallas business and political leaders had successfully promoted rail connections to the South, followed soon by an east-west line. The intersection of rail lines to the four points of the compass probably assured the future of Dallas as a major city.

Meanwhile, in 1871, the *Dallas Herald* reported that Thomas F. Crutchfield, age 68, "full of years and full of honors," had died "after a protracted and painful illness" on February 13. "He was one among the very first permanent residents here," said the newspaper, "and by his exemplary and consistent Christian course during his long residence among us won the cordial esteem and respect of every citizen."

After Crutchfield's death the reputation of the hotel gradually faded, but it continued in operation until 1888, when it once again was destroyed by fire. Later the first Masonic Temple in Dallas was built on that corner of the old courthouse square. After it was torn down, the property and immediate surroundings were developed in 1940 as a city park and christened Dealey Plaza – a place now eternally famous, or infamous, as the site of the November 22, 1963, assassination of President John F. Kennedy.

The first of six children of Thomas and Frances Crutchfield, James Oscar M. Crutchfield, was born in Franklin County, Kentucky, in 1830, and in his late teens he preceded his parents to Dallas. He obtained a grant for 329 acres in Dallas County, which he farmed. In 1851 he married Frances Patience Floyd, known as Fannie, also a native of Kentucky.

When Texas seceded from the Union, James Crutchfield enlisted in the Confederate Army in Dallas and served in the 38th Cavalry Regiment, later known as the 2nd Regiment Partisan Rangers and then as Chisholm's, or Chisum's, Cavalry Regiment. After the war he was known as Major James Crutchfield, although there were questions about whether he actually achieved that rank during his service.

Returning to civilian life, he moved with his family to Blossom, Texas, also known as Blossom Prairie, a small settlement northeast of Dallas. There he established a general store and, in the back of the same building, the community's first bank. One of his sons later recalled that James Crutchfield had a picture of one of his grandchildren, Mabel Crutchfield, printed on the checks the bank provided to its depositors.

James and Fannie had five children. The fourth was John Randolph Crutchfield, born in Dallas in 1860.

With the new rail connections, east Texas cotton growers could get their crop more quickly and more efficiently to more markets, and the boom in cotton production created new, non-farming opportunities in the economy of northeast Texas and across the American South: gins, cottonseed oil extraction, brokers, and, by the turn of the century, cotton spinning and weaving mills.

In September 1881 John Randolph Crutchfield married Mary Etta Page of Dallas. Thirteen months later their first child, Charles Harvey Crutchfield, was born in Dallas. Soon after, the family moved to Blossom, where John and Mary Etta had four more children. Later they moved farther east to New Boston, near the Arkansas line. John Randolph Crutchfield was a cotton broker

John Randolph Crutchfield

with a reputation as one of the best graders in the area. One newspaper declared that "his verdict on cotton is considered final."

Charles Harvey Crutchfield, known by his middle name, followed his father into the cotton business. In 1903 he married Frances Lowrance, known as Fannie, the daughter of George Boggs Lowrance and Katherine Gale Lowrance of Lamar County, Texas. The following year Fannie gave birth to their first child, Alice, and in 1907, a son,

Frances Lowrance Crutchfield ("Fannie")

Ralph, was born. After Harvey and his family moved across the state line to Hope, Arkansas, they had two more children: Marietta, or "Mame," in 1910, and the youngest, Charles Harvey Crutchfield, Jr., or "Chock," born on July 27, 1912.

Many years later, in the 1930s, almost a century after his great-great grandfather opened the Crutchfield House on the Texas frontier, Charles Harvey Crutchfield, Jr. became an organizer, promoter, and radio announcer for a number of "country" musicians in the Carolinas. Those talented and hugely popular pickers and singers were mostly from cotton mill towns across the Piedmont, but many of them dressed in the Hollywood version of cowboy attire for their public appearances. The western image was part of their appeal, but their boots rarely if ever touched a stirrup, and their ten-gallon hats were never powdered with prairie dust. They probably had no idea that their announcer, Charlie, was a direct descendent of real wild west pioneers who fought off Indian attacks and established successful businesses in the same Texas territory where the legendary outlaw Sam Bass and his gang were robbing stagecoaches and trains.

The Crutchfields circa 1911, clockwise, Fannie, Alice, Harvey, and Ralph

Chapter Two
Hope

By THE TIME CHARLES HARVEY CRUTCHFIELD, JR., was born, his father Harvey was doing very well in the cotton business. He had established a cotton exchange in Hope, Arkansas and, according to a newspaper account of the time, he employed "a number of experienced buyers." John Randolph Crutchfield, whose reputation as an expert cotton grader has already been noted, moved to Hope and joined his son's business.

Hope was a railroad town. Organizers of the Cairo and Fulton Railroad wanted a station in that vicinity, so they established the settlement in 1852. The town was incorporated in 1875 and became the county seat of Hempstead County and a shipping center not only for cotton, but also for other agricultural products and for timber. Later, Hope would be known for growing some of the world's largest watermelons, and as the birthplace of William Jefferson Clinton, the 42nd president of the United States. But the railroad was the original reason for its existence, and without it, Hope would not have attracted Harvey Crutchfield as a good place to establish his cotton exchange and raise, with Fannie, his young family.

It was a good time to be in the cotton business, whether growing, buying, and selling, or manufacturing. In the first decade of the century, wider use of fertilizers and improved seeds developed by experimental farmers had improved quality and yields. By late June of 1914, the price of cotton was a healthy 13 cents per pound (equal to about $2 in 2000) and a record crop was already lying like summer snow across Southern fields. That month, with both production and prices rising, Harvey Crutchfield sailed for Europe. There he spent almost two months visiting potential European markets and wining and dining new business connections in the British Isles, Belgium, France, Italy, Switzerland, and Germany.

It was a particularly interesting and historic time to be touring the continent. Within a day or two of Crutchfield's departure from New York on the SS *Celtic* in late June, a young Bosnian Serb revolutionary shot and killed Archduke Franz Ferdinand, heir to the Austro-Hungarian throne. When the SS *Celtic* landed at Queenstown, Ireland, on July 2, the assassination already had triggered a series of responses in Great Britain and across Europe that eventually led to the First World War. Austria-Hungary declared war against Serbia on July 28, and by the time Crutchfield headed back to the United States in mid-August, virtually all of Europe was at war, including Great Britain. Less than five months after she deposited Crutchfield on the southern coast of Ireland, the SS *Celtic* was withdrawn from civilian duty by the British government and transformed into an armed merchant cruiser, and then, in 1916, to a troopship.

Apparently the continent's mobilization for what would be a long, bloody, and eventually world-wide war did not interfere with Crutchfield's itinerary or his successful pursuit of new business. In a letter to his mother, written on the day of his arrival in Ireland, he reported that already, during the crossing, he had met "people on board that are going to be beneficial to us a business way…." He also expressed a touch of homesickness and closed the note by asking his mother, then living in Hope, to "keep care of my bunch."

In another letter to his mother in mid-July, from Brussels, he noted that it was 8 a.m. there and wrote, apparently referring to his wife in a sort of stream-of-consciousness shorthand: "Dreamed Fan was dead last night saw her in coffin as plain as I ever saw her anywhere in my life that she was in a runaway – little white pony to buggy." He added that he hadn't heard from Fan in two weeks and was afraid his dream meant that "something has gone bad at home." He said he planned to call home that day.

But the same letter offered his mother this glimpse of his life on the road in Europe and expressed optimism about the success of the trip: "…we pulled off another big dinner at the hotel last night with some of our friends here, then to the theater and did not break up until 1:30 last night. Am being some big dog here [and] it is costing lots of money but hope to make it a good investment in the end. We have been very successful in securing the business of everyone we have called on in that capacity and I will be disappointed if we do not have a very fine business the coming season…."

He added that he'd "had all the sight seeing I want. It soon becomes tiresome. Had rather be in Hope than any place I know." Again, he closed by asking her to "try and keep up with my bunch."

Crutchfield's optimism about his trip producing a lot of new business was quickly overturned by events beyond his control. As war spread across Europe that autumn of 1914, export markets for cotton shut down. Cotton prices fell to barely half the level that they had been just three months earlier. Many cotton exchanges across the South closed temporarily as farmers and brokers looked for places to store the cotton they could not sell. Congress quickly passed a Cotton Warehouse Act to provide more storage space.

The cotton crisis lasted more than two years, but it ended decisively when the United States entered the war against Germany in the early spring of 1917. The effect of wartime mobilization on demand sent prices soaring. Farmers started planting, warehouses were emptied, exchanges reopened to booming business, and everyone involved with cotton was enjoying a new and unprecedented prosperity.

Some years later, in an interview, one of Harvey Crutchfield's nieces remembered her uncle, probably circa 1920, as "a very wealthy man involved in cotton" and recalled that he "owned cotton mills in

South Carolina." Little else is known about Crutchfield's investments in the textile industry, but by the mid-1920s, South Carolina was producing more cotton goods than any other state in the nation.

Chock, circa 1920

While Harvey traveled across Europe, then struggled through the collapse of cotton markets and rebuilt his business and his fortune, Charles Harvey Crutchfield, Jr., known in his family as "Chock," spent his childhood and early school years in Hope. If you were a child growing up in a railroad town in the age of steam, you knew the sound of trains in the night, beginning as distant thunder, growing nearer and louder, and then the clackety-clack of wheels on rails, an iron drumbeat beneath the chug of the engine, and the wail of the whistle. You could lie in bed and imagine the sparks and smoke rushing through the darkness, coming out of the night from places you had never been, and back into the night and on to places you might go yourself someday. In the small towns of rural America in the first quarter of the 20th century, a long, long way from anywhere, even for a child whose father had traveled abroad, the railroad was a reminder of the larger world out there, a connection to places that mattered.

There were no radios bringing music, drama, and news into homes, and no phonographs or phonograph records. Children were largely dependent on their own abilities, their own imaginations, and their interaction with friends and families, for recreation and entertainment – which might not have been such a bad thing. Young Charles was a sandy-haired lad with freckles and a mischievous sense of humor. Childhood friends later remembered that in first or second grade he caught crayfish from a stream and brought them in a matchbox to school, where he would put them in strategic locations for his classmates to discover. Along with such antics, he must have developed a strong sense of independence, because he later declined to follow in anyone's footsteps. He would build his own career, not in the production of cotton crops or threads or fabrics, but in the production of sounds. For the first eight years, the primary soundtrack of his life was the rumble and whine of trains coming and going. The sounds on which he would build his career were not the sounds of trains, but they, too, would stretch across the land and connect people to distant places and inspire daydreams and bedtime fantasies. During those childhood years in Hope he could not even imagine that career. There were no radios in homes, and there were no commercial radio stations. But that would change by the time he was in his teens.

The first transmission of a human voice by radio signal was achieved at the turn of the century, but it would be two decades before someone would seize on the potential of that technology for commercial entertainment and information. That was in 1920, when a man in Pittsburgh used his radio transmitter to broadcast music played on phonograph records, which could be heard by people with nearby crystal sets. Within months, the first commercial radio stations in America went on the air, in Pittsburgh and Detroit.

(In Charlotte, North Carolina, that same year, F.M. Laxton and some friends set up an amateur radio station, WXD. Two years later WXD became the first commercial broadcasting station in the Carolinas licensed by the U.S. Department of Commerce, with the call letters WBT.)

In 1920, as the first commercial radio stations began beaming their signals in the north and Midwest, Harvey Crutchfield moved his family from Hope to Spartanburg, South Carolina. The previous eight years in Hope were almost certainly good years for Charles Harvey, Jr., and his siblings, growing up in a pleasant small town, with grandparents and an aunt and uncle and cousins for neighbors, part of a loving family supported by a successful, perhaps even wealthy, father.

It was an almost idyllic situation for a young American family in the early years of the century.

Moving to South Carolina, eight-year-old Chock had no reason to fear, and no way to know, that it was all about to change, and mostly not for the better.

Chapter Three
Spartanburg

WARTIME DEMAND BOOSTED production and profits in textile manufacturing, and the Carolinas were major beneficiaries of that trend, with existing mills thriving and new mills being established across the Piedmont. As the war ended and a new decade began, Harvey Crutchfield had recovered from the temporary collapse of the cotton market, achieved a measure of wealth as a cotton broker, and reportedly was investing in textile manufacturing in South Carolina. He bought a house in Spartanburg, at 146 Alabama Street, in a solidly middle-class neighborhood on the fringe of a busy and growing central business district, and in 1920 he brought Fannie and the children to live there. Give or take a year, Alice was 16, Ralph was 13, and Mame was ten. Chock was eight years old and headed into the third grade.

Spartanburg must have been an exciting new place for youngsters who had spent all their lives in rural Arkansas. With a population of about 30,000, it was several times larger than Hope. Its main street was part of a road that in the mid-1920s would be designated U.S. 29. It was a major north-south highway that formed the spine of the growing Piedmont textile belt of the Carolinas, and before the construction of interstate highways, was known as the "Main Street of the South."

Alongside Spartanburg's Main Street, a main line of the Southern Railway ran straight through the city, intersecting Magnolia Street and the Charleston and Western Carolina tracks at bustling Union Station. In addition to frequent trains, there were trolleys, horses, wagons, and a few automobiles crowding the streets. New shops and stores were opening their doors along the downtown streets as Spartanburg began to establish itself as a retailing center for the region, drawing shoppers from the mill towns stretching from the North Carolina line west toward Greenville.

Spartanburg was also enriched by the presence of two small but excellent liberal arts colleges: Converse, for women, and Wofford, for men.

Reflecting his financial success, and perhaps the status to which he aspired for his family in their new home city, Harvey eschewed the public schools for his oldest son and enrolled Ralph in the Hastoc School. Although it was housed near the center of the city in a modest building of no architectural or structural distinction, its students represented some of Spartanburg's most affluent and socially prominent families. The Hastoc School had been established in 1907 as a day school for boys of high school age by Hugh Thomas Shockley, son of a wealthy Spartanburg businessman. Professor Shockley, a former public high school principal with undergraduate and graduate degrees from Wofford College, emphasized character and "manliness" as well as high academic standards. By the time the Crutchfields moved to Spartanburg, the school had about 80 day students plus 20 boarding students in its dormitory, and it was highly regarded for its small classes, high teacher-student ratio, and academic excellence.

Ralph Crutchfield was a gifted student, and he apparently thrived at the Hastoc School. He began an accelerated academic schedule that carried him to a college degree when he was only 19 years old – an achievement that turned out to be very significant for his family.

The year Chock and his family moved to Spartanburg, the 18th Amendment to the U.S. Constitution went into effect, banning the manufacture, sale, and transport of alcoholic beverages. That was, ironically, the year when many Americans in the most visible parts of the nation, the urban northern states along the Atlantic seaboard, began drinking and dancing their way into what would become known as the Roaring 20s. That description never applied to Spartanburg, which sat firmly in the Carolinas' Bible Belt. In a referendum four years before national prohibition, South Carolinians had voted by a two-to-one margin to make beverage alcohol illegal throughout the state. A number of stills popped up in wooded areas of Spartanburg County to meet the demand for which there were no longer legal producers and distributors.

For those truly desperate for the effects of alcohol, bay rum, sold in drugstores as a fragrant after-shave lotion and tonic for external use only, became a potentially toxic substitute. Other drugstore substitutes for beverage alcohol during prohibition, and for sworn teetotalers, were patent medicines. Advertised as cures for almost every imaginable ailment – including some invented by the advertisers – many consisted of water, flavoring, and alcohol, often at levels exceeding wine or beer. One popular brand, originally created and manufactured by an otherwise respectable physician in Columbus, Ohio, was Peruna. It would later become a significant factor in the career of Charles Crutchfield.

Spartanburg was a socially conservative city, however, and if there was anything roaring there in the 1920s, it was the sound of trains and traffic – and the rhythm of carding machines and spindles and mechanized looms in the cotton mills. In the Piedmont Carolinas in 1920, that was the sound of money. By the end of the decade, Spartanburg would boast 35 mills and was first in the South in the number of looms and second in the number of spindles.

But the sound that caught the attention of Charles Crutchfield, Jr., was even newer. It was radio. In 1918 a young electrical engineer in New York City, Edwin Howard Armstrong, invented the super heterodyne receiver, which could recover specific information from radio waves on a particular frequency. He patented the device and sold it to

Westinghouse, which cross-licensed it to Radio Corporation of America (RCA), and it became a significant factor in the spread of commercial radio in the 1920s. (Armstrong later invented frequency modulation radio, known as FM.) Chock's family obtained a battery-operated super heterodyne radio in 1925, making theirs one of only a few South Carolina homes with radios. Chock could manipulate its three dials and pick up two of the pioneer commercial stations in the country, KDKA in faraway Pittsburgh and WBT in Charlotte, just 70 miles to the northeast. Through the goose-necked speaker came the sounds of popular dance bands, including those led by Hal Kemp, John Scott Trotter, and Johnny Long – music that surely stirred the romantic imagination of a creative 13-year-old boy. It must have seemed magical, and it was the beginning of a lifelong and lucrative love affair with radio. The following year he obtained a kit and built a crystal set.

Meanwhile, there were troubles in the Crutchfield home, and troubles on Main Street, along the Piedmont textile belt and, indeed, around the world. Not long after the move to Spartanburg, there were signs of estrangement between Harvey and Fannie Crutchfield. After moving his family, Harvey went back to Hope. Along with many others in the cotton business, he probably was suffering financially by the mid-1920s. The rapid expansion of textile manufacturing led to overextension of credits, overproduction, and shrinking profits. Mills that had run around the clock cut back to three days a week, shrinking payrolls and dumping workers into poverty. Small-town banks began shutting down. In 1926, the lieutenant governor of South Carolina declared that "almost overnight, our people were reduced from a riotous spree of making and spending to the stern reality of poverty staring them in the face." The state's economy was on the brink of depression at least three years before the stock market crash of October 29, 1929, which defined the beginning of a national and world-wide Great Depression and triggered even deeper distress across the South.

At that time, divorce was forbidden by the South Carolina Constitution, but in Arkansas, Harvey Crutchfield filed for divorce in February of 1926. The divorce was granted the following month, and five days later he married a woman named Gorda. It was not likely a whirlwind courtship. Fannie, a devout Methodist who made sure her children attended Sunday School and worship services every week, was outraged. In a letter to a lawyer in Hope three years after the divorce, she expressed "shock and grief" and called Harvey a "wicked man," who had been "living in violation of all moral laws." She asked the lawyer to help force Harvey to provide more support for the family he had left behind in Spartanburg.

Gorda's maiden name, if known, apparently was never spoken or otherwise acknowledged by Fannie or her children, and in the 1930 Spartanburg City Directory, Fannie was listed as "widow of Charles H. Crutchfield," although Harvey did not die until 1940.

Shortly after his divorce and remarriage, Harvey received what must have been an angry letter from his older son, Ralph. In his reply, Harvey wrote: "Please do not let your feelings remain toward me – don't be ever thus. I know the fire of youth, regrets of age.... I love you Ralph and shall forever, your letters cannot ever drive me to anger towards you. Am sending you a check for $75 – $50 for you and $25 for Mamie. I will in some way educate Mamie and Chock and do all I can for Alice, and would like to be of help to you if you think you would want me to.... Your devoted dad, CHC."

There's no available evidence regarding the amount of financial support Harvey Crutchfield provided for his family following the divorce. In an interview many years later, his youngest son recalled that "in the divorce settlement my father took fairly good care of the family."

Whatever the case, money was surely tight in the household on Alabama Street through the late 1920s. Ralph's early graduation from Wofford, in 1926, put him in position to help support the family. By 1928, Alice was teaching school and Ralph was working in sales for the Montgomery and Crawford Hardware Company. They were still living at home, and their jobs contributed to the household income. Chock also contributed by working part-time at Ligon's Drug Store on Main Street, selling seed and fertilizer. One year he got a summer job on a construction crew, wielding a bush ax through the hot, humid days. "I thought it was terribly hard on me," he said many years later, "but I made good money and I got myself in great condition to play football the next fall in high school."

In her letter to the lawyer in Hope, Fannie said Harvey's "persistent refusal to support his children is ruining my younger boy.... To see this boy's happiness ruined, to see him grow more bitter...every day, makes me want to do something, anything...."

Certainly his father's actions and his mother's distress – and perhaps also the financial consequences of the divorce and the times – were traumatic for Chock. He was in his early teens, which, under the best of circumstances, can be a time of awkward and confusing transition from boyhood to manhood. Although they exchanged correspondence in later years, Chock apparently never fully forgave his father for abandoning the family. Once a father himself, he never talked with his children about their grandfather Crutchfield, with one exception. He shared a brief memory of a day when Harvey had taken him along on a wagon to a general store to make a few purchases and had brought a picnic lunch, which they ate in the wagon. That wagon ride and picnic obviously made a powerful impression on the boy – perhaps because it was one of so few good times he shared with his father.

Fannie may have overstated the case a bit when she said her younger son's happiness had been ruined and described him as increasingly bitter. Chock entered Spartanburg High School the year of the divorce, and whatever his feelings about what was happening in his family, they seemed to have little effect on his status at school. By his own account he was not a very diligent student, but his good looks, personality, and energy made him one of the more popular members of the student body. He had been a "pudgy" child, but by then all the baby fat was gone, and he was growing toward a height of about five feet and nine inches, a bit above average for young men of his generation. He learned to box at the YMCA. The only traces of the sandy hair of his childhood were a few reddish streaks in the very dark, thick waves that, in a popular look of the time, he combed straight back from a center part and kept glossily in place with hairdressing. He was known among fellow students for his wit, his quick smile, his blue eyes, and his sense of style. Despite a dearth of money at home, he managed to dress well, sometimes even wearing spats to school.

He was one of the advertising managers for the school yearbook, *The Scribbler*. He played guard on the football team, which had a very successful season, winning seven of its nine games and losing only to the Clemson College "reserves" and Spartanburg's arch-rival from 20 miles east, Gaffney High School. He was not a starter, but according to one student writer's account, he "was called upon time and again to fill some gap in the old line, which he did notably."

In *The Scribbler* of 1929, among the "Senior Class Statistics," he was chosen as "Biggest Sheik," an apparent reference to the silent film of a few years earlier, *The Sheik*, starring the quintessential "Latin lover," Rudolph Valentino. As such, he was paired in a photograph with the "Biggest Flapper," Emilie Martin. He wore a white shirt, a tie, and a vested suit, with his hands thrust nonchalantly into his trouser pockets and a fedora tilted back jauntily on his head. He was also chosen "Best Looking." Posing with the "Prettiest," Margaretta Roberts, he was hatless in an open-necked short-sleeved shirt and pleated trousers, hands again in pockets.

Beneath his mug shot in the Senior Class section of the book was this inscription:

CHARLES CRUTCHFIELD
"The world looks brighter from behind a smile."

Charles is one of the best-looking boys in the Senior Class. He can play football, too, and has written a story for the Scribbler. His wise cracks are popular with 4-D and have helped many a dull hour become less so. Good luck, "Chock"!

An item in the Last Will and Testament of the Spartanburg High School Class of 1929 stated that "Charles Crutchfield bequeaths his inexhaustible jar of "Stacomb" and also his "Arrow-collar" appearance to

A.D. Cudd." The Senior Class Prophecy declared that Chock was destined to become "manager of a barber college."

More important to Chock's destiny was a petite, pretty, and vivacious girl from Miami, Florida. He met her while she was visiting an older sister in Spartanburg. After she returned to Miami for her senior year in high school, they exchanged letters. She planned to return to Spartanburg after she graduated.

Class of 1929
Voted "Best-Looking"

It had been a difficult decade for Fannie Crutchfield and her children: uprooted from their small-town Arkansas home, then essentially stranded in Spartanburg while the local economy was becoming a harbinger of the national and world-wide depression. It had been a milestone decade in the social history of the United States. It was an era defined in the urban capitals of commerce and culture by newly uninhibited and flamboyant lifestyles, unprecedented sexual candor, free-flowing bathtub gin and bootleg liquor, new money, easy credit, and undisciplined investing. Women smoked, drank, bobbed their hair, wore short skirts, and smiled sweetly at the idea of even more scandalous behavior. Men loved it and paid the bills. Then everything went bad. Rich people lost fortunes. Poor people lost jobs. Down South, in the Bible Belt, preachers and parishioners would say it was God's judgment for a decade of moral decay and immoral behavior in the sinful cities; but that would not explain why they and their neighbors were hurting, too.

In terms of young Charles Crutchfield's future, other developments of the 1920s turned out to be even more significant. One was commercial radio. Since the first signal beamed out of Pittsburgh in 1920, other stations had been popping up around the country. One was WEAF in New York City, which in 1922 offered ten minutes of radio time to anyone for $100. Following up on that proposal, a Long Island real estate firm paid the station $50 each for 15 spot announcements promoting a tenant-owned apartment complex. The result was sales in the thousands of dollars. The commercial part of commercial radio was launched.

In 1926, the Radio Corporation of America bought WEAF in New York City from American Telephone and Telegraph Co. and renamed it WNBC. Within a year it had put together the first radio network, with 19 stations, called the National Broadcasting Company. A second network, the Columbia Broadcasting System, was established in 1927.

Another was the invention of electric recording equipment and phonographs, which meant more durable recordings and better quality reproduction of music and the spoken word – important to the infant commercial broadcasting industry.

Not coincidental to those two developments, the 1920s were the beginning of the golden age of American advertising. An unprecedented assortment of new consumer products had been launched since the late 19th century – breakfast cereals, cigarettes, face creams, soaps, shampoos, hair lotions, automobiles. Artists and writers found good-paying jobs creating advertisements for those products, published in newspapers and magazines. Some of the legendary advertising agencies were established in those years, including Barton, Durstine and Osborn in 1919, Young and Rubicam in 1923, and Benton and Bowles in 1929.

With commercial radio, creative advertisers were no longer limited to the printed word or image. They could use audible and distinctive voices, and music, to promote their brands to a fast-growing mass audience, and they could multiply that audience by broadcasting the same message on several stations. In 1923 the National Carbon Co. introduced the *Eveready Hour,* the first series of broadcast entertainment by a single sponsor. The Goodrich Tire company sponsored an hour-long program on a network of nine stations in 1924. Four years later the Lucky Strike Dance Orchestra debuted on 39 NBC stations. The program later became *Your Hit Parade.*

By the time Chock and the class of 1929 graduated from high

school, the national economy was sinking into deep depression. Later that year the stock market crashed. It was not a propitious time to be taking on the responsibilities of adult life and trying to earn a living. But all the technologies, infrastructures, and innovations were in place for a career that Chock, that autumn, could not even begin to imagine.

He was only 17 years old, but he had a sense of humor, a sense of style, and a sense of values. He had ample intelligence, although apparently not of the kind that manifested itself in academic settings. He was good-looking and good-natured. All those qualities would serve him well, but perhaps the most important quality of all was a self-confidence that bordered on audacity. Where did it come from? Maybe it was genetic, stretching all the way back to those pioneer ancestors who kept pushing west to the next frontier. Maybe it was the example and influence of the erratic arc of his father's business career and personal life. Or his mother's unwavering religious faith. Or the inspiration of his academically precocious older brother. Whatever the source, or the synthesis of many sources, Chock, at 17 and for years to come, was ready and eager for the next big thing.

CHAPTER FOUR
The Voice

AS HE FINISHED HIGH SCHOOL and wondered what to do next, the most immediately obvious talent young Mr. Crutchfield brought to fore was his voice. It happens to all boys at some point in adolescence, and it had happened to Chock. His voice changed. In most cases the change is not particularly dramatic. In Chock's case, it must have been profound. The result was deep and resonant, somewhere between bullfrog and rich baritone, with the kind of texture some people – particularly radio announcers -- would smoke cigarettes for years to achieve. It was mature and manly way beyond his years, a voice that would give a nursery rhyme the ring of importance and authority. And it would be only a few months before he got the chance to put it to good use.

By the fall of 1929, his brother Ralph had moved to a sales position at Carolina Sporting Goods, which outfitted textile league baseball teams and high school athletes across the Piedmont. He was doing well enough financially to offer to pay his younger brother's tuition at Wofford College. Chock, who later said he "barely" graduated from high school, was not particularly eager to continue his formal education, but good jobs were not exactly plentiful in Spartanburg at the time, so he enrolled at Wofford.

Affiliated with the Methodist Church and established in 1854, Wofford was a venerable institution in reputation as well as appearance, with a leafy campus within walking distance of the Crutchfields' house. Ralph's offer was an impressive opportunity for Chock, but one of which he took little advantage.

Continuing the sociability and athletic interests of his high school years, he pledged the Kappa Sigma fraternity, went out for freshman football, and tried to settle into the new experience of college life. But his patience with academic discipline stretched ever thinner.

People everywhere were struggling financially. At least some of the very rich were feeling poor, and the not-so-rich were becoming desperate. With the textile industry barely limping along, Spartanburg's once-bustling Main Street probably belonged on the list when W. J. Cash wrote of that era: "…Richmond, Greensboro, Charlotte, Atlanta – all the commercial nerve centers stringing southward along the Southern Railway, took on the air of those old dead towns of Belgium and the Hanseatic League."

Perhaps to Chock it did not seem an appropriate time to immerse himself in studies that offered little in the way of solutions to the problems he and other young men could see as they looked toward the future. Or maybe it was just that four years of college seemed to him an enormous and oppressive postponement of his restless ambition. He wanted to be out in the world making some money and making his mark.

That fall and winter of 1929 into 1930, Chock probably was more interested in radio than in his college studies. Radio stations were popping up across the country, including a few in the Carolinas, and he could pick up some of the signals. At the turn of a dial he could find music, one-way conversations with faceless voices, advertisements. It was an amazing new thing, the next big thing, something to dream about, and soon it moved much closer to home – within reach, in fact. In February, Spartanburg and the South Carolina upstate got their first radio station, with the call letters WSPA and an office and studio in the Montgomery Building, not far from Wofford College and Alabama

Street. That spring, Chock occasionally stopped by the station in the afternoons as he walked to and from the campus. He would watch the announcer, Donald Sanders, talking into the microphone, and then he would go home and listen to that same deep voice on his radio. He thought it amazing that the voice from the station got into his home without benefit of wires or any other visible connection – a phenomenon that he continued to find amazing for the rest of his life.

In written and spoken accounts of Crutchfield's long career, there are several versions of what happened on one of those spring evenings. This version is the most entertaining, and given what is known about the young man, seems as credible as any others.

The announcer and an engineer, the only people at the station when Chock arrived, were both busy and the telephone was ringing, so Chock answered it. The caller, a woman, asked if the announcer could play a certain recording. Chock wrote down her name and the name of the record and handed the note to the announcer. Sanders looked at it, found the recording and played it, dedicating it to the woman who had made the request. The phone began to ring again, and kept ringing, as listeners who had heard the dedication called in to make requests of their own. Many years later, Robert Inman, author and WBTV news anchor, wrote that history was made that evening at WSPA: "It was the first radio request program in the nation."

One of the telephone calls Chock answered was from Virgil Evans, who owned the station. He wanted to know what was going on, with his announcer taking all these requests; and he wanted to know if the man with the deep voice who had answered the phone would like a part-time job at WSPA.

The negotiations that followed were simple and almost unnecessary. Chock surely would have worked for free to get a start in radio, and he almost did. His weekly pay was a meal ticket worth a few dollars at a nearby restaurant, for which Virgil Evans probably traded the restaurant a bit of advertising.

Later that spring Ralph Crutchfield realized in the shrinking economy that he could no longer afford to send his younger brother to college. He explained the situation with regret, but Chock later re-called it as "the happiest day of my life." No longer a student, he could work full time.

It obviously wasn't a good time to be launching a new business, but radio was a technology that would not wait. There were only so many frequencies available, and if you wanted one, you had to act. New stations were signing on the air in the Carolinas, and for a while it seemed that as soon as one signed on, it hired Charles Crutchfield. Just two months after taking a part-time job at the station in his neigh-borhood, Chock moved to Greensboro, North Carolina, for a summer stint at WNRC/WBIG. Four months later he was on the staff at WIS in Columbia, South Carolina. In another four months, in February of 1931, he was at WCSC in Charleston, South Carolina. That was one of his longer tenures, lasting until July. It ended in part because of the owner's insistence on playing his harmonica on the air. Apparently his playing wasn't good enough to fit into Chock's idea of quality pro-gramming. From there he moved to Augusta, Georgia, and the brand new WRDW. From the summer of 1931 until May of 1933 he appar-ently was hired, dropped (or quit), and then rehired at WRDW. He also worked for a while at an advertising agency in Augusta during that period.

Chock's explanation, years later, of his frequent jumping from one job to the next, was that he was a brash young man who thought he knew more than his boss and thus got into conflicts that either got him fired or prompted him to resign. There may be some truth to that, as in the case of the Charleston station's harmonica-playing owner. But radio was a new medium and the stations themselves were new, and the talent pool in the region was just beginning to form. Chock was part of that emerging talent pool, and thus in demand as new sta-tions looked for competent announcers. And he was always looking for a better gig, a bigger market, more responsibility and authority.

Meanwhile, in the middle of those first three peripatetic years of his broadcasting career, Chock also acquired a wife. She was the girl from Miami.

CHAPTER FIVE
Jack

JACKSONIA GERTRUDE WILLIAMS was born on the 29th of August, 1911, in Allendale, a small town in the South Carolina lowcountry, just a few miles northeast of the Georgia line.

Her parents, Pauline and William Aiken Williams, a cotton broker known by his middle name, had seven children: sons, William Aiken Williams III (Pat), Henry (Pete), and Paul; and daughters, Llewellyn, Josephine, Lucille, and Jacksonia.

When Jacksonia was about two years old, her father was shot and killed in some sort of dispute. Pauline, pregnant at the time, was left a widow with many mouths to feed. At the time of his death, Aiken had been in the process of moving his family into a house owned by his mother in Guyton, Georgia. She invited Aiken's widow to move into the white frame farmhouse as planned, and Pauline accepted. With the help of a young black man named Benny, Pauline drove a wagon full of children and belongings to Guyton. In 1914 she gave birth to the last of the Williams children, a son she named Paul.

Pauline, a bright, good-humored and resilient woman, did her best to run the farm and raise six children. To help ends meet she also taught in a one-room schoolhouse in nearby Pineora. She took Jacksonia, called Jack or Jackie, to school with her. From ages two until

Jack's parents,
Pauline and William Aiken Williams

five, Jack enjoyed being at school with the older children. It was the beginning of a love of learning that continued for the rest of her life.

Pauline's son Pat, at age nine, was deemed old enough to help run the farm. He worked alongside the family's faithful friend Benny. Pauline and her family lived in Guyton until 1917. Then Pauline married a Mr. Thompson and moved with him to another white frame country house at Bassett, near Leefield, Georgia, splitting up her family in the process.

Pauline took her sons Paul and Pete with her to Bassett, where she and her new husband raised his five children and later had two of their own, Emma and Elizabeth. Son Pat and her four daughters moved to Savannah, where their grandmother, whom they called Damma, operated an inn and tea room at 120 West Hull Street in Chippewa Square along with her daughters, Daisy and Lucy Jane. Llewellyn went to live with her Aunt Daisy, while Josephine and Lucille stayed with Lucy Jane, also known as "Aunt Tootie." Jack stayed with Damma. Later, some of her siblings said Jack was Damma's favorite, and claimed she'd been spoiled by her grandmother.

The children in Savannah enjoyed visiting their mother in the big country house at Bassett. Jack also loved living in Savannah. She loved school and had a busy account at the public library, which she visited on roller skates to check out and return books. She would always remember the two golden lions that flanked the library steps, where she sat to tighten her skates.

Physically active, Jack was a scrappy tomboy who could hold her own in sports and games with the boys. Once at a day camp she wore out a new pair of tennis shoes in a week. Her love of pranks would become a life-long talent, and some of her early ones were a bit edgy. One night she donned a black mask and crouched beneath the window of her new neighbors, a Dutch family. When the parents weren't in sight, she would rise up, and in a low voice, scare the daylights out of the children. On another occasion she pretended to choke one of her many cats just outside the window where an elderly woman sat watching, horrified and frantically rapping on the glass.

In 1923, Damma and her daughters Daisy and Lucy Jane bought land and a house in Miami, Florida, becoming part of the huge migration known as the 1920s Florida housing boom. Prior to that decade, the original south Florida settlers were largely poor, and the newcomers were often rich – wealthy northerners building winter residences, and prosperous retirees. But energetic developers began buying inland properties and subdividing them to create lots for affordable houses, and partnering with financial institutions offering low interest rates on mortgage loans with little or no down payments. Suddenly people didn't have to be wealthy to claim a place in the Florida sun and enjoy the warm winters. Middle-class Americans, perhaps picking up some of the spirit of the Roaring 20s, flooded into Miami and the surrounding area, stretching their formerly limited horizons all the way to a tropical paradise.

For Damma and her family, paradise turned out to be a bit crowded. Though Jack's sister Llewellyn moved to Spartanburg (where she attended Converse College and later married), Jack, Lucille, and Paul moved to Florida, along with Daisy and Lucy Jane and their husbands; Daisy's daughter Josie Lu and her husband and two children; and one other couple. That made for fourteen people living in one house.

By the time Damma died four years later, another house had been completed and the family was able to spread out a bit.

When the family divided into two houses, Jack and Lucille lived with their aunts, Daisy and Tootie, and their husbands. Jack, now a teenager, was something of a free spirit and had been indulged in her sometimes adventurous behavior by Damma. Aunt Daisy was strict and the girls considered her "grumpy." When Damma died, Daisy told Jack, "I can't wait to get my hands on you." Jack may have chafed a bit at her aunt's efforts to make her an altogether proper young lady, but some of Daisy's discipline and instruction had long-lasting benefits. It was she who taught Jack proper manners, and such useful lessons as how to clean house and do the laundry, how to set a table, and how to sew. She was a musician and an excellent seamstress, and under her tutelage Jack was able to make many of her own clothes, as well as curtains and other household items, as she continued to do for many years.

At some point the girl who had been christened Jacksonia Gertrude made a decision that reflected her sense of herself and foreshadowed the kind of young woman she would be, the kind of life she would aspire to live – a life and persona shaped and embellished by beauty and grace. She did not want to be Jacksonia Gertrude. She thought it an old-fashioned, unattractive name, and she resolved not to be stuck with it. She changed her first name to Jacquelin. Family and friends continued to call her Jack, or Jackie. She kept the middle name of Gertrude, but pretty much ignored it for the rest of her life.

From her earliest childhood, it had not been a promising start for Jacksonia, now Jacquelin, Williams. Her father murdered, her grieving mother already overburdened with children and another one on the way, she herself being passed off to other relatives for care. Tragedy, displacement, disconnection from her natural mother, pulling up family roots and moving to a new place where almost nobody had roots had to have taken a toll. Living as an adolescent in a house so overcrowded meant opportunities for privacy were painfully and per-haps embarrassingly scarce. But from that chrysalis of an unsettled early childhood, Jack somehow emerged not only whole and resilient, but also as lovely and buoyant as a butterfly. By the time she entered Miami High School, she was a petite, dark-haired beauty with enough charm and personality to assure her popularity among other girls – and of course among her male classmates.

Despite the depressed economy, it must have been a wonderful time to be at Miami High. The climate, the beaches, and the waterways made the city and its surroundings a year-round playground for young people. Jack was not only good-looking, but also athletic and a good diver. One year she was chosen as "Miss Grapefruit." She and some of her girlfriends appeared from time to time in photographs in the local newspaper promoting the south Florida lifestyle, wearing swimsuits and frolicking among the palm trees. With a lower percentage of stu-dents going on to college, high school was a much more important maturing, polishing, socializing, coming-of-age experience than it would be for later generations.

Before her senior year in high school Jack visited her sister Llewellyn, who had moved to Spartanburg, South Carolina. There she met Chock Crutchfield. Though he was a year younger than she, he was finishing high school a year earlier. In addition to her striking good looks and vivacious personality, she was from Miami, and to a Spartanburg boy that surely gave her an aura of glamour and sophistication. It also made things all the more difficult for him when she returned home to finish high school.

In the fall and early winter of 1929, Jack's senior year, the Miami High football team was the pride of the school and the city. The Stingarees were undefeated, going through the regular season with eight victories and one tie. On December 14, in a playoff promoted to determine the Southern championship, they defeated the Charlotte Wildcats, 12-7. One more game was then added, on Christmas Day, against Salem (Massachusetts) High School. Miami won that one, 7-6, to claim the championship of the East, and the Stingarees declared themselves national champions. Two of the stars of the team were quarterback Tommie Thompson and fullback Bud Trammell. Both were among Jack's growing cadre of beaus.

In that winter holiday season Jack's calendar was packed with social events, including an "Old-Fashioned Christmas Party" on December 23 at the Coral Gables Country Club, a Christmas Day tea dance at the Miami Beach Golf and Country Club, the Sphinx Club annual alumni dance December 27 at the Miami Woman's Club, another tea dance, this one hosted by "the Diddlers," on December 28 at the Coral Gables Country Club, and a December 30 dance at the Miramar Hotel. The Delta Tau fraternity of the University of Florida invited Miami High seniors to a holiday dance January 2 at the Miami Woman's Club.

As much as she enjoyed the parties and the attention of young men, Jack was not just a party girl. She had the inquisitive mind of a naturally good student, and that would continue to shape her attitudes and ideas for the rest of her life. Despite all the social activities, large and small, she kept up with her studies and was named to the National Honor Society on the basis of "character, service, leadership, and scholarship." It was a record that should have pointed toward higher education, but the family didn't have the resources for her to go to college as her sisters had.

The social schedule livened up again in the spring of 1930 as graduation festivities approached. One big event was the Skulls annual dance "at their Den of Death" in late May. In early June, Bud Trammell escorted Jack to a Hawaiian-themed garden party. There was also a bridge luncheon, a swimming party, and several showers honoring brides-to-be.

In her graduation scrapbook, displaying her clothes consciousness and sense of style, Jack wrote a detailed description of her outfits for two important occasions. For Class Day, she wore "powder blue organdie, with drooping circular ruffles and these trimmed with black footing. Puff sleeves and extremely low back. Pale pink linen shoes trimmed in powder blue. A natural colored straw hat filled with larkspur carried on the arm, with a big pink ribbon." For graduation ceremonies: "White or cream taffeta evening dress. Long, full skirt, tight body, double bow in back…new white slippers…."

After the 8 p.m. commencement on June 6, Jack and some of her friends partied through the night. By her own account, they eventually had breakfast and she got home at 5:30 a.m.

Among the senior accolades of the Class of 1930, Jack was chosen, along with one of her occasional dates, Tom Putnam, as "Cutest." Alongside the photo of the cutest couple in Jack's copy of the school yearbook is this handwritten message: "As long as kitty has a tail, my love for you will never fail." It was signed "Bud," but below that name some person or persons listed three others – "Tommie, C.T., Ted." To which a final note was added by the owner of the yearbook: "Bunk (J.W.)."

Whatever the bunkum quotient, in the spring of 1930 there were a number of young men in her graduating class competing, some more seriously than others, for the romantic attentions of Jacquelin Williams. But there was another suitor in the picture, probably unknown to all of the others.

That spring Chock had dropped out of college and was still living at home, working part-time, for a meal ticket, at the new radio station, and he couldn't get her out of his dreams. Meanwhile – did he know? – she was dancing happily from boy to boy, from party to party, in her tropical paradise. They exchanged a few letters, but apparently her attention waned as the tempo of spring festivities picked up in and around Miami High. Her neglect and his impatience were reflected in two telegrams she received that spring.

AM AWFULLY LONESOME AND JUST SAY I LOVE YOU. CHOCK.

The other one said:

ARE YOU DEAD IF NOT PLEASE WRITE. ALL MY LOVE. CHOCK.

Jack managed to graduate from Miami High without being snared into engagement or even steady-date status by any of her suitors. Later, to Chock's delight, she moved to Spartanburg to live with Llewellyn for a year. Chock had left WSPA and taken a summer job at WNRC/WBIG, and in the fall of 1930 he moved to Columbia and then the following February to Charleston. Somehow, despite the many moves and job changes, he managed to squeeze in a lot of courtship. There's little if any record of what went on in the personal lives of Chock and Jack during the second half of 1930 and most of 1931, while she was living in Spartanburg and he was dashing from microphone to microphone across South Carolina and into Georgia. Maybe their splintered but precious time together involved humid summer evenings in a porch swing, or twilight strolls through honeysuckle-scented neighborhoods, or swimming parties with friends. They enjoyed going to the movies, but there was no necking at a drive-in theater, because there were no drive-in theaters until a few years later. Perhaps they were able to take day trips to the nearby mountains, or spend a weekend at the beach. They listened to music, on radio or with phonograph records, and their favorite songs were the ones that began, "We strolled the lane together…" and "I'll be loving you always…."

Whatever they did, the intensity of their feelings was undiminished. On November 10, 1931, in what Charles Crutchfield, many years later, would describe as an impulsive act by a couple of kids, he and Jack were married by a Justice of the Peace in Spartanburg. Jack wore an aqua angora sweater for the occasion, and Chock was surely dressed in his dapper best. After taking their vows, they went to see a movie. Only Chock's sister Alice knew what they were doing at the time, and she kept their secret until they were ready to tell everyone else.

Jack was slim, trim, and barely five feet tall, which apparently was why, sometime after they were married, Crutchfield began to call his wife Pee Wee, and then almost everyone else did, too.

Her marriage had as unpromising a beginning as her early childhood. The Great Depression was like a cloud over every kind of ambition and prospect. Chock was living in Augusta but had lost his job at the radio station there. They set up housekeeping in Augusta, on the upper floor of a house that was the home of a Mrs. Sleigh, who knew their circumstances, liked them, and thus charged them no rent. (They had little choice but to accept the charity, but over the following months, as their finances improved, Jack paid Mrs. Sleigh, bit by bit, for the rent the landlady had initially waived.)

To avoid the cost of breakfast, Jack often slept, or at least stayed in bed, until noon. Chock would visit a nearby fruit stand and, while talking with the owner, would pick up an apple or banana or peach and eat it. The owner never charged him.

During that all but desperate period, the stern, straight-laced Fannie Crutchfield wrote a tender, compassionate, and encouraging letter to her new daughter-in-law:

> …*Try to be patient and as happy as possible, just a bit longer.… You must know I have no intention to "butt-in" – just to help. Chock really has been beside himself for some time, he's been so upset. Was not a sensible thing at all, of course, for you to get married when he had no work – but love isn't a sensible thing, and never was. There has never been a time when there were so many more men than jobs. Even men who are much older couldn't figure such a situation. We just have to do the best we can, and know that God, who is Love and Justice, rules His world. Things must come under His will some day.*
>
> *Lovingly,*
> *Chock's (and your) Mother*

CHAPTER SIX
A Swift Ascent

THINGS BEGAN TO CHANGE for the better pretty quickly. When Chock was rehired at the Augusta radio station as a vice president early the following year, he received a $50 bonus. He rushed home and suggested that they go out to dinner and celebrate. Jack said no. She insisted that they save the money.

In Augusta, Chock already was demonstrating his entrepreneurial instincts as a broadcaster and promoter. The Mills Brothers were among the top recording and performing groups in the nation, and Chock worked with some local singers in getting them to develop a sound very much like that of the Mills Brothers. He then put them on the radio, and they became so popular that they later were heard on the National Broadcasting Company (NBC) network.

The culmination of Chock's hopping from microphone to microphone across South Carolina and along the Georgia border came in May of 1933, when the Greenville News-Piedmont Company, publisher of two of the state's major daily newspapers, went into the broadcasting business by forming station WFBC. As the new station went on the air, its manager was B.H. Peace, Jr., and its program director was Charles Crutchfield.

The station was launched with considerable fanfare. On the day it first went on the air, an inaugural luncheon was held at the Imperial Hotel, with speakers that included Sen. James F. Byrnes of Spartanburg (later U.S. Secretary of State, Justice of the U.S. Supreme Court, and governor of South Carolina), Congressman J.J. McSwain of Greenville, and Governor Ibra C. Blackwood.

A glance at the station's program log, published in the newspaper, for its first two days of operation, gives an idea of what commercial radio was like in its infancy. Programs included news reports provided by the Greenville News and Piedmont, but was heavy on live music, mostly in 15-minute segments: DuPre Rhame, accompanied by Mrs. Rhame; Maury Pearson, baritone; Roddy Hudson, tenor; Mrs. D.I. Mulkey, soprano; Mrs. W.P. Barton and Mrs. C.P. Corn, vocal duet; Buford Maxwell and his Orchestra; Thomas Brockman, concert pianist; the Silver Masked Tenor (all-request program); Xylophone of the Morning; Furman University Glee Club; American Legion Drum and Bugle Corps; the Greenville Little Symphony; Organ Melodies of the Evening....

And there, in the center of all the fanfare over the new station, was Chock, with his name writ large and his photograph in the local newspapers. Still two months short of his 21st birthday, he was not only one of the best-known radio announcers in the area, he was now a broadcasting executive with a regionally significant media company. That made him an important citizen of the city and the region, and a celebrity as well, in demand for speeches before civic and business groups about the new radio station and its plans.

His publicity photo in the newspaper showed him with a neat, thin mustache that gave him a slightly more mature presence and, along with the dark, glossy hair, even more the look of

WFBC Greenville
Program Director,
Charles Crutchfiled, age 20

a 1920s or '30s movie star. The paper published this brief item assessing the new station's young program director:

> Charles H. Crutchfield, program director of Greenville's new station, is a native of Spartanburg and is widely known in this city and section. He may be expected to become a valuable addition to Greenville, possessing in addition to his radio experience a keen interest in all civic affairs.
>
> Mr. Crutchfield is a brother of Ralph Crutchfield, popular salesman of sporting goods for a Spartanburg and Charlotte concern....
>
> In his capacity as program director Mr. Crutchfield will come in contact with hundreds in this section and they will have opportunity to observe not only a smooth-working official of a radio station, but a real fellow, and a cordial individual at all times.

It had been a dizzying three years that brought him to what must have seemed at that moment the pinnacle of a young broadcaster's career. With a salary of $30 per week, Chock and Jack could afford a more comfortable lifestyle. But for all the promotion and prestige of his job at the new Greenville station, Chock's instincts told him the place to be was Charlotte, at WBT. Even as he enjoyed the status of program director in Greenville, he drove to Charlotte more than once to audition. In September of 1933, only about five months into his position in Greenville, Chock accepted an offer from WBT. His salary there would be $20 per week, $10 less than he was making in Greenville. But he believed the place and the opportunity were more important than the money. He saw WBT as the next big thing. And he was right.

From that point on, except among relatives who had known him as a boy, he would no longer be known as Chock. He was Charlie, or Crutch, and eventually, Mr. Crutchfield.

PART
2

THE MAKING OF A LEGEND

The Briarhoppers

Chapter Seven
WBT Charlotte

IN LATE OCTOBER of 1920, the U.S. Department of Commerce awarded the Westinghouse Electric Company of Pittsburgh, Pennsylvania, a license to operate the nation's first commercial radio station. At 6 p.m. on November 2 of that year the station, with the call letters KDKA, went on the air from a small studio in a shack on top of one of the Westinghouse buildings in East Pittsburgh. They immediately began reporting returns from the presidential election, supplied by a local newspaper. That milestone in the history of technology and communication was ultimately more important than the outcome of the election, in which the Republican ticket of Warren G. Harding and Calvin Coolidge crushed Democrat James M. Cox and his running mate, Franklin Delano Roosevelt. From that moment, American democracy, American commerce, American entertainment, the very experience of living in America and much of the world, was forever changed.

A few weeks later, in Charlotte, North Carolina, Earle Gluck, a Southern Bell Telephone Company employee who had been a Navy radio operator in World War I and a ham radio operator since boyhood, went shopping for ham radio components. In a store on West Fifth Street in downtown Charlotte he met two other men who were interested in building a radio transmitter. One was Fred Bunker, an engineer with Westinghouse Electric. The other man, Fred Laxton of the Tucker and Laxton construction company, had previously worked for General Electric, and was interested in that company's new vacuum tubes, which could significantly increase the power of a radio-telephone transmitter.

The three began talking about working together to set up a broadcasting station. In December they met at Laxton's home at the corner of Mecklenburg and Belvedere avenues, across the street from the entrance to Charlotte Country Club. On the dining room table the three men assembled a telephone-microphone and an amplifier, with a transmitter in an adjacent room and a receiver in what had been a chicken coop in the back yard. It all worked.

(It is somehow fascinating almost a century later, to contemplate a chicken coop in the back yard of that fine Mediterranean-style residence just across the street from a very exclusive country club.)

In March of 1921, Gluck, Bunker and Laxton acquired a license from the U.S. Department of Commerce to operate an experimental station and were assigned the call letters 4XD. In January of the following year, they applied for a commercial radio license and began moving their equipment into a room on the eighth floor of the Independence Building at the corner of Trade and Tryon streets, in the center of downtown Charlotte. (The Laxton family must have been happy to regain the use of their dining table.) The three broadcasting entrepreneurs formed the Southern Radio Corporation to operate station 4XD and sell radio components. In April of 1922 the Department of Commerce issued the license, and the South's first commercial radio station, WBT, was on the air with 100 watts of power, broadcasting daily from 10 a.m. until 11:45 a.m. and from 7:30 p.m. until 9:45 p.m.

When the owners moved the WBT studio up Tryon Street to the Andrews Music Company, Charlie Andrews became the station's announcer and pianist. Recordings would eventually provide essentially all the music played on commercial radio stations, but in the late

1920s, the recording industry, like the broadcasting industry, was still in its infancy, with very limited technology, production, and distribution. To offer musical programming, early radio stations had to bring in musicians for live on-air performances, and some even employed in-house bands, ranging from classical chamber groups, country music and jazz bands, and even string orchestras. As access to all types of recorded music expanded, live music on radio gradually faded away, although traces of it lingered on WBT and some other stations well into the 1960s.

An early live performance of some significance on WBT was by the Hal Kemp Orchestra in 1925. Kemp, an Alabama native, had formed a student dance band called the Carolina Club Orchestra while he was a student at the University of North Carolina at Chapel Hill. A key ally in that effort was a student from Charlotte, John Scott Trotter, who wrote arrangements and played piano. When Kemp left the university, he turned his student band over to a younger student and UNC cheerleader, Kay Kyser, who later had his own band and show on network radio for many years. Kemp and a few members of the Carolina Club Orchestra who were also finishing school formed the Hal Kemp Orchestra. In the big band era, there were "sweet" bands and "hot" bands, the latter also known as "swing" bands. Kemp's group evolved into a sweet band, but with a distinctively smooth sound that some listeners considered more interesting than the sounds of other sweet bands. The distinction was credited largely to the arrangements of John Scott Trotter.

The Kemp orchestra played on WBT in the mid-1920s, made recordings for Okeh Records, and became a popular touring attraction in hotel ballrooms across the country. Its theme song, "Got a Date with an Angel," was a familiar pop tune of the time. In 1932 the band moved into the Blackhawk Restaurant in Chicago for an extended stay.

(Weighing almost 300 pounds, John Scott Trotter's appetite was almost as large as his talent. He was accomplished in both classical and popular music, and his versatility and originality as an arranger earned him a job as arranger and conductor for Bing Crosby. He served

Crosby in that capacity for 17 years, on radio broadcasts, recordings, and in some early television shows.)

In 1925, the three Charlotte broadcasting pioneers, Gluck, Bunker, and Laxton, sold their station to James P. McMillan and the Carolina States Electric Company. The new owners kept it only a few months, selling it in 1926 to C.C. Coddington, who owned a Buick automobile dealership. Coddington paid about $2,000 for the station and moved it into his Coddington Building at the corner of Trade and Graham streets on the western edge of the central business district. He worked out a deal under which the Charlotte Chamber of Commerce would manage the station. One of Coddington's associates in the automobile business, Lee A. Folger, created an advertising campaign to promote the company's cars as well as the radio station. The ads announced that the station's call letters, WBT, meant "Watch Buick Travel."

The NBC Radio Network was organized in late 1926 and WBT became one of its member stations the following year. That relationship provided network programming to augment the station's local offerings. Coddington increased the station's power to 1,000 watts in 1927, and to 5,000 watts the following year, when he also moved the transmitter from the Coddington Building to his farm on Nation's Ford Road.

While WBT was increasing its power and signal range, it also expanded its broadcast schedule and the diversity of its programming. One new star on the air from WBT was Mrs. Pasco Powell who, as "Aunt Sally," read stories for children. Such was the growing range and reputation of the station that "Aunt Sally" was invited to New York to be a guest on the NBC show *Evening Star*.

A number of musical organizations entertained live on the air. There were remote broadcasts of "dinner music" from the Hotel Charlotte from 12:30 p.m. until 2 p.m., featuring Jimmie Purcell and his Dixonians, a six-piece group. The Hawaiian Serenaders, a three-piece string band, performed in the WBT studio and also recorded for Victor Records. Other groups featured on live studio broadcasts included the Woodlawn String Band, a seven-piece hillbilly band of local musicians; Joe Nesbit and his Pennsylvanians, an 11-piece band that had moved from Pennsylvania to perform on WBT; and a string band called Fisher Hendley and Carolina Tarheels. By 1928 the station had organized an in-house orchestra with flute, cello, three violins, piano, clarinet, bass, and drums. Mention of other entertainers from the late 1920s turn up in WBT archival materials including the piano-voice duo of Clemmie Reid and Billie Arthur, vocalist Robert Rhyne, and Estelle LaFrenz, who, as "Tommy, the Movie Girl," broadcast reviews of motion pictures. Larry Walker, a young singer and pianist with a vaudeville background, moved from New York to Charlotte and became one of WBT's staff musicians.

As the schedule expanded, so did the announcing staff, adding Kenneth Clapp, Tom Callahan, Donald O'Connor, and Norman Sweet.

The iconoclastic Baltimore journalist H.L. Mencken is credited with coining the term "Bible Belt" in 1924, referring to Southern states where Protestant Christianity was, probably in his view, an oppressively powerful social and cultural influence. Mencken's intent was pejorative, but Charlotte is one of a number of cities cited over the years as the "buckle" of the Bible Belt, and programmers at WBT were certainly aware of the importance of religion and churches to their growing audience. So, in 1928, they put a microphone at Dr. Luther Little's pulpit in the First Baptist Church on North Tryon Street and became the first station in America to broadcast live Sunday morning church services. Protestant ministers would continue to appear on WBT in a variety of roles over the next 40 or more years – most prominently, the Charlotte-born evangelist Billy Graham.

In 1929, following the death of C.C. Coddington, his estate sold the station to Marion Gilliam of New York City. Gilliam apparently was an agent for the Columbia Broadcasting System (CBS). When he purchased the station, NBC dropped it from its network. Within a year CBS was officially the owner of WBT. The network moved the studio and offices to the Wilder Building at the northeast corner of Third and South Tryon streets, and increased power to 25,000 watts.

The station was losing business at the time, and its reputation in the infant broadcasting industry was that of a "relay point," primarily airing material fed from elsewhere, and establishing no cultural or financial roots in its community. CBS sent William A. Schudt to Charlotte as station manager of its new property, with orders to generate more local programming and become more visible on the local media landscape. Meanwhile, Earle Gluck left WBT to help establish Charlotte's second radio station, with the call letters WSOC.

In retrospect, as important to WBT in 1929 as the new ownership, new quarters, and a major increase in signal strength was a minor programming addition: the station contracted with the city's afternoon newspaper, the *Charlotte News*, to broadcast a daily five-minute news and stock market report, and a young reporter named Grady Cole was chosen to read the reports on the air.

Cole was a native of Montgomery County, an hour or so east of Charlotte. When he was in his teens, his family moved to Charlotte, where he attended Major J.G. Baird's School for Boys. He went to work in the Charlotte office of the Associated Press, and from there he moved to the *Charlotte News*. He was still in his early 20s when he began reading the daily five-minute reports on WBT, and he quickly made himself at home in front of the microphone. The station hired him full-time as an announcer in April of the following year. It was the most important hiring decision in the station's brief history.

In 1930 there still were only about 400 radios in Charlotte and Mecklenburg County. The following year it was estimated that one in seven homes in North Carolina had a radio, and one in nine in South Carolina. However many there were, apparently most of them in Charlotte and the surrounding farms and towns along the state line were tuned to Grady Cole for the news every day.

The community that became Charlotte had coalesced early in the second half of the 18th century on a Piedmont hilltop just a few miles from the South Carolina line. It was at the intersection of an east-west Native American trading path and a part of the north-south Great

Wagon Road that was bringing Scots-Irish and German settlers from Pennsylvania into the Carolina foothills. Incorporated in 1768, Charlotte was named for the wife of King George III and was established as the county seat of Mecklenburg, which was named for Queen Charlotte's birthplace in Germany.

If the colonists' choice of names was intended to curry favor with the British monarchy, the growing unpopularity of colonial taxes and other policies imposed by the crown soon overwhelmed that impulse. On May 20, 1775, a group of rebellious Mecklenburg residents met in Charlotte and drafted and signed what became known as the Mecklenburg Declaration of Independence. The authenticity of that document has been challenged by some historians, but apparently there is no question about the Mecklenburg Resolves, drafted by the same group of citizens a few days later to establish the governing laws of the now independent county and town. During the American Revolution, British troops engaged local citizens in several skirmishes, and the outcome prompted Lord Cornwallis to condemn Charlotte as a "hornet's nest of rebellion."

A few years later, President George Washington passed through the town and described it in his diary as "a trifling place." But the city that lured 21-year-old Charles Crutchfield across the state line in 1933 no longer fit that description. Charlotte's population had grown by about 80 percent through the 1920s and was measured in the 1930 census at 82,675, making it the largest city in the Carolinas. (By 1940 it would hit the 100,000 mark.) That growth, the prestige of being the largest city, the location near the center of a two-state area that once had been simply Carolina, and the doubling of the station's signal strength to 50,000 watts the year Charles Crutchfield arrived – those were surely among the reasons he was willing to take a pay cut to get a job at WBT. It was a gamble, of course, but it produced a huge and historic jackpot for Crutchfield's career.

CHAPTER EIGHT
Medicine Shows

I N 1933, AS A NEW PRESIDENT of the United States offered a depression-battered nation a "New Deal," Charles and Jacquelin Crutchfield were making a new start in their young marriage and his young career. On a warm September weekend they arrived by bus at the terminal in downtown Charlotte. He retrieved their two suitcases from the luggage compartment and they made their way to a downtown rooming house in the city's Fourth Ward, at 225 North Church Street, owned by a Mrs. Knauff. (Her son, Billy Knauff, became a fine musician who led the best jazz and dance band in the Charlotte area through the 1940s and 50s.) Rent at the rooming house was $10 per week, half of Crutchfield's salary. The heady days of an executive title and the relative financial comfort of a $30 per week salary were over, at least for a while. Crutchfield was betting on something better. He and Jack tightened their belts and settled in.

The rooming house was within walking distance of the Wilder Building, and as instructed by Station Manager William Schudt, Crutchfield reported for work at 6 p.m. on Sunday. That night he probably met the singer Norman Cordon, who was then performing on Sunday nights on WBT, and whose bass voice eventually would take him to the Metropolitan Opera. Another future opera voice on the station that year was baritone Lansing Hatfield from Hickory, North Carolina, some 60 miles away. In addition to opera, Hatfield later starred on Broadway, including the roles of Rev. Alfred Davidson in *Sadie Thompson* and Daniel Webster in *The Devil and Daniel Webster*. Early broadcasters surely took pride in bringing classical music and musicians to their audiences, but the realities of marketing and popular taste would gradually squeeze such programming out of commercial radio.

In that autumn of 1933, Crutchfield was the newest of four announcers on the WBT staff, and thus had to take on the duties his senior colleagues didn't want. He had to be there when the station signed on in the early morning, and worked until about noon. He had afternoons off, but was due back at 6 p.m. and stayed until midnight. That was his schedule, six days a week and sometimes seven. With Crutchfield working almost every night, at least the young couple, with their tight budget, didn't have to worry about the costs of socializing or evenings out. Crutchfield would describe his duties for the rest of that year as a bit of everything. He already had considerable experience with the workings of a radio station, and as WBT evolved rapidly in technological and programming sophistication, so did Crutchfield's skills and versatility. Bill Schudt, sent from New York by CBS to run WBT, was impressed.

As an announcer, Crutchfield was a natural. Like Grady Cole, Crutchfield instinctively understood something that all successful radio announcers eventually would: that the invisible connection – between the microphone and listeners infinitely dispersed for many miles in all directions, each in the intimacy of a single home – changed everything. It was not like speaking to people gathered in a single room or auditorium. The secret, as Crutchfield explained a number of times, was not to think of an audience out there in "radio-land," but of having a one-way conversation with just one person, so that each person listening felt you were a pleasant and comfortable guest speaking directly to her or him. So although he had one of the quintessentially big and deep "radio voices" of his time, he used it in an informal, natural, conversational way. As important as the voice and the style, more important were his intelligence and articulation. He could read a script with professional polish, but he could manage well without a script if necessary. That was fortunate, because during several of his most important moments on the air early in his career, he didn't have a script.

One of the new announcer's more interesting chores, and one that provided valuable experience in ad-libbing, was broadcasting major league baseball. The Western Union wire brought pitch-by-pitch accounts of games into the studio. Crutchfield's job was to take that unadorned information as it rattled out of the wire-service ticker and create a description of the action, as if he were at the game. Crutchfield even provided sound effects. He kept a baseball bat at his side, and when he announced a hit, it was preceded by a rap on the bat with a screw driver. If there was any interruption in the Western Union transmission, he would have to fake it. One possible device was to describe a series of foul balls until the problem was corrected. (WBT was not the only station to broadcast games in this manner. During those same baseball seasons, another announcer in his early 20s was doing the same sort of baseball broadcasts, using wire reports and making up the action when necessary, from a studio in Des Moines, Iowa. Like Crutchfield, he would go on to bigger things. His name was Ronald Reagan.)

Another announcer on the staff when Crutchfield arrived was Larry Walker, whose versatile talents made him indispensable and kept him there for many years. Walker was a good singer, a competent piano player, and a good announcer.

Among the network programs on the WBT afternoon schedule that year were *The Lone Ranger* and an early soap opera, *The Romance of Helen Trent*. The syndicated newspaper gossip columnist Walter Winchell's news and commentary, delivered in dramatic, staccato style, was a popular Sunday night fixture on CBS stations. A locally produced program, the *Dixie Mammoth Minstrels Show*, was fed to the Dixie Network, which was the southern division of CBS. Another local

"The Voice" at WBT

favorite was the *Crazy Water Crystals Show*, which was a harbinger of the convergence of two developments – one commercial and one musical – that would shape Crutchfield's early career and the popularity and personality of WBT Radio in the 1930s.

The *Crazy Water Crystals Show* featured what was then known as "hillbilly" music, and was sponsored by a Texas company. The product was supposedly created by boiling down water from a mineral spring. The resulting mineral crystals could be rehydrated to create a drink that, according to the company, would cure most, if not all, of mankind's ailments and maladies. The company was one of many in the thriving patent medicine industry that discovered in the 1920s that the use of local and regional musical groups was a very effective way to advertise their cure-all potions on the new medium of radio.

The Dixie Network consisted of WBT and 11 other CBS affiliates in Atlanta, Birmingham, Chattanooga, Knoxville, Little Rock, Memphis, Mobile, Montgomery, Nashville, New Orleans, and Savannah. WBT was designated the "key station" in the network, with direct lines to CBS stations in New York and Washington, D.C. It fed CBS programming to the other southern stations in the network. It also supplied some of the programming originating in Charlotte, particularly country music shows, across the Dixie Network. That gave regional exposure to the increasingly lively country music scene in Charlotte and made WBT one of the most popular and lucrative stations for musicians to call home. That, and patent medicine.

The patent medicine business had passed its apogee by the time Charles Crutchfield reported to work at WBT, but its influence would linger a while longer, much to his benefit. The rise and fall of that industry and its influence on early radio programming is a fascinating chapter in the history of American commerce and marketing. Perhaps the most successful patent medicine of its time, and indeed of all time, was Peruna, and its story is a paradigm of that era and that industry.

An apparently successful and respected physician, Samuel Brubaker Hartman, moved from Pennsylvania to Columbus, Ohio in 1890 and began formulating several potions and tonics that he claimed would relieve various ailments and even cure serious diseases. The one that caught on in the marketplace was labeled Pe-Ru-Na. Its success was almost certainly due in large part to the fact that it had an alcohol content of about 28 percent, but Dr. Hartman advertised it as a cure for catarrh, a bronchial condition, that today would probably be called bronchitis. But Hartman developed a brilliant marketing strategy. In his advertising for Pe-Ru-Na, and in a booklet he wrote and circulated, the doctor redefined catarrh, declaring it the cause of almost every known ailment and disease. Thus, according to Hartman, indigestion was catarrh of the stomach; appendicitis was catarrh of the appendix; pneumonia was catarrh of the lungs; a canker sore was catarrh of the mouth; mumps was catarrh of the glands; etc. And Pe-Ru-Na cured catarrh!

Hartman's biggest customer was a wholesaler in Waco, Texas by the name of Frederick W. Schumacher. The doctor realized, based on his volume of sales to the Waco distributor, that Schumacher must have been a marketing genius. He hired Schumacher as his vice president. Schumacher moved to Columbus, where Hartman was building a huge manufacturing facility to keep up with the demand for Pe-Ru-Na, and he soon solidified his relationship to the company and to Hartman by marrying Hartman's daughter.

At one dollar per bottle – much higher than most of its competitors – Peruna (at some point it lost the hyphens) was the best-selling patent medicine in the United States, and through the 1890s and into the 20th century, Hartman and Schumacher were making millions of dollars. But their success produced the seeds of their eventual downfall. The highly publicized and outrageous claims of Peruna's efficacy were attracting the skeptical attention of the medical profession – and of a muckraking reporter named Samuel Hopkins Adams.

In 1904, Adams wrote a series of articles for *Collier's* magazine called "The Great American Fraud," which was an expose of the patent medicine industry. In an interview with Adams, Hartman admitted that Peruna didn't cure anything. But the doctor insisted that his product was beneficial because people believed in it; thus it made them feel better and helped them get well.

Adams' article and the concerns of scientists and medical professionals led to the Pure Food and Drug Act of 1906 and the creation of the Food and Drug Administration. That might have been expected to mark the end of the patent medicine industry, but it didn't. Sales fell sharply and the industry shrank, but some manufacturers stayed in business by scaling back their extravagant claims and even tried mixing in ingredients that had some medicinal value. Peruna was reformulated to cut its alcohol content to about 18 percent and add some ingredients that had a mild laxative effect. Some long-time users of the tonic must have been unpleasantly surprised when they discovered the changes first-hand.

Two things that really allowed Peruna and the patent medicine industry to continue for another 20 years were one, the national prohibition of the sale of alcoholic beverages, which went into effect in January of 1920, and two, the beginning of commercial broadcasting.

Peruna, for example, even with its alcohol content drastically cut, provided a legal alternative to prohibited alcoholic beverages. In the 1920s it became known as "Prohibition Tonic." Reflecting the popularity of Peruna as an intoxicant, students at Southern Methodist University (SMU) in Dallas, Texas, adopted a new fight song to the tune of "She'll Be Comin' Round the Mountain."

She'll be loaded with Peruna when she comes.
She'll be loaded with Peruna when she comes.
She'll be loaded with Peruna, she'll be loaded with Peruna,
She'll be loaded with Peruna when she comes.

The SMU Mustangs' mascot, a pony, was given the name Peruna. Then into the picture came a kind of folk music called hillbilly, later called country, then country and western, then bluegrass, and then, again, country. It evolved from the folk music that came to the New World from Scotland and Ireland, with the settlers who traveled down the Great Wagon Road and other routes into the mountains and foothills of Tennessee and North Carolina.

Hillbilly music lyrics were the plain poetry of country life: hard work, socializing with neighbors, love found and love lost, sinful Saturday nights, and pious Sunday mornings. The tunes were stitched closely to the contours of simple three- and four-chord patterns. The music could be played on stringed instruments – fiddles, guitars, banjos, dulcimers – that could be home-made or bought cheaply and carried easily from place to place. The voices of the singers – male, female, or a group – were often as twangy as the sound of the stringed instruments, with a nasal southern drawl and without any affectation of proper grammar or enunciation. The vocal harmonies, though simple, often sounded as stretched as a bow string. It was the sound of rocky mountain rivers and the north wind bending the hemlocks along the Blue Ridge, of barnyards and pastures, of hunting and fishing. It was a music of heartbreak and happiness, of slapstick humor and shameless self-pity, of true love and love gone bad, of sin and redemption. Later it would be the sound of beer joints and taverns and the down time of cotton-mill workers coming off 12-hour shifts. By the 1920s this music of the mountains had become the music of the Piedmont mill villages.

Meanwhile, swing musicians in Texas developed their own brand of western-flavored country music. By the 1930s, as motion picture theaters opened in cities and small towns across America, singing cowboys such as Tex Ritter, Gene Autry, Roy Rogers, Bob Nolan, and the Sons of the Pioneers became movie and recording stars. With the blending of southern country music and western music, a lot of southern country musicians adopted the sartorial style of the Hollywood movie cowboys, with fancy pearl-button shirts, bandanas, big-brimmed hats, and tooled leather boots.

The makers of patent medicines decided that the way to reach their large rural and blue-collar market was through hillbilly music on the radio. Through the era of prohibition, Peruna and other nostrums sponsored local and regional hillbilly bands on radio stations, particularly in the South and the Southwest.

When prohibition was repealed in 1933, the appeal of legal intoxicants such as Peruna was seriously diminished. With patent medicine profits shrinking, the young and entrepreneurial Consolidated Drug Trade Products Company of Chicago began buying up brands at discount prices, including Peruna, Kolor-Back hair dye, and Radio Girl perfume. A Consolidated marketing executive, Harry O'Neal, recalling the success of country music as a marketing vehicle for such products, contacted big-signal radio stations around the nation, looking for some who could provide the programming he wanted to sponsor.

Crutchfield, at WBT less than a year, was in station manager Bill

Schudt's office when O'Neal called. O'Neal said he wanted to sponsor a hillbilly music show, and he asked if WBT had a band available. Schudt turned to Crutchfield. "Do we have a hillbilly band?" he asked. Crutchfield must have wondered why the station manager didn't know the station had no hillbilly band. Or maybe he knew the manager was pretending not to know for the benefit of Harry O'Neal, on the line in Chicago. Whatever confusion Crutchfield might have sensed, he knew an opportunity when he heard one, and he knew how to grab it.

"Yes, sir," he replied.

He hustled out of Schudt's office and down the hall. There was no hillbilly band there, but he immediately encountered one of his colleagues, John McAllister, and asked him to round up some hillbilly musicians to form a band for a daily live broadcast on WBT. McAllister, a musician and singer, was proficient in several musical styles, including hillbilly. He played ukulele and fiddle and had a true, clear tenor voice with a range that included falsetto.

There were plenty of country musicians and singers around. Some of them worked in the mills or in retail stores and performed after hours for family and friends, or in makeshift variety shows. Others were among the Depression-era unemployed, except for occasional one-time gigs. A few worked at radio stations, including WBT.

McAllister's first recruit probably was bass player and fiddler Bill (Big Bill) Davis, who was already on staff at WBT. Other members of the original band were WBT's resident pianist, Clarence Etters, Thorpe Westerfield, who played harmonica and banjo, and fiddler Jane Bartlett. Guitarist and bassist Don White also became one of the early band members.

The band needed a name, and Crutchfield supplied it. He dubbed them the Briarhoppers, which sometimes in those early days was spelled out as Briar Hoppers. There are conflicting stories about how Crutchfield came up with the name. He apparently told an interviewer many years later that the name had come to him one day when he was rabbit hunting and saw a rabbit jumping over briars. Several

The Briarhoppers, left to right: Clarence Etters (piano); Don White; Bill Davis (bass); Billie Burton (at mic); Thorpe Westerfield (harmonica and banjo); Jane Bartlett; Johnny McAllister, Homer Drye (mandolin); Charles Crutchfield, announcer (inset).

other possible origins are noted in Thomas and Lucy Warlick's 2008 book, *The WBT Briarhoppers*. One is that the name was inspired by a story about a rabbit being chased through a briar patch. If so, maybe it was the old Uncle Remus story by Joel Chandler Harris about Brer Rabbit begging his captors, "Please don't throw me in the briar patch" – the briar patch being exactly where he wanted them to throw him.

There are other possibilities. As the Warlicks point out, Briarhoppers was a term applied to Kentucky migrants at the time, and it was used by another country band that played under more than one name to get around contractual restrictions.

What is not in dispute is that Charles Crutchfield came up with the name, and from that time forward the term Briarhoppers, to most people, referred to a band featured on a daily musical variety show on WBT called *Briarhopper Time*. The announcer for that show was himself a Briarhopper. He had hopped from station to station, from microphone to microphone, always to a better briarpatch, and now he was Charlie Briarhopper, aka Charles Crutchfield.

Chapter Nine
Hit's Briarhopper Time!

CHARLES CRUTCHFIELD WOULD WALK into the WBT studio six afternoons a week, Monday through Saturday, a few minutes, sometimes only seconds, before four o'clock, and on the hour the opening exchange went something like this:

Crutchfield: Y'all know what time hit is?

McAllister: Hit's Briarhopper Time!

Or,

Crutchfield: Pappy, what time is it?

McAllister: Why, Crutch, hit's Briarhopper Time!

At which point the band would swing into its theme song:

> *Wait 'til the sun shines, Nellie,*
> *When the clouds go drifting by.*
> *We will be happy, Nellie,*
> *Don't you sigh.*
> *Down lover's land we'll wander,*
> *Sweethearts, you and I.*
> *Wait 'til the sun shines, Nellie,*
> *Bye and bye.*

The song "Wait 'Til the Sun Shines, Nellie," by some accounts McAllister's favorite song and his choice for the Briarhoppers' opening theme song, had a long and interesting life. Composed in 1905 by Andrew B. Sterling and Harry von Tilzer, it was a big hit in the first decade of the 20th century. Thus it was almost 30 years old when the Briarhoppers adopted it, and for the next 17 years almost every afternoon WBT's 50,000-watt signal carried it across a large sweep of the United States. Meanwhile, in 1941, crooner Bing Crosby revived it as a ballad in the motion picture *Birth of the Blues*, and Judy Garland sang it in the 1949 movie, *In the Good Old Summertime*, with Van Johnson. In 1952, a year after *Briarhopper Time* went off the air, there was a movie named for the song, starring Jean Peters and David Wayne.

The Briarhoppers' version didn't include the part songwriters call the "verse," a sort of optional introductory stanza often omitted when a song is performed or recorded. The verse Sterling and Von Tilzer wrote provided this romantic and wistful context:

> *On a Sunday morn sat a maid forlorn*
> *With her sweetheart by her side.*
> *Through the windowpane she looked at the rain.*
> *"We must stay home, Joe," she cried.*
> *"There's a picnic, too, at the Old Point View.*
> *"It's a shame it rained today."*
> *Then the boy drew near, kissed away each tear,*
> *And she heard him softly say....*

The Briarhoppers' version was more energetic than wistful, more whoopee than wait-and-see. But it was a good and memorable choice for their opening theme, and its message of sunny days and happy times just ahead turned out to be prophetic. Although there were no sophisticated audience measurement techniques at the time, there was ample evidence that *Briarhopper Time* quickly became a huge hit, the most popular entertainment radio show in Charlotte and the region. The audience response was unprecedented in the station's history, and perhaps in any station's history. With WBT's 50,000-watt signal beaming the Briarhoppers to much of the country, fan mail came by the hundreds from far and wide.

By 1936, with the addition of Bill Davis' son, known as Judge, who also played bass, the first edition of the band known as the Briarhoppers coalesced. The original concept, probably developed by McAllister and Crutchfield, was of a family. McAllister was Pappy, or Dad Briarhopper. Etters was Elmer, Westerfield was Zeb, White was Sam, Bartlett was Minnie. Davis and son used their own first names or nicknames, Bill and Judge. All had the same last name, Briarhopper.

With their success on the radio, the Briarhoppers were soon in demand for live stage shows. They performed in high school, elementary school and college auditoriums, gymnasiums, and courthouses in small towns across the Piedmont and as far away as Boone, in the North Carolina mountains, and Columbia, the state capital in the South Carolina midlands.

In 1936, needing two children to complete the family, WBT held auditions to pick a boy and a girl to join the Briarhoppers. A large number of pre-teen and early teen singers responded. The winners were a 12-year-old blue-eyed blonde, Billie Burton, and Homer Drye, also 12, or by some accounts 14. They became Billie and Homer Briarhopper. Burton was billed as the "Sweetheart of the Carolinas," and her fan mail sometimes arrived at the rate of a thousand or more letters a day. Drye, with the exposure of live stage shows, quickly became a favorite of teenage girls in the audience.

Although the sponsor had asked for a hillbilly band, what he got was nothing like the pure country and bluegrass show into which the Briarhoppers, with a changing cast, eventually would evolve. According to the Warlicks' book on the Briarhoppers, there are no longer any recordings of those early shows, but a November 1936 program published in The WBT Briarhoppers indicates that *Briarhopper Time* was originally a musical variety show, with hoedowns, folk songs, Tin Pan Alley hit tunes, blues, and even Irish ballads, which were McAllister's specialty. Among the selections on that 1936 program were "Bill Bailey," "Buffalo Girls," "When My Dreamboat Comes Home," "Harbor Lights," "Frankie and Johnny," "Billy Boy," "Always," and "Waiting for the Robert E. Lee." The variety speaks well of the musicians' versatility.

The early Briarhoppers didn't adopt the Hollywood cowboy attire of later country musicians. In the studio they wore their everyday work clothes, which in those days involved a coat and tie even for blue-collar workers. In publicity photographs they are seen in country-style checked shirts, bib overalls or wide suspenders, bandanas and narrow-brimmed hats. Crutchfield eschewed the barn dance look and was, as always, debonair in a suit and neatly knotted necktie.

Almost as important as the music was the hilarious banter between Crutchfield and Dad Briarhopper, Johnny McAllister. Although the two made a great comic team, playing straight man to each other and ad-libbing jibes and jokes, there was some fundamental tension between them. Perhaps it had to do with the difference in backgrounds. McAllister, brought to Charlotte by the manager CBS sent to handle its new property, was university educated, from a well-to-do New York family, and maybe not very enthusiastic about hillbilly music. Crutchfield, a southerner with a keen sense of what would appeal to Depression-weary people in the Carolinas, thought the new show should be as down-home as possible, and the zanier the better. It isn't clear how much their disagreements were brought into the open, but the differences would soon change the program in ways that defined the Briarhoppers' legend and legacy.

Crutchfield's audacious sense of humor didn't respect the line between entertainment and commerce. He poked fun at the wondrous claims of Peruna, calling it Pee-Rooney. On behalf of Kolor-Back, he promised it would get rid of gray hair one way or another – what you didn't lose would turn black. At the same time, Crutchfield was documenting the success of his commercials. When he offered a photograph of the Briarhoppers in return for a Peruna boxtop, the boxtops poured in by the thousands every week. Harry O'Neal of Consolidated Drug Trade Products was driving from Chicago to Myrtle Beach, South Carolina, when he picked up *Briarhopper Time* on his car radio and heard one of Crutchfield's ad lib commercials. He stopped the car, telephoned WBT, asked to speak to the station manager, and wanted to know why Crutchfield was ridiculing the sponsors.

When the manager offered to take Crutchfield off the air, O'Neal, according to Crutchfield's later recollection, said, "Hell, no. He's selling this stuff by the trainload."

What was selling all that stuff were monologues such as this one, preserved on tape:

Crutchfield, at the end of a musical number:

> [You] may look kind of ratty and moth-eaten, but you sure do sing pretty. By the way, neighbors, if y'all would like to have a picture of Whitey and Hogan and Hank and all the rest of the Briarhoppers – goodness knows why you would, but if you want one – the same picture that about 18,000 folks are asking for every week, all you have to do to get one is tear off the top of the box of the stuff we advertise on this Peruny and Kolorbak program and mail it to us Briarhoppers, and we will send you one.

> Oh, yeah, this junk – I mean, these fine products sure are good, it says here. So remember, neighbors, don't go around losing your job just because you got gray hair. Douse on some of this Kolorbak concoction and that gray hair will be gone before you can say Homer Briarhopper. It don't say here on the paper how it's going to get gone, but I don't imagine so many folks would be using Kolorbak if it made your gray hair go away roots and all. Folks tell me it turns it sort of black-looking, so I reckon it must be all right.

> So go out and get yourself a bottle and send in for the picture before we run out of them, it says here. The supply is limited, the man says. (Laughs.) Truth, though, is we're up to our ears in these pictures. So if you like the Briarhoppers, for goodness sake, buy a bottle of this stuff and help us get rid of these ugly pictures....

When he wasn't trading corny jokes with the Briarhoppers and making fun of the program's sponsors, Crutchfield was establishing himself as a young executive ready for bigger and better roles. Carefully groomed, with a neat mustache, elegantly dressed, and with that deep, resonant voice, he projected a maturity far beyond his years. By 1935, firmly established as the host of a wildly popular show and demonstrating impressively entrepreneurial talents as an announcer and programmer, he was also demonstrating some organizational talent.

WBT had no program log at the time. Announcers would get a cue from the network and then grab the contract and copy for the next program or the next commercial from a stack on the desk beside the microphone, hoping the sales department had the papers arranged in the correct order. One afternoon when he was off the air, Crutchfield decided his and other announcers' task would be easier, and less prone to error, if they had a program schedule and if they had the paperwork and copy filed by date and time. He took a large sheet of paper and made out a schedule in pencil and started filing the papers.

That initiative, along with his other talents, prompted the station manager to name Crutchfield program director of WBT. He was 23 years old. In just two years he had regained the title and responsibilities he had given up to come to WBT, and at a station that would provide opportunities far beyond anything that would have been available in Greenville. With the title came a raise, and the extra money he was earning as the announcer on *Briarhopper Time* exceeded his salary. In all, it was enough for him to buy a car – a late 1920s Ford.

As important as *Briarhopper Time* was to Crutchfield's reputation and career, it occupied only a small part of his day, and it didn't distract him from other opportunities for innovative programming. In the spring of 1935, 70 years after Gen. Robert E. Lee surrendered his Confederate troops to Gen. Ulysses S. Grant, ending the American Civil War, Crutchfield tracked down eight veterans of that conflict and got them into the WBT studio. On the air, he asked one of them about the "rebel yell." As Crutchfield later recalled, the old man replied, "We did it during the war to scare the hell out of the Yankees." He further explained: "In your Bible you know about the walls of Jericho tumbling down, you know, Joshua fit the battle of Jericho. We were outnumbered by the Yankees so we screamed and hollered when we were going to invade, just like they did with the walls of Jericho."

Crutchfield asked if they could still give a "rebel yell," and they did, on the air. One of the Confederate veterans became so excited after demonstrating the yell that he screamed, "Shoot the damn Yankees!"

Crutchfield learned that crooner and songwriter Gene Austin, whose recordings had sold by the millions in the 1920s, had moved to Charlotte. Crutchfield signed him to perform every Sunday night on WBT. (A daughter was born to the Austins that year, and they named her Charlotte, for the city of her birth. A year or so later, Austin moved to Hollywood, where he had a few film roles and wrote songs for the movies. Charlotte Austin grew up to become a movie actress.)

That year, Chesterfield cigarettes sponsored a CBS network program featuring Andre Kostelanetz and his orchestra performing semiclassical and light classical music. Along with comedy shows and increasingly popular afternoon dramas called soap operas (because many were sponsored by laundry products and aimed at housewives), the networks and their stations in the major urban centers continued to aspire to cultural respectability in musical programs, with suave-sounding announcers who could articulate the names of European conductors and composers without stumbling. A few American jazz and blues artists found niches in the new medium.

WBT's new program director and Briarhoppers announcer would tell anyone who asked that he knew nothing about music. As is the case with many people, his own preference was for the music of his teens, the background music of his dating and courtship years, the popular ballads of the 1920s. But he was learning from his experience with the Briarhoppers and the response to their music.

For all their variety, what made the Briarhoppers distinctive were the hoedowns and hillbilly tunes in their repertoire. Crutchfield realized it was the down-home flavor of the show and its music that was selling so much Peruna and Kolor-Back. America was entering the golden age of Broadway and Hollywood musicals, which produced much of what came to be known as the Great American Songbook. But in the Carolinas, where, before radio brought outside entertainment into homes, people were picking and singing on their front porches and at barn dances, it was the beginning of a golden age of country music and the birth of bluegrass. Crutchfield saw, heard and sensed what was happening, and he realized how important it could be to his radio station.

He was not about to abruptly dismantle the winning combination of musicians and musical styles on *Briarhopper Time*, of course. But as some of the original Briarhoppers moved on and others moved in, Crutchfield took advantage of those opportunities to shift the emphasis more toward pure country music.

With 60-hour work weeks and schedules often stretching to midnight, he was not spending as much time at home with his wife as he would have liked. He tried to make up for that with an occasional note to let Jack know he was thinking about her even though he had to be at work. He did not always sign the notes himself or acknowledge their source. For example, Jack received correspondence, on WBT letterhead, bordered on each side with rows of small photographs of babies' faces.

> Mrs. Chas. H. Crutchfield
> Montegue Appts
> North Church Street
> Charlotte North Carolina, USA
> Universe No. 6.
>
> Dear Mrs. Crutchfield,
> Knowing as how you want a baby, I have several extras up here that I'll be glad to send down COD at your request.
> Draw a cross mark on the one you like best and I'll bring it down the chimney Sunday night providing you trust your dear husband, who is trying so hard to make you happy....
>
> Yours truly, Stork, Stork and Stork, Inc.

As it turned out, the services of Stork, Stork and Stork, Inc. were not required. Chock and Jack were young, good-looking, healthy, and very much in love, and despite the demands of his job, they found time for each other. On February 13, 1935, Jack gave birth to their first child, Richard Dale Crutchfield.

CHAPTER TEN
Encounters With FDR

PPROACHING RETIREMENT IN 1977 and recalling the motivation for his hard work and long hours as a young announcer during the Great Depression, Crutchfield said: "FDR had told us that the only thing we had to fear was fear itself, but those of us with families knew better. We feared an empty belly, and the thought that the federal government owed us a living had just never crossed our minds."

Whatever Crutchfield thought of President Franklin Delano Roosevelt's rhetoric, looking back more than 40 years later from the perspective of a highly successful, well-to-do, and politically conservative executive, FDR's popularity had helped Crutchfield establish a national reputation very early in his career. And New Deal projects in the 1930s gave a boost to WBT by helping position Charlotte to become, in the decades ahead, a paradigm, perhaps second only to Atlanta, of the "New South" city.

Crutchfield once told an interviewer that he voted for Roosevelt twice, presumably in 1932 and 1936, but not after FDR announced for an unprecedented third term.

In early September of 1936, Roosevelt, running for a second term and facing opposition to his legislative agenda from conservative Southern Democrats, decided to take a trip South to try to build up support there for his campaign and his policies. He flew into Knoxville, Tennessee, and from there went in an open limousine at the head of a motorcade of Southern Democratic governors and members of Congress across the Great Smoky Mountains to Asheville, North Carolina. After a speech in Asheville, the motorcade departed on September 10 for Charlotte and what was billed as a "Green Pastures Rally" at the brand-new American Legion Memorial Stadium.

For weeks, Democratic Party faithful and New Deal supporters from the Carolinas and adjacent states had recruited people to attend and arranged for transportation to Charlotte. It was one of the major political events in the South during that election season, and CBS asked WBT to broadcast the speech live and feed it through the network to stations across the nation. The station sent its microphones, engineers, and Crutchfield to the stadium, where he was to introduce the program to the national radio audience and describe the scene just before and after the presidential address. WBT put Crutchfield on the air and on the network a few minutes before the President was scheduled to speak. At that moment, however, the presidential motorcade was somewhere between Shelby and Gastonia, some 30 or 40 miles from Charlotte.

The President's schedulers probably had not anticipated how slow the first part of the trip would be, as the motorcade had to maneuver along narrow, tightly twisting mountain roads from Asheville down through Lake Lure. After that came a succession of foothill villages and Piedmont textile towns, where schools were closed so students could see the president. Even some of the textile mills shut down during the hours Roosevelt was expected to pass through. Despite rainy weather, thousands of people gathered to see and cheer Roosevelt along the route. When the rain stopped, Secret Service men would let the top down on the President's car. When the rain resumed, they put it back up. With the slow start, the bad weather, the leisurely pace through the cheering throngs in the villages and towns, the motorcade was running almost an hour late when Crutchfield began talking into his WBT and CBS microphone at Memorial Stadium.

For some 55 minutes he improvised, describing the crowds, talking about the extensive preparations, perhaps telling his audience about the new stadium and about the political contexts of Roosevelt's visit to Charlotte and the South. It was a virtuoso performance by the 24-year-old announcer.

As the motorcade approached Charlotte, Secret Service men were putting the top down again when a downpour began. Before they could get the top back up, Roosevelt ordered them to leave it down. Thus FDR rolled into downtown Charlotte in an open car, in a drenching rain, with a beaming smile, waving to the thousands of equally soaked people jammed along the streets. The motorcade turned down Trade Street and arrived, finally, at its destination.

The crowd waiting there was estimated at 36,000, double the capacity of the stadium. North Carolina's governor, John C.B. Ehringhaus, introduced the President, and as Roosevelt was assisted to the podium, the rain stopped, the clouds parted, sunshine bathed the scene, and a rainbow appeared overhead. Roosevelt began:

Governor Ehringhaus, Mr. Mayor, my friends of Charlotte:
Notice that the rainbow shines in the sky....

The occasion prompted a *TIME* magazine correspondent to write that FDR was "the world's luckiest politician."

Crutchfield no doubt thought that the opportunity to bring that moment to a national radio audience was ample reward for the stressful 55 minutes he had just endured.

The stadium itself and its completion were major news stories in Charlotte at the time. Construction had begun several years earlier with $70,000 from an emergency relief and civil works fund established by the Roosevelt administration. When that money was used up, the project sat unfinished for months. Then with the creation of the Works Progress Administration in the spring of 1935, the city was able to get about $52,000 more in federal assistance to complete the stadium, which it did just two weeks before the Green Pastures Rally. The city's total investment in the project was less than $5,000.

The new stadium reinforced Charlotte's position as the major sports and entertainment center of the Carolinas, but it was only one of several New Deal projects that had major impacts on the city's status, growth and prosperity. The Works Progress Administration provided $200,000 for the establishment of Charlotte's first municipal airport, which opened in 1936 and, some 70 years later, was the 30th busiest airport in the world. A grant from another New Deal agency, the Public Works Administration, provided about half the $1 million-plus cost of Charlotte Memorial Hospital, which opened in 1940 and by the end of the century, as Carolinas Medical Center, was the flagship of one of the largest public hospital systems in the nation. Although many Charlotte businesses were suffering through the Great Depression, federal assistance to the city, which included money for streets and sidewalks, a park, and an art museum, was clearly a major reason the city manager could report, in 1937, that "the city of Charlotte has never been in better financial condition than it is today."

In the election November 3, a few weeks after the Green Pastures Rally, Roosevelt won a second term with a stunning 61 percent of the popular vote and the largest electoral vote margin in American history, 523-8, over Republican Alf Landon. On November 18, the President boarded the USS *Indianapolis* in Charleston, South Carolina, for a four-week cruise to South America to dramatize his "Good Neighbor" policy. That trip led to Crutchfield's second encounter with FDR during 1936.

After speaking to the Inter-American Conference for the Maintenance of Peace in Buenos Aires, Argentina, on December 1, and stops in Brazil and Uruguay, Roosevelt headed back to Charleston, where he was scheduled to arrive at 7 a.m. on Tuesday, December 15. CBS dispatched one of its top correspondents, Robert Trout, to cover the President's arrival, but Trout's plane was delayed in Richmond on Monday night. The network wired WBT, its closest station to Charleston, and asked station manager Bill Schudt to send his best announcer to broadcast Roosevelt's arrival on CBS. Schudt was gone for the evening and Crutchfield was on duty when the wire arrived. Noting Schudt's instructions that he not be contacted at night to respond to "routine" wire messages from the network, Crutchfield declared the CBS request "routine" and answered it himself. He said WBT's best announcer, Charles Crutchfield, would be in Charleston for the 7 a.m. presidential arrival.

After signing off the air at midnight, Crutchfield drove to Charleston, a trip that probably took at least five hours. He found Pier Ten, where the *Indianapolis* was expected to dock, signed on to the network, and in the early light of a winter dawn began describing the scene to his national audience. As Roosevelt was assisted down the gangplank, Crutchfield, unaware of journalist protocol for such occasions, or perhaps simply ignoring it, walked up to meet him, put a microphone in front of his face, and asked about the South American tour. The President, who was at least as good as the young announcer when it came to ad-libbing, responded with several minutes of monologue about the highlights and accomplishments of his trip. The interview was a significant broadcasting coup, putting CBS well ahead of other media reports and official statements about the historic cruise.

Crutchfield's performance on that occasion led to an invitation the following month to be part of the CBS team covering Roosevelt's second inauguration. His colleagues that day were Robert Trout and H.V. Kaltenborn, from CBS in New York. After the ceremonies and the inaugural address, Crutchfield was assigned to ride on the running board of a car in the inaugural parade and describe the scene along the way. It was one of the few occasions in Crutchfield's early career when he didn't exactly distinguish himself, as he admitted in recollections published in 1962, WBT's 40th year on the air.

"It was a nasty day, with snow and sleet falling and the ground as slick as glass," he wrote. Raised in the South, Crutchfield wasn't accustomed to functioning in such conditions.

"I huddled down inside the official car and began bullshooting – telling people that the weather was so bad that I couldn't get outside on the running board to see what was happening. Before I knew it, I had been jerked off the air, and Kaltenborn, who must have been 65 then, put on. He was perched on the running board of the car behind me and describing things to beat the band."

Crutchfield's involvement in the CBS inauguration coverage, if not his performance itself, caught the attention of the newspaper in his home town of Hope, Arkansas, which interviewed him and published a long article gushing over his rapid rise in the broadcasting industry. One of the headlines declared that Crutchfield was "in Charge of Broadcast of Roosevelt Ceremony." The article began:

"Does anybody in Hope remember a little freckle-faced, sandy-haired boy named Charles Crutchfield, who lived here about seventeen or eighteen years ago?"

It went on to report that "the sandy-haired tyke…has gone up in the world rather fast…. In fact, Charles' voice and personality are known wherever there is a radio receiving set in the South, and it wouldn't even be exaggerating to say that his circle of acquaintance takes in most of the United States. Crutchfield is, you see, one of the ace announcers of the Columbia Broadcasting System, and he has not yet turned 25 years of age…."

There followed an account of Crutchfield's brief career, jumping from station to station and finally but quickly reaching "the goal of his early ambition," a position at WBT.

> Since Crutchfield assumed direction of WBT's program department, the 50,000-watt 'Pioneer Radio Voice of the South' has risen to first range among the major stations of the country, under the expert guidance of General Manager William A. Schudt, who recognizes in Crutchfield an able assistant.

The writer even included some observations about Crutchfield's appearance, his personal life, and his young family.

> "Chock" is a Beau Brummel when it comes to dressing, and his taste in what to wear reflects an appreciation of quality and conservative dignity. He could be, very easily, a heart-breaking Romeo, for he is a handsome fellow, in a masculine way, but he disdains flirtation. And he has an extremely good reason, which is "Jackie," or Jacquelin Williams Crutchfield, a former Miami, Fla., girl, who was one of the beauties for whom the

Florida waves break their hearts on the glistening sands.... He calls her "Pee Wee."

Finally the newspaper reported that Crutchfield had just given his wife, on the occasion of the birth of their second child, "two diamond rings, valued at more than a thousand dollars."

> One, a two and a quarter carat stone mounted on a platinum band, once belonged to his mother. The other, a fringe of brilliants, also mounted on a platinum band, belonged to Jackie's grandmother, but "Chock" had it remounted and polished.

> "Her job is much harder than mine," he said. "She brought a life into the world and will shape its destiny. All I do is make the money, which anybody can do, if they work."

> ...Crutchfield works hard and he gives much, and with that formula he is making his way to the top.

Perhaps no one could more fully appreciate just how far Crutchfield had come, and how fast, than a newspaper writer in Hope, Arkansas, during the Great Depression, who no doubt also worked hard.

Chapter Eleven
Ball Games

PRESIDENTIAL VISITS to the Carolinas weren't the only high-lights of Crutchfield's banner year of 1936. Two others were pioneering ventures into sports broadcasting.

WBT had no designated "sports director" at the time, but Crutchfield, as program director, saw sports events as a promising programming opportunity. Having broadcast big league baseball from the WBT studio by monitoring inning-by-inning teletype reports from far-away games, he recognized the potential popularity of live play-by-play broadcasts – particularly if he could have the microphone actually in the press box instead of the studio.

Probably the most celebrated sports franchise in the Carolinas in 1936 was Duke University football. Wallace Wade, already a coaching legend after winning three national championships at the University of Alabama, had shocked the sports world by leaving Alabama for Duke after the 1930 season. Duke was a private university in Durham, affiliated with the Methodist church, smaller and lacking the kind of football reputation Alabama enjoyed, but Wade quickly built a national powerhouse there. In his third season the Blue Devils won nine games and lost only one and had their first All-American player, tackle Fred Crawford. In 1935 they won the Southern Conference championship, led by another All-American, tailback Clarence "Ace" Parker. In 1936, when Crutchfield decided to try broadcasting football games live on WBT, he took a characteristically bold first step: he contacted Wallace Wade and headed for Durham.

It wasn't a new idea, but it was still largely untested and controversial. The first live broadcast of a college football game had come in 1924, when two announcers and their microphone perched in the end zone at Ferry Field in Ann Arbor to tell listeners about the Michigan-Wisconsin game. But the commercial potential of college football broadcasts was just becoming apparent in 1936. That year, the Atlantic Refining Company bought the right to sponsor broadcasts of Yale University's six home games, and from that point the concept quickly spread across the nation.

Although Crutchfield's idea put him at the crest of a rising, fast-moving wave, it was still too new to be an easy sell. Radio itself was still new, still pushing into areas of American life where people were wary of its potential effects. Colleges and their coaches and athletic directors, for example, feared that live game broadcasts would cause people to stay at home by their radios instead of buying tickets and coming to the stadium.

Crutchfield was able to persuade Wade that live broadcasts of Duke games would mean more publicity and attention for the university and its football team. Radio exposure would expand the Blue Devils' fan base even farther beyond its student and alumni core. And Coach Wade probably was confident in his team's ability to fill the 34,000-plus seats at Duke Stadium, even if the games could be heard on radio.

But Duke was a member of the Southern Conference, which prohibited live radio coverage of football games. Crutchfield would have to persuade the conference to rescind the prohibition. Not all the schools and coaches in the conference were as confident as Wade about attendance. For less successful teams than Duke, there was also the fear that football fans generally might prefer to listen to a Duke game than to come in person to a game at some other campus.

Crutchfield got an audience with Southern Conference officials in Richmond and, with Wade's help, made the case. Broadcasts, he argued, would benefit all Southern Conference teams, and college football generally, by bringing the excitement of the sport into people's homes. Hearing games on the radio, people who otherwise hadn't paid much attention to college football would be motivated to see a game in person.

Interviewing a player from Spartanburg Post 28's American Legion Junior baseball team, which had just won the 1936 national championship

But perhaps the most effective part of Crutchfield's pitch was on behalf of people who were simply unable to get to games in person – including, he pointed out, the thousands of incapacitated American servicemen in veterans' hospitals.

In removing the prohibition, the conference allowed individual member schools to decide whether or not to allow radio stations to broadcast their games. Crutchfield quickly arranged for WBT to be the first radio home of Duke football. As program director, he turned the job of calling the play-by-play action over to the station's best announcer, himself. Once again, he would learn on the job, which is what you have to do when you're doing something almost nobody has ever done.

As in the 1937 inaugural parade in Washington, Crutchfield did not exactly distinguish himself. At least that is the impression created by his self-deprecating humor in recalling his early experience as a play-by-play announcer. In a letter to Walter Cronkite many years later, Crutchfield confessed that he sometimes would "start looking at some gal in the stands, taking my mind off the game, and miss a play." Then when he turned his attention back to the game and saw that the ball had changed hands, he wrote, "I'd simply run a quick play off left tackle – no gain – Clemson gets the ball on Duke's 40."

Crutchfield manned the microphone in the press box at Duke games for two seasons, but WBT continued to be the radio home for Duke football for many more years. With the Southern Conference barrier down, radio stations in the South moved quickly to acquire rights to college games, and soon football broadcasts would become a Saturday afternoon tradition across radio dials.

Duke football wasn't Crutchfield's first experience as announcer on a live sports broadcast. In the late summer of 1936, he took his WBT microphone to Spartanburg, the town where he had grown up, for the American Legion Junior Baseball World Series. The American Legion had launched the junior baseball program only ten years earlier. The same year, 1926, Duncan Park opened in Spartanburg. Over the intervening years it had hosted textile league, high school, minor league, and college baseball games. Meanwhile, Spartanburg's American Legion Post 28 fielded a team that quickly became one of the best in the nation. In 1936 the team, the ballpark, and the climax of the American Legion Junior Baseball season converged.

Duncan Park's wooden bleachers could accommodate only about 3,000 spectators, but newspaper accounts of the Junior World Series there that year put attendance at 20,000. Crutchfield was there describing the action to WBT's audience, which sprawled across the Carolinas and much of the eastern United States. Much to his and the host town's delight, the home team, Spartanburg Post 28, defeated a team from Los Angeles to win the national championship.

Shortly after broadcasting Post 28's victory, Crutchfield had to return to Spartanburg, this time not to cheer but to mourn. His sister Alice Crutchfield Johnson, just 32 years old, died September 18.

But perhaps Crutchfield's most vivid memory from 1936 did not involve presidential visits or sporting events, but the wedding of two former slaves – a 97-year-old man and a 92-year-old woman, both getting married for the first time. Crutchfield read about the wedding plans in the *Charlotte Observer* while working at the station on a quiet Sunday afternoon. He wrote this account for the WBT archives in 1962.

> It being Sunday, and little else happening, the spare engineer and I decided to cover this big event. Loading our equipment, we hopped into my car and headed...toward Pineville.
>
> What we thought would be a rather routine assignment suddenly developed complications when the Board of Deacons – after a hurried huddle – decided that it would be sacrilegious to broadcast from the church. Things were looking pretty bleak until the chairman of the board, a lean, white-haired old fellow, admitted that he "jest mite" crack one of the windows for a little "consideration."
>
> Poorer by two dollars, I climbed a plum tree outside the window, stuck the mike inside, and aired the entire ceremony. Then I jumped in the car, pulled up to the front steps, jumped out, opened the door, and told the couple that this was the official wedding car.
>
> They climbed in, and we got an interview with the couple – both of them toothless and both of them grinning from ear to ear.
>
> When I asked the groom what his plans were, he came out with this classic: "I'm gonna quit running 'round, settle down, and start raising a big family." And you know, after talking with that old buck, I wouldn't be a bit surprised if he did just that.

While her husband was off on one adventure after another, building a national reputation and enhancing his value and status at WBT, Jack was getting ready for the birth of their second child. In anticipation of an addition to the family, the Crutchfields went shopping for more living space. They found it in a duplex at 1404 East Boulevard, just south of downtown in Dilworth, the neighborhood developed by Edward Dilworth Latta in the late 1890s as Charlotte's first "streetcar suburb." Their new home was shared with the Scholtzes, who owned a commercial nursery with greenhouses and a small fish pond on the property.

Crutchfield also upgraded in the automotive department, giving up his old Ford and buying a big Oldsmobile sedan.

The baby was expected around the end of the year or early the next. Newspapers in those days made much of announcing the first baby born at a local hospital in the New Year. When New Year's Eve of 1936 passed without a new arrival in the Crutchfield family, they thought perhaps theirs would be the first newborn in Charlotte in 1937, but the baby girl came an hour or so too late for that honor. They named her Leslie Alice Crutchfield, and their family was complete.

CHAPTER TWELVE
We'll Have Manhattan

THE GLOOM AND MISERY of the Great Depression lingered into the mid-1930s. There were strong signs of economic resurgence by 1935, but a year later the recovery seemed to be losing steam. Crutchfield's career at WBT was off to a fast start, but he worked long hours, often at night and on weekends. Jack, at home, was taking care of a new baby and a toddler. For all that, the Crutchfields were, in appearance and attitude, a glamorous young couple. Photographs of them in the 1930s, individually or together, have the look of Hollywood publicity photos of movie stars. Jack had acquired some of that aura as a popular teenager in Miami; and for all his success as a country music announcer and straight man for the cornball humor of the Briarhoppers, in other aspects of his life, and with Jack, Crutchfield was a very consciously urbane young man.

Both of them smoked cigarettes, as did almost everyone they knew. At Jack's urging, Crutchfield gave up cigars, apparently the smoke of choice on the WBT staff, and began smoking a pipe. He handled it with the same panache that characterized so many of his activities.

As with many bright people of their generation, their style, in look and outlook, was born of the aesthetic, social, and behavioral revolu-

Pee Wee and Crutch, circa 1937

tions of the 1920s. Cubism and surrealism transformed the definitions and standards of visual art. Composers of serious music abandoned the old tonal centers and harmonic rules. Art deco changed the look of buildings, interior design, and graphics. Young women shocked their elders by bobbing their hair, smoking cigarettes, drinking illegal liquor, and with uninhibited dancing to jazz rhythms out of New Orleans and Harlem. Young gentlemen were still expected to practice conventional good manners, but they also wanted to be witty, suave, urbane, shockproof, and stylish.

Then the stock market crashed and the national economy went into depression and thousands of Americans were out of work and queuing up for free soup and bread. The superficiality of Roaring Twenties glamour and values became obvious. Hollywood responded with noir melodramas and realistic, gritty depictions of poverty. But hard times made people even more eager for escapist entertainment, and in response, movie makers and broadcasters also preserved some of the humor, glitz, and romance of the previous decade. Thus some of the scandalous sparkle of the 1920s survived as a bright thread into the popular culture of the otherwise grim 1930s.

A paradigm of that style and manner was the 1934 film version of Dashiell Hammett's slender mystery novel *The Thin Man*, starring William Powell and Myrna Loy as Nick and Nora Charles. Just a year after the repeal of prohibition, the movie's humorous glamorization of Nick and Nora's uninhibited, round-the-clock drinking was considered shocking. They were a very contemporary, witty, beautifully stylish, and often intoxicated couple, and the movie was distinguished less by its murder mystery plot than by Nick and Nora's funny and edgy banter.

In an early scene, Nora, who has been shopping, joins Nick in a bar and orders a drink. Noting Nick's condition, she asks, "Say, how many drinks have you had?"

He replies, "This will make six martinis."

"All right," says Nora. "Will you bring me five more martinis, Leo?"

Later in the movie, when Nick is involved in a murder investigation, Nora says, "Nicky, take care of yourself."

He laughs and says, "Why, sure I will."

"Don't say it like that," she says. "Say it as if you mean it."

"Well," says Nick, "I do believe the little woman cares."

"I don't care," says Nora. "It's just that I'm used to you, that's all."

It was an extremely popular movie, and the Crutchfields probably saw it. They were too busy, too responsible, and too ambitious to emulate Nick's and Nora's drinking habits but, to the extent his working hours permitted, they enjoyed socializing and social drinking. And a letter from Crutchfield to his wife a few months after their second child was born reveals some of the same wit and attitude epitomized in films such as *The Thin Man*.

In early June of 1937 Jack left young Dicky and baby Leslie with their grandmother – they called her Bamma – in Spartanburg and went to New York. Crutchfield would join her there a few days later for a vacation, but while he was still in Charlotte he wrote her a letter on June 9 that reads, in part:

My very Dear Mrs. Crutchfield:
    This is to advise that I have something to do besides write letters….
    Yours (all of them) arrived on schedule and if I don't have time to read them, I guess you'll tell me what you said when I get there. Else I'll take them with me and spend my vacation scanning their superb content.
    …About your chart. It was most interesting but what the hell is it. I know, you did it when you were tite one night; you're just full of little pranks, you little bugger. Anyhow, I'll be there late Sunday afternoon and you won't have to meet me at the

Holland Tunnel. After all YOU'RE the one who has never been anywhere before. Maybe you should come down to Concord and show me the way...

Oh yes, I almost forgot. The Duke Power Company replaced those two busted glasses in our car, touched up all the scratched places, and gave me a swell waxing job all because I stopped for a red light on the square the other day and their street car didn't. Kinda brushed my left rear fender but, you know old chizzling Charlie. I was ready to get in a wheel chair or suffer severe reactions if they didn't be nice. Made me mad, tho. It's a wonder I didn't take over one of their Power Plants or something.

I love you Jack, damyou.

Chock

Scrapbook pages packed with souvenirs suggest that the Crutchfields had a great time in the big city, reinforcing their sense of their own sophisticated tastes and style. According to that scrapbook evidence, their Manhattan itinerary included the Metropolitan Museum of Art, the Café Promenade at Rockefeller Center, Radio City Music Hall, and its RKO Gateway Restaurant, which beckoned patrons to "stop in for a cocktail at the bar before and after the show" and offered drinks for 25 cents and dinner entrees at prices starting at 50 cents. On Broadway, at the Winter Garden theater, they saw Vincente Minnelli's new musical, *The Show Is On*, starring Beatrice Lillie and Bert Lahr, with music by, among others, Vernon Duke, Hoagie Carmichael, the Gershwins, and Rodgers and Hart.

Back in Charlotte, now with two children under his roof, Crutchfield was determined to be the kind of father he'd never had – attentive, accessible, playful.

Old photographs from earlier that year, in late February, show them playing in the snow with Dicky and Leslie outside their East Boulevard home – Crutchfield in a handsome, belted polo coat, a fedora on his head and a pipe in his smiling mouth, Jack in dark jodhpurs and tall boots. In September the family traveled to the picturesque High Country town of Banner Elk, near the Tennessee

Riding horses in the mountains

line, to enjoy the crisp air and long views across the Blue Ridge mountains. The following spring there was an Easter egg hunt on the Crutchfield lawn, with Leslie toddling about in her Easter dress, wearing a big bonnet, and hugging a white stuffed bunny.

Bamma often visited and took care of the children to give Chock and Jack some time on their own, and the children enjoyed spending time with her and with Ralph and his family in Spartanburg.

The Crutchfields were a good-looking, fun-loving young family, enjoying life and anticipating an ever brighter future. But as well-informed people aware of the larger world around them, they were concerned, as were their country's elected leaders, about events across the Atlantic, where Nazi Germany was building a frightening war machine and making threatening gestures toward its neighbors.

CHAPTER THIRTEEN
Talent Scout

BY THE MID-1930s, WBT's announcing staff consisted of Crutchfield, Clair "Shad" Shadwell, Bill Bivens, Reginald Allen, who was probably the station's first "Esso reporter," and Caldwell Cline, who also played the violin. As program director, Crutchfield was cutting back his own announcing duties. He worked with Bill Schudt to build a staff of quality announcers and a roster of talented entertainers, consistent with the station's goal of adding more and better local programming and expanding its broadcast schedule. Crutchfield turned out to be a good judge of people and of talent, as evidenced by the number of hires who either established long and impressive careers at WBT or moved on to national recognition as broadcasters.

One who stayed was Lee Kirby, a slim Texan, hired in 1936. Kirby was enthusiastic and knowledgeable about sports and quickly became one of the pioneer sports broadcasters in the South. For many years his was the play-by-play voice on WBT's broadcasts of Duke football games. He could also handle a newscast and sometimes filled in for Crutchfield on the Briarhoppers show. Kirby finished his career at WBT.

For others, WBT was a stepping stone to bigger things. Sandy Becker, a very young New Yorker when he was hired as a WBT announcer, moved back to New York and played the lead role in a popular CBS Radio daytime drama, *Young Doctor Malone*. In the 1950s and 60s he became an innovative and much celebrated star of children's television programs.

Russ Hodges, a native of Dayton, Tennessee, was hired as a sports announcer in 1939, but soon headed north to broadcast major league baseball games. In 1949 he became the radio voice of the New York Giants and eventually moved with the team to San Francisco.

Jack Knell joined the station in 1939 after gaining national attention in May of that year with his coverage of what has been called "the greatest submarine rescue in history," off the New Hampshire coast. The submarine *Squalus* sank when a ventilation valve was left open, either through human error or mechanical failure. Many crew members were killed as water gushed into the sub, but 33 survived the initial trauma and eventually were brought to safety by boats using a new device called the McCann Rescue Chamber. Crutchfield and Schudt were looking for a real journalist to beef up WBT's news department and, based on Knell's reporting of the submarine rescue, they offered him a job. Knell had a long career at WBT and eventually went to CBS.

Crutchfield also found time to take on a major task for the Roosevelt administration. In 1938, President Roosevelt and his postmaster general, James A. Farley, designated May 15-21 as National Air Mail Week, a promotion designed to bolster the 20-year-old but sputtering air mail service. Charlotte Postmaster Paul Younts was named general chairman of the event, which may have had something to do with the selection of Crutchfield to serve as national publicity chairman.

Publicity was no problem. In the months leading up to that week in May, Crutchfield and others dreamed up a variety of activities certain to attract attention. One was a race from Washington, D.C. to New York City between an Eastern Airlines transport plane and four carrier pigeons. (The pigeons had a head start and won.) The week began with the issue of a new six-cent airmail stamp framed in dark blue with an eagle in carmine red, based on a rough sketch by

President Roosevelt himself. Every American was urged to send an air mail letter during the week, and every town was invited to create a cachet – a design or slogan to be printed on all envelopes mailed from that location on May 19. There was a student essay contest, with winners to be invited to Washington for lunch with the president. Crutchfield persuaded WLS in Chicago to fly a recording disk to various capitals around the world and record messages from their heads of state, congratulating President Roosevelt and the American people on their air mail accomplishments.

Crutchfield later became convinced that National Air Mail Week had been dreamed up by Roosevelt and Farley as a way not only to promote air mail, but also to put together a national network of people for the President's next reelection campaign. But he said that even if he had been aware of any such secret motive at the time, "it wouldn't have made any difference, because I was so excited about the postmaster general asking me to be the national publicity chairman."

Through the late 1930s and into 1940 Crutchfield strengthened WBT's increasingly important country music and gospel music programming with the addition of the Rangers Quartet, the Golden Gate Quartet, and the Johnson Family Singers. For some years the Johnsons, accompanied by veteran WBT pianist Larry Walker, were probably second only to the Briarhoppers in popularity. A mother, father, and four children, they sang gospel songs, and WBT put them on the air on Sunday mornings, as listeners were putting on their "Sunday best" to go to Sunday School and church services. One daughter, Betty Johnson, later became a jazz and pop music singer working in major markets and made several successful recordings.

Country and gospel ensembles were eager to perform on the radio for very little compensation, because the exposure led to lucrative live performances across the Piedmont and beyond.

The Dean Hudson Orchestra, a popular dance band, was also added to the schedule in 1940.

Crutchfield turned over his early morning announcing duties to the already popular Grady Cole and, recognizing the importance of agriculture across the Carolinas, he added farm reports to Cole's schedule.

"I went down to Spartanburg, where I was raised," Crutchfield later recalled. "The county farm agent down there had a library full of books on farming and gardening and all that sort of thing, so I got the back end of my car full of those, put them in an office, put some shelves up, and we made Grady Cole the farm editor.... He would answer questions on the air from those books that I brought. If you'd write in, he'd read the question one day, and the next day he'd have the answers. He started the Grady Cole Farm Club. He sent a little button if they'd write in and say they wanted to join."

The decision to put Cole in the morning slot turned out to be one of the most significant Crutchfield would ever make. Cole's farm reports earned the station a *Variety* magazine Farm Service award. More important, Cole was now signing the station on the air in the early mornings, getting his listeners through their coffee and breakfast and out the door to work, and staying around a bit longer with the housewives left behind. He related the news, including farm reports, commodities prices, and weather forecasts, all seasoned with his own peppery opinions. He also played a variety of recorded music on his program, and occasionally had live music from the Rangers Quartet.

Grady Cole's radio persona was that of a man sitting in a rocking chair on your front porch, chewing the fat, shooting the breeze, offering plainspoken, unsophisticated opinions about whatever was going on, and tossing in a few descriptions of products he thought you ought to try. His commercials were like recommendations from a friend or neighbor. His credibility as a salesman for his sponsors would make him and the radio station a lot of money. His voice was gravel and molasses, his accent was Piedmont Carolinas but without the deep country twang of many of his listeners. He predated Arthur Godfrey, one of the most important radio and television personalities of the mid-20th century, in eschewing the stentorian sound and manner of most radio announcers of his time and in telling his listeners, in a

Three legends of Southern broadcasting – Arthur Smith, Grady Cole, and
Charles Crutchfield – captured by legendary photographer Hugh Morton

friendly, almost confidential one-on-one manner, why they should buy
his sponsor's products.

As radios became increasingly ubiquitous in American homes,
Grady Cole soon had, arguably, the best-known name and voice in the
Piedmont Carolinas. For the next three decades, his would be the most
popular and influential voice on radio in the Carolinas, and as WBT's
signal strength continued to increase, far beyond his home market.
Meanwhile, the home market itself was growing impressively.

There were no audience measurement services at the time, but
the farm club gave the station a measure of Cole's audience.
Crutchfield said the membership in the Grady Cole Farm Club eventually reached 50,000, and as the numbers rose to that level, the
station took the letters and membership figures to Chicago and New
York advertising agencies and companies marketing to farmers. That
produced contracts with International Harvester and fertilizer companies, and soon the station was earning more advertising dollars
during Cole's 6 a.m. - 9 a.m. program than during all the other hours

of the day and night combined.

Cole also demonstrated his audience appeal in early 1937, after the Ohio River flooded large areas of Kentucky, including the city of Louisville. The flood took 385 lives, destroyed some $500 million worth of property, and left a million people homeless. When Cole asked listeners to send contributions to aid victims of the flood, they responded with $44,000. It was an impressive amount of money, and President Roosevelt sent Cole a plaque in recognition of his efforts.

The most interesting of Crutchfield's early initiatives as program director was the decision in 1939 to put Dr. Joseph Samuel Nathaniel Tross, PhD, DD, on the air every Sunday morning. Tross, a minister of the African Methodist-Episcopal Church, ranked as one of the more interesting citizens in the city. He was born in British Guyana in 1889, attended Oxford University in England, lived for a while in Canada, and in 1914 moved to Boston and enrolled at Harvard. He continued his education at two African-American universities, Lincoln, in Oxford, Pennsylvania, and Howard, in Washington, D.C., and then earned his doctorate at the University of Pittsburgh.

In 1919 Tross began teaching religion and philosophy at Livingstone College in Salisbury, about 40 miles north of Charlotte. He wrote a book, *This Thing Called Religion*, in 1934. When he began his radio broadcasts on WBT he was serving two African Methodist-Episcopal churches in the Charlotte area and building a reputation as an important leader and spokesperson in the local African-American community.

The messages he wrote for his radio program were thoughtful, professorial in style, focused primarily on relations between the races, and delivered in an accent that reflected his multicultural heritage and diverse educational background. It was not his purpose, and certainly not Crutchfield's, to advocate racial desegregation. In 1939, Charlotte, like the rest of the South, was racially segregated. There were separate schools for blacks and whites, separate water fountains, separate public restrooms, separate residential neighborhoods. Most of the jobs, public or private, that white people might want were not available to black applicants. Much of the segregation was a matter of law. Virtually all

Charlotte's white citizens and, no doubt, a good number of its black citizens, considered segregation the natural and appropriate order of things and not to be challenged, even though its consequences were clearly and in many cases cruelly unfair to the racial minority.

More than half a century later, after the court-ordered desegregation of public schools, after the Voting Rights Act, after legislation prohibiting segregation in employment, public accommodations, and real estate transactions, it may be difficult to appreciate the unlikely partnership of Charles Crutchfield and J.S. Nathaniel Tross. The constant theme of his radio broadcasts, Tross once said, was "interracial goodwill." He preached good will and mutual respect between the races. Later it was said that his Sunday morning messages over the decades deserved some credit for the city's relatively peaceful acceptance of school desegregation. Others doubt that it had that much impact, because the civil rights movement in the 1960s so radically changed the climate and the dynamics of race relations and the expectations of black citizens.

In the early 1940s Tross was president of a group called Community Crusaders that, among other things, successfully urged the city council to install streets lights in black neighborhoods as a way to reduce crime. Later Tross had less success lobbying the council to employ black police officers and truant officers.

He chaired the Charlotte Rationing Board during World War II, and in 1949 he became publisher of the *Charlotte Post*, a newspaper primarily serving the African-American community.

In the 1960s his influence waned as more aggressive black leadership emerged, advocating desegregation of public schools and public accommodations. Tross was bothered by the sit-ins, marches, and other confrontational tactics of the civil rights movement and feared they would create a violent white backlash. As a result he was largely dismissed as an "Uncle Tom" by younger black leaders. But in the middle years of the century his broadcasts may have laid some of the foundation for desegregation in Charlotte, by constantly reminding the city of the common humanity of the races and the importance of interracial harmony and civility.

Years later, Crutchfield would point with pride to the fact that WBT had been broadcasting weekly messages on race relations from a black minister for more than two decades before the civil rights movement became a transforming force in Charlotte and across the south.

As more and more Americans made their living talking or otherwise performing on the radio, some of them felt the need to organize for collective bargaining with their employers. The model had been set by workers in American manufacturing during the previous century after the Industrial Revolution, and just before the turn of the century by the American Federation of Musicians. The American Federation of Radio Artists was created in August of 1937 through the merger of two smaller organizations formed shortly after passage of the 1935 National Labor Relations Act. With important support from performers who, in the first decade of commercial broadcasting, had become nationally known stars, including Eddie Cantor, Edgar Bergen, Jack Benny, and Bing Crosby, AFRA successfully negotiated contracts with the two major networks, CBS and NBC, providing large raises for its members. Over the next few years, local units of AFRA were established to represent announcers and performers on individual stations. By that time, Crutchfield was program director at WBT and considered part of management, not labor. As an announcer, he could have joined the union, but he chose not to. Others on the WBT announcing staff joined AFRA and some became active in the leadership of the AFRA local in Charlotte. They persuaded the local to approve of Crutchfield's continuing role as announcer for the Briarhoppers even though he was not an AFRA member.

By the end of the decade, Adolf Hitler's aggressive policies seemed ever more likely to draw the United States into war. In March of 1939 Nazi Germany took over Czechoslovakia, and on September 1 German troops invaded Poland. Two days later, fearing that Hitler's goal was the conquest of all of Europe, Britain, France, Australia, and

New Zealand declared war on Germany. On September 5, the United States proclaimed its neutrality. The Roosevelt administration probably realized American involvement was inevitable, but there was still strong public and political support for isolationism. On September 10, Canada, with its strong British and French connections, also declared war on Germany.

Hitler responded to those declarations with more aggression. Poland surrendered in late September, and the following April the Nazis invaded Denmark and Norway. On May 10, 1940, they attacked France, Belgium, Luxembourg and Tthe Netherlands. The same day, Winston Churchill became British prime minister, and took office with a roar of defiance against Nazi aggression. The English Channel protected Britain from a ground attack, but by midsummer, German aircraft were bombing British factories and airfields, and in late August the bombs were falling on London.

In part because of radio, Americans were more immediately and intensely aware of those events than earlier generations would have been, and in Charlotte and across the nation, the idea of U.S. neutrality or isolationism was losing credibility. American armed forces were gearing up for war. Governor Clyde R. Hoey, in a speech in Charlotte on October 1, declared:

"Very soon we shall call 400,000 men in North Carolina to come in for a year's training.... We value our heritage of liberty and freedom.... In order that we shall safeguard it for ourselves and our children, and our children's children, we must make full and complete preparation for the defense of America...."

Even before it became a world war, the conflict was transforming American commercial radio, a still relatively new, entertaining novelty, good at playing music and getting laughs and selling soap, into an urgent, indispensable medium of communication, information, and inspiration.

In 1914, as what would become World War I was spreading across Europe, Charles Harvey Crutchfield, Sr. toured the major cities of the continent, wining, dining, and signing up customers for his cotton business. Now, 25 years later, with Europe engulfed in what would be World War II, he was living in Hope, 57 years old and ailing.

He had abandoned his family many years before, leaving his children with that bitter memory of him and few good ones. But when his sons, Ralph and Charles, Jr., learned that he was ill, they went to Arkansas in 1939 to visit him. When Charles, Jr., returned to Charlotte, he sent his father a letter bringing him up to date on his success at WBT and his family and enclosing photographs of the children, Dick and Leslie.

The senior Crutchfield responded in early September with a letter written in pencil on four sheets of ruled paper from a small tablet. He thanked Chock for his letter and the photographs. "That boy of yours is a 'dead ringer' for you at his age," he wrote, and continued:

> Hope you and yours are well. One seems to learn later in years, that's the main thing. I have been having fever...to 102 degrees right along with some infection in my guts somewhere.... Have been to town several times to see Dr since you were here but am too weak to stay any length of time....
>
> Got your card from Roanoke, Va. Chock, I don't guess you know as I had never said anything about it but Virginia Dare is a old time kinswoman of yours. You are a direct descendant of her on my grandmother Crutchfield's side of the family.... There is a kinsman of ours lives in Garland, Texas, a man around 88 years of age now, who has many of her things, even an old flintlock gun she used herself defending... from Indians etc. Thought I'd mention this, didn't know if you would care a d--- or not.
>
> Also, you are a direct descendant of Gen. Sam Houston who won Tex. Independence from Mexico, was president of the Republic of Texas and after the state joined the Union was first Gov. of Texas. Just thought I'd mention those facts, because if I did not the chances are your kids would never know – and it surely hurts nothing to know things, whether it does any good or not.

Well I am going to have to stop. Remember me to your wife and children.

Your Dad,

CHC

He died five months later, on February 9, 1940.

Chapter Fourteen
The Sounds of War

H E WAS BORN EGBERT ROSCOE MURROW in April, 1908, to Quaker parents in a Society of Friends community along Polecat Creek in Guilford County, North Carolina. His first five years were spent in a house without electricity or plumbing. Then the family moved to the state of Washington to take advantage of free land available to homesteaders. During high school summers he worked in logging camps. He attended Stanford University, the University of Washington, and finally Washington State College, earning his way by washing dishes in a sorority house and unloading freight trains. By the time he graduated in 1930, with a degree in speech, he had been elected class president, named top cadet in the campus ROTC program, and had changed his name to Edward R. Murrow.

At a convention of the National Student Federation he made a speech urging students to become more involved in public affairs. It so impressed the other delegates that they elected him national president of the organization. That took him to New York City to run the national office of the NSF and financed visits to hundreds of American as well as European colleges and universities.

Intrigued by the new medium of radio, Murrow came up with the idea of a "University of the Air," a program that would feature notable academics and intellectuals. He presented it to the infant Columbia Broadcasting System, which liked the concept and assigned Murrow to recruit the guests.

Meanwhile, CBS President William Paley was establishing an independent news division. In the network's first few years, H.V. Kaltenborn and Robert Trout had been the news announcers, reading stories acquired from wire services and newspapers. Kaltenborn, previously a newspaper journalist, had traveled extensively abroad, and he used his knowledge of foreign affairs and European politics to add analysis and commentary to his news reports. In 1930, Paley hired another newspaper veteran, Paul White, to build and head the network's news staff.

White hired Murrow in 1935 as Director of Talks and Education, responsible for lining up people for Robert Trout to interview on his daily news program. Trout was also a North Carolina native, born Robert Albert Blondheim in Wake County in 1909.

CBS sent Murrow to London in 1937 to broadcast cultural programs, but Nazi aggression soon commanded his and his network's attention. As Hitler pushed Europe toward the brink of war, Murrow began recruiting reporters to monitor the situation first-hand and keep American listeners informed. Probably the first was William L. Shirer, former European correspondent for the *Chicago Tribune* and then in Berlin for International News Service. Murrow, remaining in London, established a European Bureau in Vienna and asked Shirer to cover the continent from there.

On Sunday night, March 13, 1938, after Hitler used military intimidation to annex Austria, Trout and Murrow put together a program of live reports from correspondents in several European capitals, including Vienna. To transmit the reports from various points on the continent across the Atlantic to the United States, they used the short wave radio technology that had largely replaced cable in transoceanic communication. It was a revolutionary programming concept and became the model for the *CBS World News Roundup*, which would set the standard for radio news broadcasts for decades.

Other Murrow recruits were Eric Sevareid, Charles Collingwood, and Richard C. Hottelet. They became known within the network as "Murrow's boys." Their reporting in the late 1930s helped erode American resistance to joining the war against Nazi Germany. The incessant static and frequently poor reception of those long-distance broadcasts only added to their dramatic impact and caused people to listen more intently. Within a few years their names and voices were familiar to hundreds of thousands of American families, who sat by their radios each evening to get the latest news from foreign battlefields.

But it was Murrow himself who became the best known and most celebrated radio journalist of the era, beginning in the late summer and early fall of 1940 during the Battle of Britain. As Germany attacked England from the air, Murrow's live, first-hand reports gave Americans a cool, unvarnished but vivid account of the terror and destruction being inflicted on their Mother Country. His opening line – "This (pause) is London" – his plainspoken writing and somewhat clipped delivery set the perfect tone for his somber stories, and listeners could hear air raid sirens and bombs exploding in the background.

Late the following year, with America clearly gearing up for war but not yet officially a combatant, Murrow returned to the United States for a visit and a dinner at the Waldorf-Astoria Hotel hosted by CBS in his honor. More than 1,000 people attended, and CBS broadcast the event nationally. Archibald MacLeish, the lawyer, poet, writer, editor, and, at that time, Librarian of Congress, paid tribute to the honoree:

"You burned the city of London in our houses and we felt the flames," said MacLeish. "You laid the dead of London at our doors and we knew that the dead were our dead…were mankind's dead, without rhetoric, without dramatics, without more emotion than needed be. You have destroyed the superstition that what is done beyond 3,000 miles of water is not really done at all…."

A few days later Japanese bombers attacked Pearl Harbor, and a few days after that Germany declared war on the United States, and the war became a world war – the second in the first half of the 20th century. Murrow returned to London and hired more reporters, in-

Crutchfield with Edward R. Murrow
at the Charlotte airport

cluding Howard K. Smith, Mary Marvin Breckinridge, and Winston Burdett. Murrow himself reported from European battlefields and from the air, on Allied bombing raids.

In a very real sense, the war made commercial radio matter much more to Americans than it would have otherwise. Eventually it may have become as important as a source, not just of entertainment, but of information for a mass coast-to-coast audience, but the war accelerated the process. And correspondents such as Murrow and his "boys" established a quality and culture of radio journalism that would serve the nation well and carry forward into the age of television.

All of that also mattered to Charles Crutchfield and WBT. Already the dominant station in the Carolinas, WBT now had what many people regard as the most credible and distinguished network news programming of its time. Families across the Piedmont Carolinas, including many with husbands, fathers, or sons on faraway battlefields or distant oceans or flying combat missions, were listening intently to CBS News on WBT.

The quality of network news coverage of the war also demonstrated the importance of news programming in attracting listeners, encouraging many radio stations, including WBT, to devote more resources to local and regional coverage by their own news departments.

Chapter Fifteen
On the Home Front

WHILE WAR SPREAD ACROSS Europe and Americans debated whether to stay out of the conflict or join the effort to stop Nazi aggression, the U.S. government continued its peacetime functions, which in 1940 included counting the population. The 1940 census was of particular interest in Charlotte, where civic boosters and business leaders were hoping the city's population had moved past the 100,000 mark. If so, Charlotte would be the first city in the Carolinas with that distinction, which would help attract more new business and strengthen the city's position as the state's most important urban center.

An early count that spring, however, showed Charlotte coming up short of 100,000. The Chamber of Commerce, in effect, called for a recount. The afternoon *Charlotte News* offered to provide census takers with names of uncounted residents. These would be provided by publishing coupons that uncounted residents could fill out, clip, and mail to the Census Bureau. The morning *Charlotte Observer* took up the cause, offering similar coupons. Both newspapers waged vigorous campaigns that spring, asking readers again and again, "Have You Been Counted?"

A final count in June put Charlotte's population at 100,337, setting off a celebration at the Chamber of Commerce and among WBT and other local media that competed with other markets for national advertising dollars. It had taken Charlotte 172 years to attain a population of more than 100,000. It would take only 20 more years to gain the next 100,000, and then 20 more for another 100,000.

But the celebrants were also keeping wary eyes on the war, as it became increasingly clear that American involvement was inevitable. Further evidence that year was the Selective Training and Service Act, which Congress passed in 1940 and Roosevelt signed on September 16. It created the first peacetime military draft in U.S. history. The act made men age 21-35 eligible for the draft. After the United States entered the war, the age range was widened to 18-45.

Whether a man in that age range was drafted depended in part on his physical and mental fitness for military service, and also on his occupation. At 29, Crutchfield was almost in the bullseye of the age target, and he was physically and mentally fit, but as a broadcasting executive he was exempt from the draft. Broadcasting, like a number of other occupations, was considered important to national defense and the war effort, particularly in the case of a clear-channel 50,000-watt radio station. As the war began, the Federal Communications Commission designated WBT as a "key station" to serve as the communications center for a group of 25 stations in case of a national emergency.

WBT broadcast programs created specifically for men and women in military service across the Atlantic and received a large number of mail responses from those battlefields, particularly in North Africa.

There were ample opportunities for civilians to cooperate and assist in the war effort. Donations of newspapers and waste paper, rags, and scrap metal provided raw materials for production of goods needed by the military. Civic clubs assisted in such efforts, and school systems staged competitions among schools for turning in the most paper or metal or whatever was needed. Radio stations promoted those activities and kept citizens informed about what they could do to help win the war. Crutchfield was named chairman of the Public

Relations Panel of the local rationing board.

In 1942 WBT became the first station to win two *Variety* magazine awards in one year. One was for its contributions to the war effort and the other was for fostering racial good will and understanding. The next year, WBT was one of 12 stations nationally to receive *Variety* magazine's "Showmanagement" awards for demonstrating "how the American radio industry…used its head, its heart and its cosmic tools to serve the people during the second year of the war."

Even as the nation went to war, Americans maintained a measure of normal activity. Businesses, including broadcasting, were still serving their customers and pursuing income and profits.

With his salary as program director plus compensation for the Briarhoppers show, Crutchfield was prosperous enough in 1941 to build a house – two stories, four bedrooms, a circular staircase, and a bay window. It was on a spacious lot on Mecklenburg Avenue, just a short walk from Charlotte Country Club and near the house where, some 20 years earlier, Gluck, Bunker and Laxton had set up the radio transmitter that would become WBT. The new home provided Mr. and Mrs. Crutchfield and their two children more space and comfort, and proximity to the country club was a fine amenity. WBT gave Crutchfield a club membership in lieu of a raise one year, and in the sweltering Carolina summers, the Charlotte Country Club swimming pool would become an almost daily treat for Dick and Leslie. An open field next door to the house became a playground for all the neighborhood children, as did the nearby woods with a creek full of crayfish.

The house also gave Crutch and Pee Wee more room for entertaining, and they took full advantage of it. Weekend gatherings, mostly of friends in the neighborhood, with plenty of liquid refreshment, ample ashtrays, laughter, and good conversation, were a regular occurrence at 2331 Mecklenburg Avenue. They became known for hosting great parties and telling great stories. As a raconteur, Crutchfield had timing and dramatic skill, and he loved to relate humorous anecdotes and experiences, sometimes elaborating a bit to make them even funnier.

Crutchfield now had the space and opportunity to take advantage

The Crutchfields' home on Mecklenburg Avenue, built in 1941

of his handyman talents. He enjoyed fixing things, building things, growing things. He took great pleasure in his new workshop. He often didn't have the right tools for the job at hand, but instead of going out and buying what he needed, he would improvise, using whatever he had and usually making it work. He also was known to sharpen an old knife so many times there was little of the blade left.

Trick or Treat: Leslie, Pee Wee, Crutch, and Dick as Batman

He enjoyed the outdoor part of home maintenance – the lawn, planting and pruning shrubbery, building a brick terrace. He planted trees, azaleas, camellias, boxwoods, and roses, pouring on plenty of fertilizer and taking great pride in the results. He also planted what was known in the war years as a "victory garden" to provide some of the food the family needed. And he raised a few chickens.

Perhaps his favorite part of the new home was the screened back porch, where he loved to sit and relax, listening to music from the phonograph. In warm weather the family often had supper there.

Providing food and clothing for the troops and weapons and other equipment for battle meant rationing at home and led to scarcities in some consumer goods, including bicycles. One Christmas in the early 1940s when Dick Crutchfield was at an age when a boy ought to have a bicycle, Pee Wee located an old one in poor condition. She bought it and hid it in a neighbor's garage where, over several weeks prior to Christmas, she and Crutchfield repaired it and applied a coat of shiny new paint. On Christmas morning, Dick was delighted.

Meanwhile, Crutchfield continued to recruit a strong announcing staff and outstanding performers, largely in the fields of country and gospel music. In 1941 he signed the Carter family, primarily a gospel group with mother, father, and several daughters. One of the daughters, June Carter, later married and performed for years with the country music superstar Johnny Cash. That same year he brought in Claude Casey, a handsome ballad singer and yodeler, for the Briarhoppers and other country music programs. The Southland Jubilee Singers, an African-American vocal group, came on the following year.

Arthur Smith, a guitar player and songwriter, was signed in 1944. He was with the Briarhoppers for a while, and then developed his own show at WBT. His band was known as the Crackerjacks, with brothers Ralph and Sonny Smith and Tommy Faile. Arthur Smith and the Crackerjacks became one of the most popular musical groups in the Carolinas and successfully moved their radio show onto television after WBTV went on the air a few years later.

Increasingly, the emphasis in hiring announcers was on "personalities" instead of indistinguishable "radio voices" who simply read the news and announced the next program. One of those personalities, in the mid 1940s, was Fletcher Austin, a versatile announcer who was a fixture on WBT for many years.

The network also was building and improving its entertainment offerings, even as its news operation was adding able reporters and setting the standard for broadcast coverage of the war. CBS hired away three of rival NBC's most popular attractions: Jack Benny, Edgar Bergen, and Amos 'n' Andy. CBS President William Paley also began asserting more network control over content. In the pattern established in the early years of commercial radio, advertisers and their agencies would buy blocks of air time and create programs to fill them. In the 1940s Paley steered CBS into program development and eventually the network sold one-minute or 30-second advertising spots within its programs. Among the popular and long-running programs that came out of the process were *The Adventures of Ozzie and Harriet*, *Our Miss Brooks*, and *My Favorite Husband*, starring Lucille Ball. That last one was later reincarnated on television as *I Love Lucy*.

CBS News again distinguished itself with its coverage of D-Day, June 6, 1944, when 160,000 American, British, and Canadian troops landed on the coast of Normandy, France. Almost 10,000 of them died in the effort, but it began the march across the continent that would bring down the Nazi regime and end the war in Europe. By the following spring Allied troops had liberated Paris and moved into Germany. Along the way they took over one of the notorious Nazi concentration camps, Buchenwald. Edward R. Murrow was with them, and his report from Buchenwald was typical of his blunt style of reporting and its powerful impact. He offered graphic descriptions of the terrible condition of prisoners who were still alive. Those who hadn't survived, he said, were "stacked up like cordwood." He concluded his report by saying:

"I pray you to believe what I have said about Buchenwald. I have reported what I saw and heard, but only part of it. For most of it I have no words. If I've offended you by this rather mild account of Buchenwald, I'm not in the least sorry."

A rapid sequence of events was beginning that would lead to the end of World War II, and in those same weeks and months another sequence of events changed the ownership of WBT and thrust Charles Crutchfield into the upper echelons of American broadcasting.

First, with victory in Europe now in sight, President Franklin

Delano Roosevelt died on April 12 at Warm Springs, Georgia. The train carrying his body to Washington rolled up the Southern tracks through the Piedmont Carolinas, through the heart of WBT's immediate coverage area. Vice President Harry Truman was sworn in to succeed Roosevelt, and it would be up to him to finish the war.

In early 1945, in order to comply with a Federal Communications Commission rule, CBS put WBT up for sale. The announcement brought 18 bids, which the CBS board opened on May 2. Among the bidders were the Jefferson Standard Life Insurance Company of Greensboro, which owned a small Greensboro station, WBIG; Charlotte investment banker R.S. Dickson; and the *Charlotte Observer*, the city's morning daily newspaper, owned by Curtis Johnson.

WBT's relationship with the *Observer* had been up and down. In the early days of radio, newspapers had covered local stations as part of an interesting new phenomenon, provided news to be read on the air (and in the case of Grady Cole, a reporter to do the reading), and as stations began to develop reliable program schedules, newspapers published them. Then, as newspaper publishers realized that radio was becoming a serious competitor for advertising dollars, the relationship changed. The American Newspaper Publishers Association suggested that publishers should stop promoting radio. The *Observer*'s Curtis Johnson was one who took that advice. He instructed his news staff to ignore radio, apparently hoping that would make the new medium go away. The *Observer* no longer published program schedules. Newspaper photographs of events such as news conferences, in which radio microphones were present, were doctored to remove the microphones. At one point, Johnson tried to get his editors to keep the word "radio" out of the newspaper.

Given that attitude on the part of the *Observer*, Crutchfield was alarmed at the prospect of Curtis Johnson owning WBT. At lunch one day that spring at the Charlotte Country Club, he encountered one of the directors of Johnson's organization and asked about the seriousness of the *Observer*'s interest in buying WBT. The director responded that his company was quite serious and would go as high as $1.5 million to get the station. Crutchfield said he had not heard of any other bids that high, and said the *Observer* probably could get the station for that much money.

Back at his office, he telephoned Julian Price, head of Jefferson Standard, and said he admired the insurance company's reputation for integrity and hoped it would be successful in its bid to buy WBT. He also said he believed the highest bid would be $1.5 million, and if Jefferson would offer $5,000 more it would win the bidding. Price apparently took Crutchfield's advice. On May 2, CBS accepted Jefferson Standard's bid of $1,505,000, against several bids of $1,500,000. The sale still required approval by the Federal Communications Commission.

Meanwhile, on April 30, with his mad dreams of conquest shattered and allied troops moving in on his hideaway, Adolf Hitler committed suicide. A week later, Germany unconditionally surrendered.

During the war, the United States and Germany both had been rushing to develop a nuclear bomb, which scientists said would be the most devastating weapon in history. By the summer of 1945, the United States had such a bomb, ready to deliver. Although the surrender of Japan seemed inevitable at that point, President Truman decided to use the weapon in order to prevent the indefinite extension of the war in Asia and the loss of thousands more American lives. On August 6 the United States dropped an atomic bomb on Hiroshima, and on August 9 it dropped another one on Nagasaki. Japan surrendered on August 14, and World War II was over.

A week later, CBS and A.D. Willard announced that Charles H. Crutchfield would become acting general manager of WBT effective September 1, when Willard was leaving the station to become executive director of the National Association of Broadcasters.

The next day, Aug. 21, 1945, the FCC approved the sale of WBT to Southeastern Broadcasting Company, a subsidiary of Jefferson Standard Life Insurance Company created to own and operate the radio station.

During the transition, North Carolina Gov. Gregg Cherry appointed Crutchfield district chairman of the North Carolina Symphony

Society fundraising campaign, responsible for Mecklenburg, Lincoln, Gaston, Stanley, Cleveland, Cabarrus, and Union counties.

Julian Price put his son-in-law, Joseph M. Bryan, in charge of Southeastern Broadcasting. Bryan and Edney Ridge, manager of Jefferson Standard's station WBIG in Greensboro, came to Charlotte to look at WBT's studios in the Wilder Building. Crutchfield also took them on a tour of the transmitter site south of the city. There was a safety door on the transmitter cabinet that would automatically shut down the station if it was opened. Not knowing the purpose of the door, Bryan opened it before Crutchfield could stop him.

"Joe," said Crutchfield, "your first official act as president was to knock the station off the air."

Before they returned to Greensboro, Crutchfield took Bryan and Ridge to his home to meet his wife and have a drink. Bryan told Julian Price that Crutchfield, already tapped to be acting station manager starting September 1, was the right choice to run WBT.

Southeastern Broadcasting completed the takeover of WBT on September 23, 1945, and Charles Crutchfield was named general manager. Just 33 years of age, Crutchfield was the youngest head of a 50,000-watt radio station in America.

PART
3

PEACE, PROSPERITY, & TELEVISION

Crutchfield with television personality Arthur Godfrey, circa 1950

CHAPTER SIXTEEN
Morning in America, 1944-1949

ADVERTISING FOR PRESIDENT RONALD REAGAN'S successful 1984 reelection campaign was built around the theme of "morning in America." Its intention was to make voters feel good about their country and their own immediate circumstances, and even better about the future. It was an appealing and effective metaphor. Whether it was altogether accurate in 1984, it would have been unquestionably appropriate 40 years earlier.

In 1944, America was being reborn. As it led the allies toward their now inevitable victories in Europe and Asia, its military power was unprecedented and unmatched, and considered sufficient to keep despots in check and deter future aggression of the sort that had led to two world wars. Its economy, the largest in the world, seemed only to grow stronger as it responded to the challenge of the war. Its democratic values and principles were admired around the world, with the major exceptions being the Soviet Union, Japan, Nazi Germany, and China.

After three years of sacrifice, in 1944 the American people knew victory abroad was only a matter of time, and American business and government were already making postwar plans. In Charlotte that February, the City Council approved a long and ambitious list of infrastructure improvements and expansions, some delayed since the beginning of the war. The list included a cross-town boulevard, other street improvements, expansion of the airport and the water-sewer system, a new municipal auditorium and civic center, and a new library. As those plans were implemented, they became critical elements in the city's dramatic growth through the late 1940s and the 1950s.

Having achieved victory in a conflict widely regarded as the epitome of a just war, the country also experienced a sense of moral superiority, even perhaps of divinely ordained invincibility. Such views deserved the skepticism of thoughtful Americans and became a basis for questionable policies in years to come. But in 1945 those presumptions were benign in their innocence, gilded with good intentions, and were only a minor element of the buoyant optimism that was energizing the nation and lifting its spirits.

Men and women were coming home from military service to resume careers, reunite with families, marry sweethearts. Some went to college with financial assistance from the Servicemen's Readjustment Act of 1944, better known as the G.I. Bill, which also provided low-cost loans to veterans to buy homes or start businesses.

Wartime America had been a model of disciplined patriotism, hard work, faith, secular as well as religious, and sacrifice. Postwar America became a triumph of government largesse in the service of free-enterprise capitalism for the benefit of its people.

For all those reasons and more, it was a wonderful time to be running a radio station. It was even more wonderful to be running the dominant radio station in Charlotte, a city poised giddily on the brink of unprecedented growth and prosperity. That was where Charles Crutchfield found himself.

In 1944 WBT began 24-hour-a-day operation, the first station in the Southeast to stay on the air around the clock. In those immediate postwar years, people were beginning to hear about something called television, a sort of radio with moving pictures. But for many it remained, like Dick Tracy's two-way wrist radio, a preposterous science-fiction invention that would never actually materialize. In the late 1940s and well into the 1950s, radio remained the primary medium of in-home news and entertainment. Even as television stations began to pop up around the country, advertisers remained wary of the high cost and limited programming of the new medium, and put most of their dollars into tried and true radio.

It was in that brief era of postwar, pre-television radio ascendancy, and shortly after Jefferson Standard Life won its bid to purchase WBT, that Julian Price, president of the insurance company, summoned Charles Crutchfield to Greensboro to get better acquainted.

Price had started work at age 17 and for the next 20 years had gone from railroad telegraph operator to Southern Railway dispatcher to snuff salesman in his native Virginia. In 1905, when he was 38 years old, he moved to North Carolina to join the sales force of the Greensboro Life Insurance Company. He was an effective salesman and used some of his earnings and borrowed money to buy stock in the two-year-old company. Seven years later he represented Greensboro Life in successful merger negotiations with Security Life and Annuity Company of Greensboro and Jefferson Standard Life Insurance Company of Raleigh.

Price was named vice president of the merged companies, which took the name of the Raleigh firm but established headquarters in Greensboro. In 1919 he was promoted to president and became one of North Carolina's wealthiest and most influential citizens.

Price was 77 years old when Crutchfield visited his Greensboro office, but he was still a shrewd, aggressive businessman. He was conservatively dressed in the style of a mid-century American executive, but two of his eccentricities, very familiar to the people of Greensboro, were an unnecessary walking cane, which he had carried since he was a young man, and a hat, which he wore indoors as well as out. The day of Crutchfield's visit, Price was sitting in his office wearing his hat. At one point in their conversation he looked out his 14th floor window and said, "All that air out there, and I just paid a million and a half dollars for some of it. Do you think it will ever pay out?"

"Yes, Mr. Price," said Crutchfield, "I think it will. I think it will within your lifetime."

From the beginning, the station was a spectacularly good investment for the big insurance company. The following year, on October 25, 1946, Price was on Highway 421 just east of Wilkesboro, traveling from Greensboro to his mountain house in Blowing Rock, when he was killed in an automobile accident. At that point, Crutchfield later recalled, WBT had earned its parent company about $1.5 million, fulfilling Crutchfield's prophecy.

In 1946 the company changed the name of its broadcasting subsidiary from Southeastern Broadcasting Company to Jefferson Standard Broadcasting Company, promoted Crutchfield to vice president of the subsidiary, and moved the broadcasting company's headquarters to Charlotte. Joe Bryan, president of Jefferson Standard Broadcasting, remained in Greensboro. Things were off to a good start.

After Julian Price died, his son Ralph moved into the president's 14th floor office and moved Bryan from an adjacent office to one three floors below, signalling that Bryan would not be part of the new president's inner circle. But the broadcasting subsidiary Bryan headed quickly became an important source of corporate earnings, thanks largely to Charles Crutchfield. That gave Bryan his own power base to build on as long as it continued to be successful. To his credit, Bryan recognized how important Crutchfield was to that continued success.

However, the relationship between Crutchfield and Bryan was a bit prickly at first. Crutchfield attributed that to Bryan's experience as a sergeant in the military, which made him inclined to be hands-on and bossy with his new subordinate. He was a sometimes brusque New Yorker who had come into a company of soft-spoken Southerners as the boss's son-in-law, which did not make him very popular with his colleagues in the executive offices of Jefferson Standard. And that probably made him all the more determined to make a financial success of the new broadcasting subsidiary under his direction.

Crutchfield appreciated Bryan's determination, but he didn't want or need to be managed. He had always been his own man, taking initiatives, confident in his decisions, leaving jobs when he and the boss didn't agree. He didn't like to be second-guessed, particularly by someone who didn't know nearly as much as he did about the radio business. A collision was probably inevitable. But each of the two men was so important to the other's success that they managed to cooperate with mutual respect and without open conflict.

As long as things were going well.

And in those early postwar years, things were going very well at WBT. Although it was no longer owned by CBS, it was still affiliated with the network, and CBS entertainment programs overall were the most popular network radio shows in the country. CBS News continued to set the standard for broadcast journalism. After the war, Edward R. Murrow returned to the United States as CBS Vice President of News, Education and Discussion Programs, and he continued to recruit talented journalists whose names and voices, along with those of the original Murrow's Boys, would become familiar to Americans. They included Alexander Kendrick, David Schoenburn, Robert Pierpoint, and Daniel Schorr. Murrow would resign that position two years later to return to what he did best, reporting and commenting on the news.

Some of WBT's local programming, particularly in country or bluegrass and gospel music, was comparable in quality, production values, and audience appeal to the network's. National awards affirmed the status of WBT programs and personalities. The N.W. Ayer advertising agency in 1946 honored Lee Kirby for "best all around individual performance in play-by-play broadcasting of college football." Later in the 1940s *Billboard* magazine gave first-place awards in its Music, Folk and Western division to three WBT programs. Two of the programs featured Arthur Smith. The third was *Fun by the Fireside*, with some of the WBT regulars.

The Briarhoppers' popularity was undiminished in the mid-1940s, and WBT's big signal brought them a national audience. When some of Hollywood's popular singing cowboys, including Gene Autry and Jimmy Wakely, were touring the Southeast, they would take advantage of a chance to appear on the Briarhoppers program. (Autry once

Dick and Leslie with Gene Autry at the Armory Auditorium

broadcast his weekly radio show from Charlotte's Armory Auditorium, converting that venerable venue into "Melody Ranch" for an evening. But Gene had laryngitis and wasn't able to sing.)

Even some classical musicians were fans of the Briarhoppers and wanted to appear with them. In an interview with Thomas and Lucy Warlick for their book on the Briarhoppers, Whitey Grant recalled a visit from noted violinist David Rubinoff:

"I thought surely that he would play some opera stuff that would be way over our heads. Rubinoff looked me straight in the face and said, 'Do you know *Bile Them Cabbage Down?*' You could have knocked me over with a feather…but he played it just like Fiddlin' Hank did. He had that Stradivarius fiddle, you know."

Jose Iturbi, the classical pianist who appeared in a number of movie musicals of that era, played a concert in Charlotte and asked to be on the Briarhoppers program. Crutchfield and the Briarhoppers were happy to accommodate him.

Some of WBT's local programs were broadcast nationally on CBS. One was the *Carolina Hayride*, which WBT launched in late 1944. It was recorded weekly before a live audience at Charlotte's Armory Auditorium and featured many of the country musicians already performing on the station, including the Briarhoppers, Larry Walker and the Rangers Quartet, the Tennessee Ramblers, Arthur Smith and the Crackerjacks, Fiddlin' Hank Warren, Claude Casey, Fred Kirby, Big Bill Davis, the Johnson Family, and the Southland Jubilee Singers.

Charlie Briarhopper himself was master of ceremonies and announcer, thanks to a decision to waive in his case a union prohibition against management, including program directors, working as announcers. On December 5, station manager A.D. "Jess" Willard received this message:

"We, the announcers of WBT, hereby request that you consider the selection of Mr. Charles Crutchfield as the announcer to emcee the forthcoming *Carolina Hayride* hillbilly network show to be originated by WBT… Asking you to voluntarily overlook the clause in our AFRA contract which forbids any announcing by the program director…because we are unanimous in our opinion that Mr. Crutchfield is best qualified to handle such an assignment, as proved by his work on the Briarhoppers…."

The letter was signed by J.B. Clark, Howard Turner, Alan Burke, Fletcher Austin, and Lee Kirby. Thus Crutchfield continued his announcing career as a master of ceremonies on country music shows, despite union contract prohibitions. It was a tribute not only to his talent as an announcer, but also to his popularity with the announcing staff.

After he became general manager the following year, his management responsibilities inevitably cut into his announcing schedule. As he phased out his role as Charlie Briarhopper, every other announcer at the station wanted to be his replacement, and over the rest of the Briarhoppers' tenure at WBT, most of them were, at one time or another, including Lonzo Squires, Kurt Webster, Lee Kirby, Bill Bivens, and Fletcher Austin. Grady Cole often went on the road with the band to serve as announcer on their live shows.

As general manager, Crutchfield had to handle contract negotiations with the American Federation of Radio Artists local, which represented his former colleagues on the announcing staff. It was a potentially adversarial relationship, but Crutchfield's announcing background and the good relationships he maintained with the staff served him and the station well in that role.

On a national scale, union negotiations could be more difficult, in part because of the complexities of the broadcasting industry, with its random pattern of networks, independent stations, network-affiliated stations, and network-owned stations. For example, at 10:18 p.m. on Nov. 14, 1946, Crutchfield received a telegram at his home from Howard Hausman, director of personnel relations at CBS, warning him to be prepared for a walkout if CBS negotiations with AFRA broke down. The dispute had nothing to do with the usual industrial union concerns such as wages or working hours or fringe benefits. AFRA was demanding that networks refrain from supplying programs to local independent affiliated stations that had not signed AFRA contracts, and CBS was resisting. That dispute was eventually resolved without silencing America's radios.

Management's hand was strengthened considerably by the Taft-Hartley Act, passed in 1947 over President Harry S. Truman's veto. It prohibited the "closed shop," in which an employer agreed to make union membership a condition of employment. It permitted employers to agree to "union shop" contracts under which employees would be required to pay union dues after a certain initial period of employment, but it allowed individual states to prohibit that practice. The same year North Carolina did exactly that when it became one of a number of states, mostly in the South and West, to enact Right to Work laws. Labor organizations moved quickly to challenge the state laws as unconstitutional, but without success.

Those issues had surfaced in Crutchfield's negotiations with the AFRA local earlier that year. Following the national organization's lead, the local wanted WBT to agree to a closed shop or union shop.

Apparently most of the WBT announcers, although they were represented by AFRA, were not particularly enthusiastic about the proposal. They had joined the union in the hope that membership would mean more income and better career opportunities. But many of them had grown up with Southern traditions and were offended by the idea of telling anyone they had to join a union, just as they would object to someone telling them they had to belong to a particular church.

Crutchfield objected to establishing either a closed shop or union shop, as did his bosses in Greensboro. He managed to successfully conclude negotiations on his terms by agreeing to reopen discussions on that issue if the state's Right to Work law were declared unconstitutional. It wasn't.

His handling of the matter earned praise from the network. In a letter to Crutchfield, Howard Hausman wrote that he was "impressed with the job you did" in AFRA negotiations. "It looks to me, Crutch, that you did an extremely good job all around."

Carolina Hayride aired coast-to-coast on CBS every Saturday afternoon at 2:30, and it was a huge success far beyond its home market. One of the audience measuring services of the time, C.E. Hooper, estimated that during one rating period one of every four listeners was tuned to the *Hayride*.

WBT initiated other, similar barn-dance shows carried on CBS or its Dixie Network in the 1940s, including *Carolina Calling* and *Dixie Jamboree*. The station had become a major incubator and home base for country music talent, and recording companies periodically set up shop in Charlotte to capture their music for possible commercial distribution.

It was one of the few times in his career that Crutchfield, by his own admission, failed to recognize and seize an opportunity. Nashville's WSM was broadcasting the *Grand Ole Opry* with a signal heard across most of the country, making that Tennessee city a magnet for country music performers and writers. But the talent at WBT and the power of its signal at the time put Charlotte on at least an equal basis for claiming to be America's country music capital.

Some country music archivists and historians believe the only reason Nashville eventually won that title was that WBT and Charlotte didn't stay in the game. While the *Opry* became a permanent fixture on the American folk and pop culture landscape, WBT failed to sustain its country music programs.

Wade Mainer, one of the top banjo players of that era, said in an interview years later that "Charlotte could have been Nashville. Crutchfield told me that he let it all slip through his fingers. I don't think that he really liked our type of music, and that he thought country music would never put Charlotte on the map. Crutchfield was wrong."

As a broadcaster, he obviously appreciated the appeal of country music, but he didn't take it home with him. He and Pee Wee enjoyed listening to Guy Lombardo's orchestra, Bing Crosby, Perry Como, Jo Stafford, and popular singing groups such as the Ink Spots. "Til Then" by the Mills Brothers was one of his favorite recordings. When entertaining guests, he loved to play comical records such as "I'm My Own Grandpa," "Who Threw the Whiskey in the Well?", and Spike Jones' takeoffs on well-known popular and semiclassical pieces. He also liked to sing around the house, whatever else he might be doing: "Dear Old Girl," "Precious Memories," "Easter Parade," and Christmas carols. And he loved old hymns and spirituals.

Whatever his personal tastes, it was Crutchfield who recognized the appeal of country music to WBT's audience, who created and nurtured and became one of the Briarhoppers, who recruited so much country music talent to WBT. But he admitted in a newspaper interview after he retired that he "just didn't realize that bluegrass and country music would become as popular as they did."

Maybe so. But he also had other things on his mind, things Charlie Briarhopper would never think about. He was taking on more management responsibility, dealing with new ownership that included some of North Carolina's most prominent businessmen, becoming part of Charlotte's business and civic leadership. And, having seen the important function of broadcast journalism, national and local, during the war, he was surely spending more time pondering WBT's role as a community, state, and national institution and a participant in the critical dialogues about policies and principles in postwar America. It was time to shed the Charlie Briarhopper persona.

One of the subjects that engaged his attention was Soviet communism and the growing military power and expansionist tendencies of the Soviet Union. On March 5, 1946, Winston Churchill, the World War II British leader whose words had stirred the conscience and courage not only of his own people, but also of Americans, received an honorary degree from Westminster College in Fulton, Missouri. His speech on that occasion included these words:

> I have a strong admiration and regard for the valiant Russian people and for my wartime comrade, Marshal Stalin. There is deep sympathy and goodwill in Britain – and I doubt not here also – toward the peoples of all the Russias and a resolve to persevere through many differences and rebuffs in establishing lasting friendships.

> It is my duty, however, to place before you certain facts about the present position in Europe. From Stettin in the Baltic to Trieste in the Adriatic an iron curtain has descended across the Continent. Behind that line lie all the capitals of the ancient states of Central and Eastern Europe. Warsaw, Berlin, Prague, Vienna, Budapest, Belgrade, Bucharest and Sofia; all these famous cities and the populations around them lie in what I must call the Soviet sphere, and all are subject, in one form or another, not only to Soviet influence but to a very high and in some cases increasing measure of control from Moscow....

> In a great number of countries, far from the Russian frontiers and throughout the world, Communist fifth columns are established and work in complete unity and absolute obedience to the directions they receive from the Communist center.

Except in the British Commonwealth and in the United States where Communism is in its infancy, the Communist parties or fifth columns constitute a growing challenge and peril to Christian civilization....

I do not believe that Soviet Russia desires war. What they desire is the fruits of war and the indefinite expansion of their power and doctrines. But what we have to consider here today while time remains, is the permanent prevention of war and the establishment of conditions of freedom and democracy as rapidly as possible in all countries. Our difficulties and dangers will not be removed by closing our eyes to them. They will not be removed by mere waiting to see what happens; nor will they be removed by a policy of appeasement.

"Iron Curtain" was a powerful, ominous metaphor that resonated across the United States and the other Western democracies, signaling the beginning of what became known as the Cold War. The response of American government and popular opinion to the challenge Churchill described would be the strongest single influence on U.S. foreign and military policy for the next 40 years. It also would exert significant influence on Crutchfield's concept of patriotism and on his political views.

Meanwhile, as he thought about radio's responsibilities as part of important community and national dialogues, Crutchfield was quick to respond to critics who considered it nothing more than a vehicle for advertising, with its content shaped exclusively by commercial concerns. He was sufficiently articulate and rational to hold his own with the editorial writers in the local newspapers. For example, in response to an editorial in the *Charlotte News*, he submitted a letter to the editor, which the *News* published at length and which read, in part:

...you undertake to condemn radio for its commercial practices. An interesting study, sir, the lurching of your logic. You rise to such a crescendo of indignation, in eight paragraphs, that you arrive at the bland conclusion that radio is disappearing anyway (all of which nullifies the usefulness of your foregoing indictments against it).

Let me take some of your statements, which I presume you offer as factual, and mirror them against the actual circumstances.

You say: "Radio is the only one of the media which is completely and unashamedly commercial."

There are over 1,000 broadcasting stations on the air. About 20 percent of them have no network affiliation at all. Those who do devote an approximate average of 30 percent of their time to network programs. It is safe to say that 60 percent of what you hear on the air is produced by radio station staffs. (Do you know of one show originating in Charlotte that is produced by an advertiser or agency?) And you cannot cite a single network production which goes on the air without the supervision of a network production expert.

You say, "The successful radio programs are prepared, not by entertainment or information experts, but by advertising experts."

Is this intended to imply...that such programs as Information Please, Bob Hope, Fred Allen, the NBC Symphony, Quiz Kids, DuPont Cavalcade, Kate Smith, the Hit Parade...are produced by advertising men? If such is your implication, where are you getting your information? For it is completely fallacious....

You say, "A man who objects to a radio commercial can defend himself only by shutting off the entire program."

That's better than he can do with a newspaper, of course, and I defy you to find on any radio station advertising as noxious as some of the body odor-depilatory copy that appears in the press. There is a strong inference to be drawn from this part of your discussion that advertising, per se, is objectionable – since you state that in a newspaper a reader can overlook the advertising, while in radio a listener cannot. I call this to the attention of all advertisers now employing space in your good newspaper, to any of whom I will be happy to forward a WBT rate card with a list of availabilities.

You say, "Our measurement is totally unscientific, but we seem to note a pronounced trend away from radio listening."

...[L]et me tell you that there are over 60,000,000 radio families in the United States today; ... that federal officials predict there will be twice as many radio stations in the United States by January 1948 as there were in January 1947; ...that studies have shown that people spend more time listening to radio than they devote to any other pursuit excepting working and sleeping....

I believe most listeners would agree with me that radio has come a long way in 25 years from a standing start; that its service, as developed in a short quarter century, at least matches the service of the press of this nation, which has been operating for over two centuries.

— CHARLES CRUTCHFIELD
General Manager, WBT

CHAPTER SEVENTEEN
Magic and Power

B Y THE 1940S, DISC JOCKEYS – a term reportedly coined by Walter Winchell to describe a well-known New York City radio announcer a decade earlier – were fixtures on many American radio stations. They played popular recordings, read or played recorded commercials, sometimes read a brief hourly news report or a weather forecast, all interspersed with humorous chatter or comments about the music. The recording industry soon learned that disc jockeys, or deejays, could make a record a hit by choosing to play it, and that eventually led to illegal record industry payments to individual disc jockeys or station music directors, and the payola scandals of the 1950s and 60s. But in the more innocent years of the 40s, most disc jockeys played records of their own choice, based on their own tastes, and not all of them were new. There probably was never a better example of the power of a popular deejay on a far-reaching station to create a hit record than Kurt Webster's resurrection of "Heartaches" on WBT.

Webster, like most of the WBT announcers, was a versatile performer. He hosted a morning variety show with a live audience, called *What's Cooking?* But he holds a distinctive spot in WBT's history as a disc jockey on the *Midnight Dancing Party*, which aired Monday through Saturday nights from 11:05 p.m. until 1 a.m.

One day in 1946 a local record dealer gave Webster a stack of Decca label records that had been sitting on the shelves, unsold, for several years. Webster played them off the air and apparently was hooked by one called "Heartaches." The song was written in 1931 by John Klenner and Al Hoffman. This particular recording had been made in Los Angeles in 1938 by the Ted Weems Orchestra, nationally known from its appearances on Jack Benny's popular network radio show beginning in 1931. A crooner named Perry Como got his start singing for the Weems band in the mid-1930s, but he wasn't on their recording of "Heartaches." Instead of a vocalist, there was a whistling solo by Elmo Tanner. Webster began playing the record on his *Midnight Dancing Party*, and what happened next got him and WBT on the front page of the *New York World-Telegram*, under the byline of staff writer Ed Wallace:

> The past 60 days have shaken a lot of piano-pecking New Yorkers around in their unabridged shoulders and knee-length pleats. An old song called "Heartaches" has bounced back from oblivion, bringing bands and composer along with it.

> The company which owns the copyright will make a gentle $150,000 through the accident of having acquired "Heartaches" among 400 other tunes it bought from an inactive firm for $10,000.

> Three months ago, "Heartaches" was a long-dead ditty. Today the phonograph industry expects to sell four million records. Sixteen bands have made hasty recordings. John Klenner, who wrote it, has had his hand wrung and his back embraced with great warmth all along Broadway. In words lyrically chosen, he says; "Everybody is speaking to me again – and nobody's got more friends than a guy with a hit."

> Al Hoffman wrote the music, and he is not sad.

> Ted Weems made the original recording long ago, and had gone back West and was modestly playing the countryside. Now his band is on top again, deluged with dates, getting

$2,500 a night guaranteed....

Most amazing aspect of all is the strange, unfocused gaze one finds in Tin Pan Alley. The old order has changed, somewhat. The forgotten song backfired from Charlotte, N.C., and there is some confusion at the moment over just who wears the high button shoes, and who is a bumpkin.

A young man named Kurt Webster plays records at night on Station WBT in Charlotte. Several months ago a record dealer... gave him a pile of old Decca recordings.... Among them was "Heartaches" by Ted Weems.

It thumped out through the Carolina night and people loved it. It had a fraternity house sort of rhythm, corny but nice, and the whistling solo by Elmo Tanner was extra good....

Frantic and perplexed telephone calls came back to Lou Levy of Leeds Music Corp., to airmail orchestrations. Ted Weems heard the news, then listened to his ancient record and was embarrassed. He no longer plays that way, heavy with the banjo, wire scrapers, skirling reeds and thump thump.

Mr. Weems was not discomfited, however, to find himself hurled back to the top of the heap, making about five times as much money per night....

It all proves something pretty important to the music industry, Mr. Levy explained. Vaudeville was once the supreme song maker. Then the honor passed to big name bands. Now it is possible for a disc jockey, an obscure little guy playing records at night, anywhere in America, to bring back an old song and make it a great success. In this case it was a Carolina boy who showed Broadway how the hog ate the lettuce.

Mr. Levy, in an expansive mood, has invited Mr. Webster to come to New York as his guest, and with $150,000 from "Heartaches" filling the till, the man from Charlotte will be unlikely to taste frankfurter or see the Mills Hotel.

Time magazine, in its March 10, 1947, issue, also took note of the revival of "Heartaches," but was less effusive, crediting "a disc jockey in Charlotte, N.C." without naming him. Kurt Webster fans were irate over his anonymity in the *Time* article, and Crutchfield himself wrote a letter to the editor that was published in the March 24 *Time*. He criticized the magazine for its failure to identify the disc jockey and added, "Even the Charlotte press, not given to plugging radio, compares your story to reporting discovery of America by 'local sailor'."

Such was the magic of radio in those last few years before the advent of television, in the era of powerful signals that reached across most of the country. It could bring a Grady Cole into people's homes before they were out of their pajamas, a presence so comfortable that listeners felt they knew him almost as well as they knew their next of kin, and they needed that familiar voice as much as they needed their first cup of coffee. It could bring the sound of bombs falling on London and Ed Murrow's gritty, plainspoken descriptions of the horrors of war into American living rooms. A famous dance band playing in an elegant hotel ballroom in New York or New Orleans would also be serenading a Midwestern housewife as she cleaned up the supper dishes – and shaping the musical tastes of a teenager listening in the dark to a bedside radio in a South Carolina mill town.

A lone person sitting in a small studio in the Wilder Building in downtown Charlotte at midnight could draw thousands of people across the country, unknown to each other, in their individual homes – large or small, urban or rural – into a single, intimate audience hearing an old record that suddenly sounded new again.

Chapter Eighteen
New Signals, New Visions

AS KURT WEBSTER WAS MAKING Ted Weems' "Heartaches" a national hit, WBT's 50,000-watt signal was converted to directional, beaming north and south and heard, as WBT would boast for years to come, from Canada to Cuba. That included New York City and other major media markets throughout the eastern United States. The impact of Webster's resurrection of "Heartaches" earned him the designation of third-ranked disc jockey in the nation. It also probably had something to do with Crutchfield's invitation from the National Association of Broadcasters (NAB) to speak at their annual convention in Atlantic City in 1947. Crutchfield addressed some 2,500 program directors, station managers, and other media representatives at the NAB Program Directors Clinic on the use of recorded music in station programming.

In February of that year Crutchfield was named North Carolina Radio Chairman for Brotherhood Week, sponsored by the National Conference of Christians and Jews. A local newspaper story announcing the appointment noted that Crutchfield was "long recognized for his work in interracial relations." In 1948 he was elected Chairman of the Board of the Charlotte Salvation Army.

Through the late 1940s, Crutchfield took advantage of WBT's

prosperity to strengthen the on-air staff with new personalities. Clyde McLean was one, and he would later become best known as "Cloudy" McLean, giving nightly weather forecasts on television. Pat and Harry Snook read the *Charlotte Observer* comics on the air each Sunday morning. Pat, under her maiden name of Pat Lee, later had her own morning show on radio, a variety program aimed primarily at women, and then moved successfully into television. Snook became business editor of the *Charlotte Observer*. Jim Patterson, a versatile announcer and actor who would take on many radio and television roles, joined the station in 1949.

A significant addition to the WBT sales staff in 1948 was Wallace Jorgenson. Thirty years later, Jorgenson would succeed Crutchfield as president of Jefferson-Pilot Broadcasting.

The latest radio technology was frequency modulation, or FM, which didn't have the range of high-powered AM signals such as WBT's but provided a clearer sound within a more limited, circumferential area. In announcing the Southeastern Broadcasting Company's application to the Federal Communications Commission for permission to establish a 50,000-watt FM station, Crutchfield explained the differences between AM and FM:

> The most obvious advantage of FM broadcasting...from the listeners' standpoint, is FM's freedom from noise and static....
>
> "FM broadcasting is a revolutionary development in radio that will afford listeners far wider choice among programs, provide greater access to the microphone for groups who now feel they are inadequately represented on the radio, and put competition among stations and networks almost entirely on the basis of their respective program offerings....

Crutchfield also cited a statement by CBS President Frank Stanton, who said: "We believe that aural broadcasting of the future will be identified, almost entirely, with FM broadcasting."

Stanton's predication eventually turned out to be accurate, but not for at least another 50 years.

WBT-FM went on the air in 1947, broadcasting from a temporary tower on Spencer Mountain, about 17 miles west of Charlotte, with a signal that reached much of the Piedmont Carolinas. It carried some of the same local and network programming as WBT, with improved reception within its smaller coverage area. The WBT auditorium on the first floor of the Wilder Building was renovated to house a studio for the FM station.

The permanent transmitter and tower on Spencer Mountain were completed in 1948, and WBT-FM's effective radiated power was increased to 54,600 watts. On its hilltop location, the 500-foot tower stretched to 1,867 feet above sea level, giving the signal a radial range of about 100 miles.

Even before the new radio technology had time to have any significant impact on the broadcasting industry, WBT was moving quickly into an even more dramatic new era of communication, with profound implications for the marketplace of goods, services, ideas, entertainment, sports, culture, and politics. On February 2, 1948, the company – now Jefferson Standard Broadcasting – was granted a television construction permit by the Federal Communications Commission. It was one of the last permits awarded before the FCC, running out of Very High Frequency (VHF) channels, froze the process. The freeze would last until 1952. Crutchfield announced that WBT's television antenna would be installed atop the FM tower, and transmission was scheduled to begin the following year.

Crutchfield was appointed acting chairman of the Southern Regional Committee of the Television Broadcasters Association, created in 1945 as a sort of parallel organization to the National Association of Broadcasters to serve the emerging television industry.

Crutchfield accepted another appointment in 1948, little noted but perhaps more significant. Gov. R. Gregg Cherry named him to a committee studying the possibility of establishing a statewide educational FM radio network.

Although, as Frank Stanton had predicted, FM eventually became the standard broadcasting technology, most people through the late 1940s, the 1950s, 1960s, and into the 1970s continued to tune to AM stations. For all the publicity it generated, the first WBT-FM attracted few listeners and few advertisers. Most radios in homes and cars had no FM reception, and early FM programming gave consumers little reason to invest in new radios.

After four unprofitable years of FM broadcasting, the company in 1952 gave up its WBT-FM license. It donated all its FM equipment, valued at about $85,000, to the University of North Carolina at Chapel Hill, where it was used to establish an educational station, WUNC-FM.

CHAPTER NINETEEN
"And Now Television"

I N THE LATE 1940S the decision to establish a television station in Charlotte might have been seen as premature and ill-advised. The first television sets cost enough to impede consumer demand. A set with a screen the size of a dinner plate could cost half as much as a new automobile, or a month's income for an average family. Available programming might not be appealing enough to potential viewers to overcome the price barrier. It might be many years before the television audience in the market area grew large enough to attract significant advertising revenues. Meanwhile, the equipment required to send out a television signal also carried the high price tags that come with new technology. The talent and know-how to operate the equipment and create programs were all but nonexistent in a market the size of Charlotte. There might well be big operating losses in the early years, and there were still otherwise sensible people around who didn't think television would ever really catch on.

Crutchfield was not one of them. On a business trip to New York City in 1946 he had watched several hours of television reception and, according to a newspaper report, described the experience as "remarkably clear and free of eyestrain." He had an instinctive sense of timing, of positioning himself just the right distance ahead of the curve, and

Joe Bryan had learned to trust it. Crutchfield understood that being the first radio station in the Carolinas had given WBT an early and continuing competitive advantage. He did not intend to be among the also-rans of television in the WBT market.

In Greensboro, Bryan had his own reasons to seize the moment. He knew that WFMY, owned by the same people who now owned the Greensboro newspapers that once had belonged to Julian Price, was getting ready to build a television tower there. It was a question of which company would be first in the Carolinas to put out a television signal, and Bryan wanted it to be Jefferson. He and Crutchfield moved quickly to make that happen.

As soon as the FCC granted a construction permit in 1948, the company began moving television transmission equipment into WBT's Spencer Mountain facilities. A television antenna was installed atop the 500-foot WBT-FM tower. The new television station was assigned the call letters WBT-TV, but Crutchfield asked for and got permission to change the designation to WBTV.

In early 1949, Crutchfield spoke at a luncheon meeting of the Advertising Club of Charlotte (on the upper deck of the Ship Ahoy restaurant) about plans for the new television station. He brought WBT's chief engineer, Marvin J. Minor, to help with any technical questions the audience might have.

On April 20, the *Charlotte News* reported that WBT would have a television station on the air by August. The story was headlined: "And Now Television."

The first contract for television advertising in the Carolinas was signed later that year in anticipation of WBTV's first telecast, scheduled for July 15. The advertiser was Carolina Appliance Company of Charlotte, a distributor of Motorola products. The planned campaign was already being produced for Motorola by the Walter J. Klein Company of Charlotte in order to be ready for the first day of transmission. The historic signing was held at the Selwyn Hotel, where Carolina Appliance was displaying the latest Motorola television sets.

As technical preparations continued, Crutchfield, who would be general manager for television as well as radio, put together the management team and staff for WBTV. Long-time WBT fixture Larry Walker, assistant general manager of WBT, was named program director of the television station. Charles Bell, who had been in radio management in Chester, South Carolina, following military service as an electronics engineer, would be production manager. The business manager would be Kenneth Spicer. The sales staff would be headed by General Sales Manager Keith Byerly and Local Sales Manager Wally Jorgenson. WBT News Director Jack Knell would take on the same role for television, and Bob Covington, WBT promotion manager, would be promotion manager for WBTV. The chief engineer was Marvin J. Minor.

On July 1, WBTV began transmitting a test pattern from noon until 7 p.m. daily. It was an inert image that included a line drawing of the head of a Native American in full feathered headdress and an arrangement of various circles and parallel lines. It was an early television version of what in the computer age would be known as a "screen saver." Viewers also could use it to adjust their television sets for clarity. In those few Carolina homes that had television sets, friends and neighbors would be invited in to see the test pattern. On downtown streets, furniture and appliance stores displayed television sets in their windows, and people walking by were known to stop and stare, transfixed, at the test pattern.

In the Armory Auditorium on July 14, WBTV staged a television preview show, inviting the public to come in and see actual television programs. Just as they had with radio, newspapers would experience a lot of painful ambivalence regarding the new medium. They had an obligation to treat the arrival of television as an important news story, but they also were concerned that it might become a serious competitor for advertising dollars. But on this occasion the *Charlotte News* and the *Charlotte Observer* were obviously caught up in the excitement of the birth of the first television station in the Carolinas, and both newspapers published special editions to mark the occasion and signed on as co-sponsors of the preview show. The show continued for three days, and WBTV estimated that 12,000 people visited the Armory to see television.

Meanwhile, on the morning of July 15, a 25-year-old WBT announcer named Jim Patterson became the first face and voice on television in the Carolinas. According to some accounts of that historic moment, Patterson drove to Spencer Mountain and signed the station on live. In an interview many years later, Wallace Jorgenson, who had succeeded Charles Crutchfield as president of the company, said WBTV filmed Patterson's announcement before transmitting it. Either way, at noon that day viewers of the few television sets in the Charlotte area, tuned to channel 3, saw an American flag flying and heard the National Anthem. Then they saw Jim Patterson and heard him say: "This is WBTV, Charlotte, North Carolina, signing on Channel 3 television."

Chapter Twenty
Firing the Engineers

AFTER ALL THE excitement over the birth of the Carolinas' first television station, reality intruded. As with so much new technology, the early television sets were very expensive, and the programming initially available on WBTV provided meager incentive for consumers to buy them.

The coaxial cable from New York network studios didn't reach as far as Charlotte, so there was no way to feed live network programs to WBTV. The only way WBTV could broadcast national news film and network entertainment programming was by kinescope, produced by positioning a motion picture camera in front of a television screen while live programs were being telecast. The films of the programs on the screen were known as kinescopes and were shipped to stations in distant markets such as Charlotte, which could then put them on the air. There was no color television, of course, and the black-and-white programs on kinescope were mostly gray. Early television watchers in the Carolinas were prepared to forgive the poor quality, at least for a while, because the moving pictures were coming into their homes and they didn't have to go to a theater and buy tickets to see them. But the choices were very limited, the pictures on the screen were fuzzy, and the sets required frequent adjustment.

There was not much of an initial viewing audience to attract advertisers, and many advertisers, particularly local companies, didn't know how to use television. It required pictures, preferably moving pictures, along with the words, and most advertisers were unprepared and unequipped to produce television commercials. Given those circumstances, it probably wasn't surprising that WBTV was losing about $10,000 a month during its first few months of operation. And almost as soon as it was on the air, it became entangled in a very public labor relations controversy that made advertisers even less inclined to invest in commercial time on Channel 3.

Jefferson Standard Broadcasting's contract with the International Brotherhood of Electrical Workers was due to expire on January 31, 1949. Negotiations for a new contract began in December of 1948 and were at an impasse when WBTV went on the air in July of the following year. According to information filed with the National Labor Relations Board, the issue blocking agreement on a new contract was the union demand that all discharges from employment be subject to arbitration. The company insisted that it should determine whether there was adequate cause for discharging an employee.

Some years later, Crutchfield had a different recollection. In a 1986 interview for the Southern Oral History Program of the University of North Carolina at Chapel Hill, he said, "I would not agree to a contract that guaranteed a two-week sick leave. The reason I wouldn't guarantee it is because we had had, in the last two years, one engineer who was out a year and a half, another one who was out six months. We paid them every minute they were out. We didn't have hospital insurance, but we paid them salary. I resented the national union people coming in and saying you've got to sign this contract with a two-week sick leave clause. That was the main argument."

Given the records of the National Labor Relations Board passed on to the U.S. Supreme Court, the official reason for the impasse was the arbitration issue. But Crutchfield may well have resisted any effort by the national union to impose a two-week sick leave clause in what to him was a matter of trust and confidence between him, his company, and its employees.

When the contract expired at the end of January, WBT and WBTV technicians who were members of the IBEW continued to work at the station. Negotiations resumed in July but broke down after a few days. The employees still did not strike, but on July 9, during their off hours, they began picketing in front of the station, carrying placards, and passing out handbills accusing the company of being unfair to its technicians.

On August 24, with contract negotiations still stalled, the union employees launched a new strategy. The picketing technicians, still employed by and working for WBT and WBTV, distributed thousands of handbills on the sidewalks in front of the studios in the Wilder Building and for blocks in every direction in uptown Charlotte, and in barbershops, restaurants, and buses. Handbills also were mailed to local businesses. All of them bore the same message:

> Is Charlotte a second-class city? You might think so from the kind of television programs being presented by the Jefferson Standard Broadcasting Company over WBTV. Have you seen one of their television programs lately? Did you know that all the programs presented over WBTV are on film, and may be from one day to five years old? There are no local programs presented by WBTV. You cannot receive the local baseball games, football games, or other local events, because WBTV does not have the proper equipment to make these pickups. Cities like New York, Boston, Philadelphia, Washington, receive such programs nightly. Why doesn't the Jefferson Standard Broadcasting Company purchase the needed equipment to bring you the same type of programs enjoyed by other leading American cities? Could it be that they consider Charlotte a second-class community, and only entitled to the pictures now being presented to them?

The handbills were signed "WBT Technicians" and included no reference to contract negotiations between Jefferson Standard Broadcasting and the electrical workers' union or any conflict between the union, its members, and the company. Ten days later, on September 3, Crutchfield, with Joe Bryan's approval, fired 10 of the technicians identified as distributing the handbills. The IBEW charged the company with unfair labor practices. In a letter to each of the 10 technicians, Crutchfield stated the company's position:

When you and some of our other technicians commenced early in July to picket against this Company, we felt that your action was very ill considered. We were paying you a salary of ___ per week, to say nothing of other benefits which you receive as an employee of our Company, such as time-and-a-half pay for all work beyond eight hours in any one day, three weeks vacation each year with full pay, unlimited sick leave with full pay, liberal life insurance and hospitalization for you and your family, and retirement and pension benefits unexcelled anywhere. Yet, when we were unable to agree upon the terms of a contract with your Union, you began to denounce us publicly as 'unfair.'

And ever since early July, while you have been walking up and down the street with placards and literature attacking us, you have continued to hold your job and receive your pay and all the other benefits referred to above.

Even when you began to put out propaganda which contained many untruths about our Company and great deal of personal abuse and slander, we still continued to treat you exactly as before. For it has been our understanding that, under our labor laws, you have a very great latitude in trying to make the public believe that your employer is unfair to you.

Now, however, you have turned from trying to persuade the public that we are unfair to you, and are trying to persuade the public that we give inferior service to them. While we are struggling to expand into and develop a new field, and, incidentally, losing large sums of money in the process, you are busy trying to turn customers and the public against us in every possible way, even handing out leaflets on the public streets advertising that our operations are 'second-class,' and endeavoring in various ways to hamper and totally destroy our business. Certainly we are not required by law or common sense to keep you in our employment and pay you a substantial salary while you thus do your best to tear down and bankrupt our business.

You are hereby discharged from our employment. Although there is nothing requiring us to do so, and the circumstances certainly do not call for our doing so, we are enclosing a check payable to your order for two weeks' advance or severance pay.

Very truly yours,
Jefferson Standard Broadcasting Company
By: CHARLES H. CRUTCHFIELD
Vice President

During the picketing of the station, there were no incidents of hostile confrontation or violence. But late the following year there was at least one unsuccessful attempt, possibly related to the IBEW-Jefferson Standard Broadcasting dispute, to blow up WBTV's transmission tower. There was more than property damage at stake; there were people working at the site who could have been killed if the bombers had succeeded. One man was charged with conspiracy to bomb the tower. When police, acting on a tip, went to the tower, they saw another man tossing dynamite sticks with burning fuses toward the tower. The fuses burned out before they reached the dynamite, and the man was arrested.

For some time during and after the period of labor unrest, Charlotte police kept a guard at the Crutchfield home on Mecklenburg Avenue.

Meanwhile, the IBEW took its case to the National Labor Relations Board. The company responded, in part, by charging that the handbills deliberately avoided any mention of contract negotiations or employment issues; and therefore that the distribution of the handbills had nothing to do with labor relations, but was an act of disloyalty to their employer, with the intent to damage the company's reputation with the public and potential advertisers. The board ruled in favor of Jefferson Standard Broadcasting.

Crutchfield's letter was, typical for him, thoroughly reasoned and carefully and clearly worded, and it turned out to be influential in the National Labor Relations Board's decision, which included this statement:

> The company's letter shows that it interpreted the handbill as a demonstration of such detrimental disloyalty as to provide 'cause' for its refusal to continue in its employ the perpetrators of the attack. We agree.

The board found that the employees' "ultimate purpose – to extract a concession from the employer with respect to the terms of their employment – was lawful. That purpose, however, was undisclosed; the employees purported to speak as experts, in the interest of consumers and the public at large. They did not indicate that they sought to secure any benefit for themselves, as employees, by casting discredit upon their employer."

The union then took its case to the courts and eventually to the U.S. Supreme Court, which in December of 1953 ruled in agreement with the NLRB and Jefferson Standard Broadcasting. But in 1949, the controversy spilling across the streets and sidewalks of uptown Charlotte and into executive offices across the region did not make the new television station's difficult early months any easier.

In contrast to the IBEW controversy, Crutchfield continued to enjoy good relations with local chapters of the announcers' union and the American Federation of Musicians. Unlike those corporate executives who dealt with union representatives on an arms-length or even adversarial basis, Crutchfield took advantage of his own background as an announcer and his warm personal relationships with members of his staff to encourage friendly and cooperative negotiations. A good example of that approach was a letter in March of 1951 to Jack S. Paschal, president of Local 342, American Federation of Musicians:

> Dear Jack,
>
> This is just a note of thanks, not only for the cooperation we

have been receiving and are continuing to receive from your Local but for the spirit in which this cooperation is given.

Now that our new contract is signed, sealed, and delivered and that our negotiations were so pleasant, I simply want to assure you and all your members that we will do everything in our power to employ and keep in our employ as many boys from your Local as we possibly can.

It was of course a big disappointment to us to have to sever connections with the Briarhoppers, but I am happy that we have been able to take care of Elmer Warren and Fred Kirby, and that Whitey seems well satisfied with his new job. I hope that in the not too distant future we will be able to bring the Briarhoppers as a unit back into the family, or at least take care of the guys who have been so faithful through the years – like Claude Casey and the others.

By the way, Jack, I hope you won't wait for next negotiation time to pay us a visit. We are always glad to see you – so the next chance you have to shake yourself loose, please give me a ring and let's at least have lunch together.

Television remained financially shaky, but more and more people were realizing the new medium wasn't a passing fad and wasn't going away. It was quickly working its way into the fabric of their lives and their communities, making a television set an all but essential home appliance.

Grady Cole, the first and still the leading radio personality at WBT, apparently had no interest in being on television and remained a skeptic. He said he couldn't call television "illegitimate, because radio gave birth to it and is still supporting it."

Then, in a scramble of metaphors that may or may not have been deliberate, he added: "I'll tell you what TV is doing. It is leading the hams to slaughter. Personally, I'm going to wait until the rest of the hams are slaughtered, and then I'll have the field to myself."

CHAPTER TWENTY-ONE
The Young Executive

WITH WBTV ON THE AIR, Charles Crutchfield, still more than three years short of his 40th birthday, found himself in charge of a broadcasting empire that consisted of one of the most powerful radio stations in the United States and the only television station in the growing and prosperous Charlotte market. No longer best known as a radio personality trading corny jokes with the Briarhoppers and hosting barn dance broadcasts, he was now a young executive shouldering significant responsibilities.

As vice president of Jefferson Standard Broadcasting, he was a very public and visible representative of one of the state's corporate powerhouses. As general manager of WBT and WBTV, he was increasingly influential in national broadcasting circles.

Such a rapid ascent might have left such a young and relatively undereducated man wrestling with an inferiority complex. But rapid ascents had been the mark of Crutchfield's career, in large part because he had always projected confidence and assertiveness and had the ability to back up the image. He relished the new challenges and enjoyed the recognition, respect, and prestige that came with them.

He looked the part, of course. He always had. Even in high school he was known for being well groomed and well dressed. Looking the part may have been one reason he got the part. He enjoyed good clothes and believed in dressing appropriately for whatever he was doing. He wore suits to the office every day, kept his coat on even at his desk, and expected other men in management positions at the two stations to do the same. The only exception was when he sometimes came to the office on a Sunday. On those occasions he usually wore a sport coat and an open-necked sport shirt with the collar worn outside the coat collar.

Outside of work he also dressed for the occasion, whatever it might be, from black tie to attractive, well-made casual clothes. For yard work at his Mecklenburg Avenue home, and while building a patio there, he wore a khaki shirt and trousers. He could have left the patio and stepped right into an African safari.

There was still that basso profundo voice, which commanded attention whenever he spoke, but it now came with a touch more edge of authority, and he probably carried himself with a bit more swagger. Offsetting that was sensitivity to others' feelings and a knack for self-deprecation that softened the edge – when he wanted to soften it.

A good example of that equilibrium was a memorandum he wrote to Herb Carlborg and Wilbur Edwards of Radio Sales, which represented WBT nationally. He began by noting that he had been in his "alleged position" only a few years. "I realize of course that I am still a green station manager," he wrote, as if to suggest that their experience was far more extensive than his own, and that he might not know what he was talking about. He assured them that he was not unhappy with their performance, but he then proceeded to gently point out that too many good shows were unsold.

With bigger responsibilities came tougher decisions. Changes in the consumer marketplace and the public's tastes in entertainment were demanding new thinking about radio programming. Some of it was difficult for Crutchfield, none more so than the future of the Briarhoppers on WBT.

It was the show that, more than any other single entity, had propelled Crutchfield's career in Charlotte, and it was arguably the station's "signature" program. But advances in pharmacology and increased regulatory attention from the federal Food and Drug Administration had all but destroyed the patent medicine market and with it the advertising support for "hillbilly" music on most urban radio stations.

In an effort to salvage the program, Crutchfield persuaded Pilot Life Insurance Company, part of Jefferson Standard Life, to sponsor the Briarhoppers. That arrangement, Crutchfield later acknowledged, "went over like a house on fire." Commercials for life insurance were hardly a good fit for the spaces once occupied by Peruna and Kolor-Back. The Briarhoppers continued to tour and perform, and their surviving members were still picking and singing into the 21st century, but 1950 marked the end of their legendary program on WBT radio.

It was a difficult year in his personal life as well. On November 21, Fannie Crutchfield died in Spartanburg, just 11 days after her 66th birthday. Crutchfield's father had died 10 years earlier but, in effect, he had lost his father long before that. His mother had raised him through boyhood and well into his teens and, just over an hour's drive apart, they had remained close over the years. In that time of grieving he could take some comfort in the outpouring of sympathy in his adopted city. Some of the cards and letters, many handwritten and expressing obviously genuine and personal feelings, came from people who worked for him – janitors, engineers, announcers, sales people. Others, just as personal, from many of the more prominent citizens of Charlotte. Collectively they constituted an impressive demonstration of the Crutchfield family's status in the community, and the community's affection for Charlie, or Crutch, and Pee Wee.

Among those expressing their sympathy were two of Crutchfield's best friends, both physicians – Dr. Elias Faison and Dr. Paul Sanger. Faison, an internist, was a Davidson College graduate and captain of the football team there in the 1920s. He was one of the young doctors whose efforts led to the 1940 establishment of Charlotte Memorial Hospital, the predecessor of the Carolinas Healthcare System. Paul Sanger, a cardiologist, had been chief surgeon in the legendary 38th

Evacuation Hospital that served in England, North Africa, and Italy during World War II. After the war, with Dr. Francis Robicsek, he pioneered in heart surgery and transplants. Faison and Sanger represented heady company for a young man of Crutchfield's background, but their friendship demonstrated the appeal of his personality and his intellect.

Crutchfield with two of his best friends, cardiologist Paul Sanger and internist Elias Faison

In the Wilder Building in uptown Charlotte, Crutchfield was the boss. But his boss was in a tall building in Greensboro, as were his boss's bosses, and Crutchfield much preferred being boss to being bossed. Each December he had to bring his proposed annual budget to Greensboro for Joe Bryan's approval, and it was an ordeal he did not enjoy. Bryan questioned item after item and insisted on cuts. He still knew little about radio and television, but he could read a financial statement and he was under pressure from Jefferson Standard management and directors because of WBTV's large operating losses. Crutchfield felt the pressure of the losses, too, but he knew it would take good programs and good people to maintain WBT's standards and make the television station profitable.

On one such occasion Bryan was objecting to pay raises Crutchfield wanted to give his employees. Crutchfield had enough. He threw the budget papers across the desk, made a crude suggestion about what Bryan could do with his radio station, and walked out. Back in Charlotte, he cleaned out his desk and then went home to wait for word that Bryan had fired him.

That may have been Bryan's first impulse. If so, he quickly had second thoughts. Perhaps he didn't want that $1.5 million investment adrift without leadership while he tried to find a replacement for

Crutchfield. Or maybe he still believed, as he had from the beginning, that Crutchfield was the best person to run the radio station, and he was not going to let his anger overwhelm that judgment.

What happened next is part of the Crutchfield legend. Bryan drove to Charlotte, knocked on Crutchfield's front door, and apologized. Crutchfield was surely smart enough to respond in kind. From that day on, until Bryan retired in 1961, they were a mostly compatible and very effective team.

Crutchfield was also an executive of sorts at home and on the road with his family. He enjoyed being in charge, especially in dealing with any sort of problem or crisis. He took great pride in being able to take good care of his family, not only as a handyman and problem-solver, but also as a provider. He and Pee Wee never discussed finances in any detail within hearing of their children, and he never talked with Dick or Leslie about money. Maybe he remembered family worries about financial insecurity when he was growing up and wanted to make sure his children never felt insecure or worried about money. The parents were disciplined regarding spending for or by the children, but the issues were always about what was reasonable and appropriate, as well as affordable.

He was attentive and nurturing with the children, but it was not a child-centered home. Pee Wee was his priority. He was always affectionate with her and supportive of her interests and activities. If they sometimes had a serious disagreement or argument, it was private and without any apparent damage. Their public arguments were more humorous than rancorous. Leslie remembers them having what seemed to her a long argument about how long a slice of lemon had been in the refrigerator. He was a careful driver, not inclined to speed, and she would call him "an old fuddy-duddy" and urge him to go faster. When she was driving, he would caution her to slow down.

They gave their two children a lot of freedom to make their own choices as to how to spend their time away from school and rarely applied any pressure on them to perform up to some parental standard. The parents set the standards more by example than by edict, and

Leslie and Dick understood what was expected: responsible behavior at school, at home, and elsewhere, and a reasonable respect for social standards in conduct and appearance. The family attended Myers Park Presbyterian Church regularly, although Pee Wee, an independent thinker who had developed her own philosophy of life, sometimes expressed a bit of cynicism about organized religion. Dick recalls "her solid, home-spun wisdom" and the many times she offered friendly advice, encouragement, and commentary on life's ups and downs.

With his wife and children, Crutchfield was patient in the long view. But he was impatient in terms of immediate time. His early career as a radio announcer gave him a sure sense of when five minutes – or other designated periods of time – were up. He was always prompt, and he expected others to be prompt, too – including his wife and children.

With the children he was slow to anger, but when he let it out, which was rare, it was explosive. Leslie remembers once when she and Dick were playing Parcheesi, one accused the other of cheating, and they began to argue. Their father heard them and told them to "quit fighting." But they continued, and he burst into the room, grabbed the game board, and ripped it apart.

Both parents encouraged and supported their children's hobbies and enthusiasms, and Crutchfield took particular interest in some of Dick's activities, encouraging his bird-watching and building a taxidermy workshop for him in the basement. He tried to instill in both children his love of the outdoors, taking them camping, fishing, hunting, and even frog-gigging.

He taught Dick how to shoot and to handle firearms responsibly and safely, first with an air rifle and later a .22 rifle, and then with his own deer rifle and a shotgun. They hunted doves and quail in the fields beyond Charlotte Country Club and once went bear-hunting on Grandfather Mountain. Other hunting grounds included land south of Charlotte owned by Crutchfield's friend James J. Harris, and a South Carolina plantation owned by Dr. Elias Faison.

Crutchfield also owned a carbine given to him by Charlotte Police

Chief Frank Littlejohn, which he was told had belonged to the infamous gangster John Dillinger, and a .32 police special pistol, which he kept by his bed.

Dick became, in his own words, a "nature boy." He made good use of his taxidermy table in the basement, keeping his specimens in cigar boxes. When Crutchfield went hunting he sometimes brought home a dove or a duck for Dick to stuff and mount. During that period, Leslie, her mother, and the maid never knew what to expect when they opened the refrigerator door. On many an occasion it was mouse tail hanging out of a cigar box. Later Dick became interested in nature photography, and his father provided equipment and instruction to help him with that hobby.

With Dick in his teens, Pee Wee began accumulating information about summer camps and prep schools. In the summer of 1949 Dick spent a few weeks at Camp Chewonki, in Maine, and the following year he enrolled as a 10th grader at the Loomis School in Windsor, Connecticut.

Leslie's summer hours at the Charlotte Country Club pool led her into competitive swimming when she was 11 years old, and later she became a member of the Charlotte Aquatic Team, swimming backstroke and butterfly in statewide meets. Both parents came to her early country club swim meets to cheer her on and were delighted to see her working hard at something that was so good for her. Her favorite movie star at the time was Esther Williams, the champion swimmer who appeared in the late 1940s in a series of very successful musical films that featured her as the smiling centerpiece of elaborately staged synchronized swimming exhibitions.

Crutchfield loved taking the family to the beach. He loved fishing in the surf and from rented fishing boats – and getting a suntan. Nobody at that time had seriously sounded the alarm about skin cancer, and a trip to the beach for him meant buying suntan lotion, not sunscreen – or mixing baby oil with iodine to promote a tan. Pee Wee's skin was delicate, and she always protected herself from the sun. But he had the kind of complexion that took the sun well, turning more brown than red, and when he came home from the coast and put on his white shirt and tie, his appearance was even more striking and dashing. (In his 80s he developed several skin cancers that required surgical removal.)

The Crutchfields often vacationed in the North Carolina mountains at Linville or Blowing Rock and at Wrightsville Beach and Pawley's Island. Sometimes he rented a beachfront house and sometimes they stayed at one of the old inns at Pawley's – Newcastle or Mrs. McGregor's – where family-style meals were served to barefoot guests on the screened porch, with the children at a separate table.

Crutchfield also liked to cook. Pee Wee had primary responsibility for buying and preparing food, but for her it was simply part of her job as wife and mother. For her husband it was another outlet for his restless and wide-ranging creativity. His culinary repertoire was limited but tasty. He enjoyed spicy foods, including canned hot tamales. He especially loved to cook fresh fish and game, including frog legs from gigging expeditions to a South Carolina lake. His daughter's appetite was squelched when she saw a set of frog legs twitch as he sprinkled salt and cornmeal on it.

He enjoyed shopping for groceries and, much to his wife's consternation, often bought more than was needed, duplicating cans and jars that were already in the pantry at home. His shopping habits also created duplication in the medicine cabinet: several bottles of aspirin, several cans of bug repellent, for example. It was as if he were afraid he would run out of something he needed. Maybe he remembered running out of things as a boy, or in the first year of their marriage, and never wanted to have that feeling again.

Chapter Twenty-Two
Choo-Choo and the Redskins

WITH THE CABLE BRINGING direct network access to WBTV in place, the station's fortunes improved quickly, as did its programming, which now could include live sports events. As a pioneer in putting football and baseball games on radio, Crutchfield was quick to appreciate the even greater potential of sports on television. Thus, appropriately, the first live network telecast in the Carolinas was the football game between the University of North Carolina and Notre Dame on September 30, 1950.

The previous autumn – the final year of what became known in North Carolina as the "Justice Era," because of UNC's All-American tailback Charlie "Choo-Choo" Justice – Notre Dame, on the way to a national championship, had trounced the Tar Heels in a much publicized game in Yankee Stadium. The game was televised nationally, but with no cable to the state's two television stations – WBTV and WFMY in Greensboro – North Carolinians couldn't watch it. But in 1950 they could watch the rematch – which UNC also lost – if they had access to a television set. Those who didn't were increasingly feeling left out.

That telecast and subsequent live network programming persuaded more and more Carolinians that a television set was worth having, even though prices were still high and some families simply couldn't afford one. Another boost came the following football season when WBTV began carrying weekly Sunday telecasts of Washington Redskins games.

The Redskins were the closest thing to a Southern team in the National Football League (NFL), and team owner George Preston Marshall's strategy was to take full advantage of that proximity. He hired star players from Southern schools, including "Choo-Choo" Justice, quarterback Harry Gilmer from Alabama, and halfback "Bullet Bill" Dudley of Virginia. He arranged charter buses to bring fans from Southern cities to the nation's capital for Redskin games. Not wanting to offend fans in the still segregated South, Marshall was the last owner in the NFL, years later, to hire African-American players.

With television stations signing on in Southern markets, Marshall organized a regional network to televise Redskins games, and WBTV was part of it. Sports fans in the Charlotte area had yet another reason to want television sets.

Major league baseball games soon became a regular feature on network television. Legendary players of that era were previously known to most people only through newspaper accounts, radio play-by-play broadcasts, and brief newsreel film clips at movie theaters. Now fans in their own homes on summer Saturday afternoons could see Ted Williams, Stan Musial, Bob Feller, Willie Mays, Mickey Mantle, and all the other stars of the game, all live in action from baseball diamonds across America.

And college basketball, which traditionally had attracted little interest in the Carolinas, soon would grab the attention of television viewers across the two states in one incredible weekend; but that came a few years later.

As it began bringing live sports events, national news programs, and the world's most popular entertainers into people's living rooms, the new medium quickly came of age.

CHAPTER TWENTY-THREE
Greece

U.S. SECRETARY OF STATE Dean Acheson contacted Charles Crutchfield in 1951 and asked him to go to Greece as part of a State Department mission to restore functional and dependable public radio communications there. A decade earlier, the German invasion and occupation had destroyed much of the Greek transportation, communications, and electric power infrastructure. The occupying forces required citizens to register their radios, which were then sealed so they could receive only the signal from a government station controlled by the Nazis. When German troops withdrew in 1944 they destroyed one major transmitter and tried with limited success to disable the rest of the network.

Greece was a major beneficiary of the Marshall Plan in the late 1940s, but there were few radios in Greek homes and no reliable broadcast source of news to link the citizenry. Many Greeks had no access to up-to-date accounts of events in the capital and actions of a sometimes unstable government. Soviet-backed Greek communists spread their propaganda unchecked and unanswered. The Greek government asked the United States for technical and executive assistance in establishing better radio communications across the country.

The choice of Crutchfield for the mission began with a screening process by the National Association of Broadcasters, which provided the names of several finalists. The fact that Crutchfield had not been publicly associated with any political viewpoint or party was a point in his favor, because Acheson and the Truman administration did not want any political fallout from the appointment or the mission.

Crutchfield got Joe Bryan's approval to take two months away from the job and go to Greece. With WBTV just beginning to get a bit of traction after a slippery start, Bryan wasn't very happy about the decision, but it probably would have been difficult to deny Crutchfield an opportunity to serve his country and the recognition of his status in the industry. Later he told someone, "Charlie was always looking for a government job," and claimed that "when we started that TV station it was Larry Walker and I who did the job."

Bryan's sarcasm probably wasn't intended to be taken literally, and certainly what he said wasn't literally true. But there may have been a bit of metaphorical truth in his comment about Crutchfield wanting "a government job." After changing jobs seven times during his first two and a half years in broadcasting, Crutchfield had now been at the same place for 18 years, but still looking for the next big thing, moving quickly from bottom-of-the-order announcer to top-of-the-order announcer to program director to station boss and corporate executive. At 39, he was still restless, still looking for a new challenge. If not literally a "government job," it wouldn't be at all surprising if he wanted to do something that mattered in the larger scheme of things.

Crutchfield's arrival at his hotel in Greece, as he later described it to his son, must have been a bit unsettling. There were fresh bullet and shelling holes on many of the surrounding buildings. When he got to his room he found a radio, tuned it to Radio Moscow, and heard a voice, in flawless English, expressing a hearty welcome to "Charles H. Crutchfield of the Voice of America." If he had hoped to slip quietly into the country and accomplish his mission without attracting too much attention from Soviet agents, it was immediately obvious that it wasn't going to happen that way.

With an engineer named Ed Kerrigan to handle technical details,

Crutchfield had a successful and eye-opening two months in Greece. He saw first-hand the lingering devastation of war, even several years after it had ended. He certainly gained a greater appreciation for the blessings of American democracy and a greater fear of any kind of tyranny. He visited villages still impoverished by the war and the occupation, where the memory of atrocities was kept fresh by bullet holes in the walls of buildings and the debris left by shelling. One was Kalavatra, where the invading Nazis met fierce Greek resistance. After finally taking control, the Nazis rounded up all the surviving men and boys of fighting age, more than 1,200 in all, and killed them.

In a later interview, he described what they had found and what they had done.

> They had one haywire station in Athens and a worse one up in Salonika.... Until 1951, or until we got this network established, the government in Greece, like so many unstable governments, would change hands and it would be weeks before distant places like Delphi and Salonika and Corfu learned of the change in the government. Sometimes it would be even months before the Greeks down in the Peloponnese, and far away places like that, would hear the news. So this was a very important job that I'm very proud of. We did it and we did it effectively....

> In addition to putting in transmitters where they could hear them, we had to supply radios. A lot of these places didn't even have radios. Little towns like Kalavatra up in the mountains, where the Germans killed all the male population because of one of their soldiers getting killed, were without news sources....

> My job was negotiating with the Greek government and going to these places.... One idea I had...was in some of these little towns like Kalavatra they didn't have the money to do anything, so we put up, right in the center of town, tremendous loudspeakers with one radio, and we taught a drug store operator how to turn it on and off. It would literally blast you out

of bed. But the Greeks loved it even if it disturbed their sleep or anything else. They loved it because some of them would be two or three miles away up on a great mountain, and it was a marvelous thing. They could hear what was going on in government. They could hear regular news bulletins...."

The Voice of America had been launched before the United States entered World War II to broadcast American news and advocate American democratic principles in areas controlled or threatened by Nazi aggression. After the war, the VOA continued to operate, but its primary propaganda rival was now Soviet communism, which was attempting to spread its message, overtly in some places, and by clandestine means elsewhere, across the continent and even in the United States. Communists tried, with some success, to jam the VOA signal.

A Greek citizen politely advised Crutchfield that the language being spoken on the VOA broadcasts was not contemporary Greek, but an archaic dialect. Crutchfield promptly passed that information back to the State Department.

That year, President Truman and the Joint Chiefs of Staff announced a seaborne initiative to transmit Voice of America (VOA) broadcasts deeper into Europe and beyond the Iron Curtain. The new initiative involved stationing the Coast Guard Cutter *Courier*, with the most powerful radio transmitter ever installed on board a ship, just off the Greek island of Rhodes. The *Courier* arrived the following year in July, 1952 and continued to operate there for many years. It is unclear now whether there was any connection between that operation and the network Crutchfield established on land in Greece.

While in Greece Crutchfield saw how Soviet-backed indigenous communist elements maneuvered. He witnessed the threat of communist infiltration and possible takeover of shaky governments that were American allies in the so-called "free world."

Dick Crutchfield, then a student at the Loomis School, heard his father express concerns that the Soviet Union was a military threat to its neighbors and perhaps even beyond, in a speech he gave at the school in 1951. Communism was painted as a political threat to the democratic traditions and institutions of Western Europe and the United States.

When he returned home, Crutchfield was recruited for a position with the Voice of America. Despite his boss's comment about Crutchfield wanting a government job, he turned it down.

Chapter Twenty-Four
Mid-Century

THE LONG CHINESE CIVIL WAR ended in 1949 with the Communist Party of China establishing the People's Republic of China on the mainland. The communist political and economic system that Americans understandably feared as hostile to their security now reached from Russia across the northern tier of Eurasia, ruling a large part of the world's land mass and population. The same year, the Soviet Union detonated its first atomic bomb, several years earlier than American intelligence had expected, and missiles capable of delivering nuclear warheads were in development on both sides of the Iron Curtain. Now the Cold War included a nuclear arms race and was more ominous than ever.

American diplomacy and foreign policy now were shaped almost completely with the goal of stopping the expansion of communist influence and communist territory, making communism an ever larger political issue in the United States. Some American politicians made much of their own militant anti-communism and accused their opponents of having links to communism or being "soft on communism." One such politician was Richard M. Nixon, a Republican member of Congress from California who won a seat in the U.S. Senate, and two years later became vice president of the United States as running mate to General Dwight D. Eisenhower.

Anti-communist politics climaxed when Republican Senator Joseph McCarthy of Wisconsin claimed to have evidence of communists and communist sympathizers in the military, the State Department, and elsewhere in the federal bureaucracy, and in academia and among writers, artists, actors, and other prominent categories of American culture. McCarthy's accusations brought him enormous publicity but eventually disgusted his colleagues, resulting in a Congressional censure.

Even before the extremes of McCarthyism, there was a growing conviction among right-leaning politicians and voters that political liberalism was the threshold of socialism, and socialism was the penultimate step toward communism.

Though there were communists and communist sympathizers in the United States, in most cases their motives and intentions were far less threatening than McCarthy would have Americans believe. Some Americans had cheered the Russian revolution of 1917 as a triumph of a populist movement over antiquated and oppressive tyranny. Later some of those same Americans were appalled by the new and often crueler tyranny imposed by the victorious communist revolutionaries. The Great Depression also had caused many Americans, particularly in academia and the arts, to become disillusioned with capitalism and sympathetic to socialist or Marxist economic and political theories.

By 1950, most American socialists and communists were more naïve than dangerous, more concerned with economic fairness and social justice, which they found rooted in the founding documents of the United States, than with foreign ideologies. Few had any interest in overthrowing the government, and only wanted it to promote what they believed were basic American principles and ideals.

A number of loyal, patriotic American citizens believed in economic theories and systems other than pure, unregulated capitalism, and their right to advocate their beliefs was protected by the Constitution.

There were a few loyal to a hostile foreign power and working to overthrow the American government by subversion or force.

After World War II, the FBI, under the direction of J. Edgar

Hoover, devoted increasing attention to communist subversion and infiltration in the United States. Hoover compiled large files on citizens whose loyalty to the United States was absolute, but who were considered suspect by the FBI. Politicians who might be inclined to question Hoover's methods or motives never knew what he might have on them.

In the South, "conservative" white politicians attempted to discredit the first stirrings of the civil rights movement by suggesting that it was infiltrated and promoted by communists, and early civil rights leaders were soon on the FBI suspect list.

A popular CBS Radio program from 1944 until 1958, *The FBI in Peace and War*, was produced with Hoover's blessing and helped enhance the image of the bureau. Ironically, its dark, steely-edged theme music was a march from the opera *The Love for Three Oranges*, written in 1919 by Russian composer Sergei Prokofiev.

Such was the political atmosphere to which Crutchfield returned from Greece. While he had grown up in the Democratic "solid South" and had admired President Franklin Roosevelt, prevailing conservative rhetoric and the Republican Party's strident opposition to communism pulled him more to the right politically. In addition, his own corporate management opposed organized labor and liberal politics.

Crutchfield took pride in having had an African-American commentator on the air for many years, and in his reputation as an advocate for mutual respect and understanding between the races. But he also seemed to find some credibility in right-wing warnings that communists were trying to inflame racial tensions by encouraging and taking advantage of the emerging demands for desegregation and civil rights.

For example, his suspicions were aroused when his son, home for a visit from Loomis in 1952, talked about a lecture he had heard at a student assembly earlier that year. The speaker was a civil rights activist named Bayard Rustin, and Dick was impressed with his message about human rights, non-violence, and world peace. Implicit in Rustin's talk was his opposition to the militant anti-communism at the heart of U.S. foreign policy.

Rustin, like some other young civil rights leaders, had a brief flirtation with communism in the 1940s. (The Communist Party USA had been supportive of the early civil rights movement.) After becoming disillusioned with communism, Rustin continued to support pacifist and socialist causes.

Five years after speaking at Loomis, Bayard Rustin became one of the founders of the Southern Christian Leadership Conference. He was an important ally of Dr. Martin Luther King, Jr., and was the primary organizer of the historic 1963 March on Washington, where King delivered the "I have a dream" speech.

Crutchfield contacted J. Edgar Hoover, questioning whether Rustin was an appropriate speaker to be influencing the minds of American prep school students.

Soon after Crutchfield and Hoover spoke, the Loomis headmaster, William Speer, was fired mid-term.

Discussing the incident many years later, Dick said if he had known that his father might have been responsible he would have been upset and would have felt betrayed. "I happened to be very much impressed by both our headmaster and Mr. Rustin," he said.

The year of his mission to Greece, Crutchfield was named president of the Charlotte Better Business Bureau. That year he also hired Doug Mayes.

Born 30 years earlier in a log house north of Nashville, Tennessee, Mayes had grown up with a father who played fiddle and an uncle who played five-string banjo. He learned to play guitar and bass, and in his teens he worked in various country music groups in the Nashville area, in concerts and on the radio. After he finished high school he got a job at WKPT in Kingsport, Tennessee. On the morning of Sunday, December 7, 1941, he tore off a piece of news wire copy for announcer Bob Poole, and asked, "Bob, where's Pearl Harbor?" Poole joined the Navy and Mayes got his announcing job. (Poole later had a very successful radio announcing career in Greensboro.)

Mayes then volunteered for service in the Navy, and after the war used G.I. Bill money to spend two years at High Point College. He dropped out and worked in other radio jobs and in 1951 auditioned for a position at WBT-WBTV. About 40 people tried out for the job. One of three finalists, along with Mayes, was a teenager named Charles Kuralt, but he was going to college the following year. Mayes was hired, and a few months later, in 1952, he tried out for and won the job of WBTV Esso Reporter, inaugurating the station's first regularly scheduled locally produced news program. In an interview many years later, he recalled that it was "the greatest thing that ever happened to me." He became one of the most popular and respected news announcers in the station's history, anchoring news broadcasts on WBTV for the next 22 years.

After an eye-opening and busy two months abroad, Crutchfield's life was back to normal at his office in the Wilder Building and his home on Mecklenburg Avenue. But normal is a relative term. The definition was about to change.

Just two years earlier, when WBTV signed on for the first time, there were about 1,000 television sets in its coverage area. As Crutchfield returned from Greece, the number was approaching 100,000, and in another two years it would pass 400,000. Television was going to transform life in America. It would transform marketing, advertising, journalism, education, entertainment and popular culture, amateur and professional sports, even family life. At the mid-point of the century, it had not yet achieved any of that, but in barely a blink it moved from a cloudy test pattern to a central component of the residential and commercial environment. But that was not the only change that some people didn't see coming in the American way of life. Things were only temporarily on hold.

Radio was still the most important function of Jefferson Standard Broadcasting, and much of the daily fare on radio had remained unchanged since before the war. Daytime programming was aimed at the women who were at home while their husbands were at work. Staples still included the "soap operas," those serial dramas launched in the 1930s and sponsored primarily by Lever Brothers, Proctor and

Gamble, and other companies that manufactured and marketed soaps and other household cleaning products. Shows such as *Our Gal Sunday*, *Life Can Be Beautiful*, *Ma Perkins*, *The Romance of Helen Trent* continued into the 1950s, and some later became daytime television shows.

Late afternoons featured after-school programs for a younger audience: adventure serials such as *Terry and the Pirates* and *The Sea Hound, with Captain Silver and Jerry*. *The Lone Ranger*, first broadcast the year Charles Crutchfield joined WBT, continued until 1954. There were still the nighttime musical, drama, and comedy shows such as *Your Hit Parade*, *The Kate Smith Show*, *The Jack Benny Show*, *The Shadow*, *Mr. Keene, Tracer of Lost Persons*, and *Casey, Crime Photographer*.

The venerable Grady Cole still began the day for many thousands of WBT's listeners, with his rural-flavored commentary and recorded music that was probably most appreciated by people who were middle-aged or older. Late night was Kurt Webster playing recordings of current popular music, and occasional "oldies" such as "Heartaches," for a huge audience up and down the East Coast.

Popular culture, which had been transformed by the drama, emotions, and sentiments of the war years, was returning to other interests and themes. The best-selling novel of 1950 was *The Cardinal*, by Henry Morton Robinson, about "an American prince" of the Catholic Church struggling with personal issues, including his libido. Other best-selling fiction included several historical novels, *Across the River and into the Trees* by Ernest Hemingway, and a powerful but now largely forgotten book by Budd Schulberg, *The Disenchanted*, a fictional treatment of the drunken disintegration of F. Scott Fitzgerald.

Atop the non-fiction list was Betty Crocker's *Picture Cook Book*, followed by *The Baby*, *Look Younger, Live Longer*, and *How I Raised Myself from Failure to Success in Selling* – all reflecting the preoccupations of a society readjusting to peacetime norms.

The Academy Award for best motion picture of 1950 went to *All About Eve*, starring Bette Davis as an aging Broadway star and Anne

Baxter as a young, ambitious, and manipulative fan. Somewhere down in the cast was a young blonde named Marilyn Monroe.

The top five recordings in popular music that year were "Daddy's Little Girl," by the Mills Brothers, "Mona Lisa," by Nat "King" Cole, "Music! Music! Music!" by Teresa Brewer, "Tennessee Waltz," by Patti Page, and "A Bushel and a Peck," by Perry Como.

There was nothing particularly challenging, abrasive, or otherwise discomfiting going on. With the exception of the dissonant tones and fractured rhythms coming out of a few Harlem jazz clubs, to which the general public was mostly oblivious, it was a very comfortable social and cultural environment. (*Life* magazine took bemused notice of the jazz genre called bebop in a 1948 article that focused more on Dizzy Gillespie's horn-rimmed glasses, goatee, and beret than on his musical genius. Few people actually listened to the music, and some who had didn't care for it.)

In 1950, Jack Kerouac was somewhere on the road, scribbling notes that would become a famous novel, but it would not be published until 1957. Hugh Hefner, on the staff at *Esquire*, was dreaming about starting a magazine of his own.

A young teenager named Elvis Aaron Presley had just moved with his parents to Memphis from Tupelo, Mississippi. In England, John, Paul, George, and Ringo were children. Rhythm and blues music, with its pounding pulse and sometimes suggestive lyrics, was still largely confined to black audiences and juke boxes in black restaurants and bars and to the "R&B" or "Race" sections of record stores. (But in 1951 there was a harbinger on the Pop music charts. "Sixty-Minute Man," by Billy Ward and the Dominoes, banned by many radio stations for its salacious content, made it to Number 17. Some historians of American popular music now consider it the first rock-and-roll record.)

In 1951, a reproductive physiologist named Gregory Pincus obtained a small grant from Planned Parenthood to begin the hormonal contraceptive research that would lead to birth control pills, which came on the U.S. market in 1960.

Khakis and crew cuts had moved comfortably from military bases to college campuses. Outside the shadowy, smoky world of jazz musicians and hipster junkies, marijuana and more serious illegal drugs were all but unknown.

Troops from Communist North Korea invaded South Korea on June 25, 1950, and on July 1 a U.S. infantry unit arrived on that distant little peninsula between the Yellow Sea and the Sea of Japan – perhaps not so much to protect South Korea from an aggressive neighbor to the north, but to protect it from communism. Even that was only a vaguely ominous distraction for most Americans, many of whom thought U.S. forces would clean up the situation pretty quickly.

America was enjoying a prolonged moment of comforting conformity, poised at mid-century on the brink of chaos.

African-Americans who had served in wartime were angry to find the same old discrimination waiting for them when they came home. The crusade for desegregation and civil rights was about to challenge America's character and conscience. The age of television was just beginning, and that would have been change enough, but the age of sex, drugs, and rock-and-roll was just ahead.

Charles Crutchfield was still a young man, but he and others of his generation soon would encounter a future that would make them feel a lot older.

PART
4

REVOLUTIONS

Crutchfield in Berlin during the late 1960s

Chapter Twenty-Five
Race and Rock & Roll

THE REVOLUTION GETTING underway in American popular music at mid-century was of a kind and a magnitude that some-one of Charles Crutchfield's generation never would have expected, although commercial radio was a significant part of it and would be reshaped by it.

With television in more and more homes, and increasingly the focus of family gatherings in the evenings, radio programming was becoming dominated by music. Unlike the early days of live band performances from the studio, or the 1940s, when stations broadcast network musical programs, music on the radio in the 1950s consisted mostly of recordings played by disc jockeys. That change transformed the market for commercial music, and the marketing of it. Listeners could hear the latest songs and decide what records and sheet music to buy and take home. Given that opportunity to listen and choose, their preferences, not the informed taste of critics or the judgment of musically educated experts, increasingly determined what was performed and recorded.

The other significant medium for presenting and marketing recorded music was the coin-operated phonograph known as the juke-box, an all but ubiquitous amenity in taverns, diners, cafes, canteens, and even some respectable restaurants from the early 1940s into the early 1960s. By the 1950s, machines aglow with rainbow colors, made by Wurlitzer, Seeburg, Rock-Ola, and a few others, could be stocked with as many as 50 vinyl 45 rpm records, representing 100 selections. From that huge inventory, usually consisting of some new material, the current hit records, and some old favorites, a listener could choose one to play for a nickel, or five for a quarter. (Later it was 10 cents per play and three for a quarter.)

Most jukeboxes were owned and maintained by companies that placed them in eating and drinking establishments for a negotiated share of the weekly proceeds. The machines were equipped with meters, so companies could tell how many times each record had been played during the previous week. The more popular selections were left on the machines longer, while less popular ones were replaced. Thus listeners voted with their nickels and, as in radio, it was a process that put the listener in charge of determining the success or failure of individual songs and performers. In offering a relatively large but limited number of selections and a method of evaluating their popularity, jukeboxes would become an important influence on radio programmers.

A jukebox operator of that era once remarked that it was the wrong business to be in if you really cared about music. His point was that if you wanted the nickels to keep pouring into the slots, you had to provide music that patrons of particular establishments wanted to hear, whether you liked it or not. A machine in a rural or small-town Southern "beer joint" would be stocked with records by such country music stars as Hank Williams, Roy Acuff, Hank Snow, and Eddie Arnold. In an African-American neighborhood cafe, the jukebox needed rhythm and blues records by black artists such as Joe Turner, the Clovers, Ray Charles, and Fats Domino. To appeal to the patrons of a family-style restaurant, the jukebox owner would stock the machine with the popular hits of the day, many of them written for Hollywood movies or Broadway musicals and performed by the likes of Frank Sinatra, Jo Stafford, Patti Page, Eddie Fisher, and Bing Crosby. If you were a jukebox operator who loved Beethoven or Artie Shaw or the Morman Tabernacle Choir, it made no difference. What paid the bills were "Your Cheatin' Heart," "Work With Me, Annie," and "How Much Is That Doggie in the Window?"

Jukebox operators were assisted in their programming decisions by the "Top 100" charts in Billboard magazine, which influenced what recordings got into jukeboxes and were influenced by how often they were played. The Billboard charts were divided into three categories: Popular, Country and Western, and Rhythm and Blues (labeled "Race" in Southern record shops). Although recordings in one category sometimes became successful in another category, those three genres corresponded quite accurately to the basic differences in jukebox locations – at that time.

The assumptions, probably accurate, were that nobody drinking beer in a rural roadside tavern would pay a nickel to hear Mario Lanza, and no white family in the Carolinas, out for a meat-and-three supper at a local restaurant, wanted to hear someone like Rosetta Howard singing "Men Are Just Like Streetcars" or "Ebony Rhapsody." But those assumptions would soon lose their validity, and if the white family included a teenager, there was a good chance he or she would be listening to rhythm and blues on the radio later that night, and maybe even had danced to "Ebony Rhapsody" on a pavilion at the beach the previous summer.

That division of the world of commercial music into three categories was also becoming the pattern in radio programming. As AM stations proliferated across the dial, more of them aimed for particular segments of the market, narrowing and focusing their programming toward particular demographic or ethnic or racial target audiences. On the leading edge of this new theory or philosophy of radio programming was Todd Storz of Omaha, Nebraska, who had an epiphany of sorts while sitting in a local café observing the jukebox.

Storz and his father, heirs to a brewing fortune, bought an Omaha radio station, KOWH-AM, in 1949. The station, like most at the time, offered soap operas, adventure series, a variety of musical selections, news, and farm reports. Its identity, and its appeal to any particular listener, depended on the time of day. Young Storz was installed as general manager of KOWH, and one day in a neighborhood café he became fascinated with the pattern of play as customers put their nickels in the jukebox and punched the buttons for a particular selection. The jukebox probably contained 25 or more records, providing 50 or more choices, but Storz noticed that the same few tunes kept playing over and over. As he continued to sit and watch and listen, he continued to hear the same handful of recordings. Most of the records on the machine were never played.

Based on that experience, Storz cleared out the existing blocks of varied programming on his station and replaced them with recorded music played by disc jockeys. The playlist was based on the "Top 40" recordings in any given week, apparently as measured by record sales and juke box play. The list would include the current top hit records plus recent hits and perhaps a few "oldies" that had been hits in years past.

The success of WKOH with its new format led other stations to make similar changes, using the "Top 40" of the particular genres that would appeal to their target audiences. Within a few years Storz owned a number of successful stations in various markets. Meanwhile, stations across the country switched to "Top 40" formats. Some of them shrunk their playlists down to a handful of records in hopes that any time a listener tuned in he would hear a favorite song, and would never hear anything unfamiliar enough to tempt him to turn the dial.

It was not a chance coincidence that the spread of Top 40 programming coincided with the proliferation of radios in automobiles. As more families were turning on TV sets instead of radios at home, teenagers in cars (some getting drivers licenses at age 14) became an increasingly important part of the radio audience.

So as the 1950s began, the era of eclectic radio, when one might hear the *Longines Symphonette*, *The Lone Ranger*, *Our Gal Sunday*, *Carolina Barn Dance*, and the CBS News on the same station, was ending. WBT was slow to change and only gradually evolved from varied programming and middle-of-the-road musical offerings. Well into the 1960s, for example, the station still featured local programs such as the *Pat Lee Show*, a sort of radio version of newspaper "women's pages." WBT's resistance to change was understandable. The station had both the gravity and momentum of a long-established, successful institution. It also had an able, creative staff, and was buttressed in that regard by its sister television station.

As more stations followed the jukebox model, the jukebox operator's advice about it being no business for someone who really cared about music would apply to radio, as well. Charles Crutchfield probably would have agreed. He certainly cared about music for its own sake, but only in a personal and casual way. He loved Guy Lombardo, the Mills Brothers, Spike Jones novelties, old hymns, and he sang a lot around the house. But radio was his business, and if a patent-medicine company in Chicago wanted to sponsor a hillbilly band on the radio, Crutchfield would provide a hillbilly band, and even become its announcer. Later he was considerably slower to respond to what amounted to the racial desegregation of the music business. In the 1950s, new trends in popular music, particularly with no advocates on his staff or among his contemporaries, were of little or no concern to him. He presided over a venerable and successful radio station and the only television station in the market. As Chock, Crutch, or Charlie Briarhopper, he had always been on the lookout for the next big thing. But not now.

Another big signal CBS affiliate that was sticking with its traditional block programming in the early 1950s was WLAC-AM in Nashville, Tennessee. But what it did with one of its blocks added considerable momentum to the changes in broadcasting and the record industry that Top 40 radio represented.

Around 1950 WLAC, with a clear-channel signal that reached much of the Midwest and eastern United States, started devoting its nighttime block to rhythm and blues music. Its target market was African American, and it had considerable success with advertisers whose products were aimed at that market. Among its major nighttime sponsors were record shops that packaged blues, rhythm and blues, and Gospel records for sale by mail. Its disc jockeys, Gene Nobles and John R., were white announcers who developed a style of patter that was energetic, sassy, and often suggestive. Whatever the station's success with the African-American audience, its programming produced a fringe benefit, perhaps unexpected: Southern white teenagers, probably by the thousands, were tuning to WLAC at night.

There were several apparent and possible reasons for the appeal of such quintessentially black music to white adolescents. Two closely related styles of music had emerged from African-American experience, culture and creativity. One was jazz, which by mid-century was becoming increasingly complex and demanding of serious musical talent. The other was blues – basic, almost primitive three-chord material with simple, repetitive lyrics. When played to a somewhat faster tempo, with drums, rhythm guitar, perhaps a bass and piano or even a horn or two, blues became rhythm and blues, and it had a powerful visceral appeal that obviously crossed racial lines.

Teenagers, white as well as black, enjoyed dancing to that throbbing, shuffling beat, and they also enjoyed the occasionally salacious lyrics. Another likely reason for the music's appeal to Southern white teenagers was that in many cases their parents would not approve of it. It was something they couldn't listen to at home, which made it all the more exciting to listen to it in a car, in the dark, with friends.

Maybe it was part of the teenage rebellion phenomenon that was about to explode into America's consciousness in 1955. In films it took the form of James Dean as the torturously misunderstood adolescent in *Rebel Without a Cause*, or the switchblade-wielding urban high school students in *Blackboard Jungle*, raising hell to the rhythm of "Rock Around the Clock."

Many teenagers identified with the characters from those movies, but far fewer actually put the idea of rebellion into practice. It was more the idea of it that was appealing, and somehow energizing. They could dress, walk, pose, act the part, without doing anything that might have real consequences. The media dramatized and even romanticized it, and in a few years people were talking about a "generation gap."

Music was very much at the core of it, and music was the part of it in which every kid could be included, whether he had anything to rebel against or not.

Crutchfield could not have been happy about the images and sounds of teenage rebellion, but he was not personally in its path. The Crutchfield kids were almost out of reach, by age and to some extent by circumstances, of that wave that was building. It was no more than a marginal influence on Dick as he graduated from the Loomis School in 1953 and enrolled at Washington and Lee, in Lexington, Virginia. Leslie, off to prep school at Mount Vernon, in Washington, D.C., would make it through college just before denim replaced khaki and the scent of marijuana replaced Old Spice and Chanel.

Meanwhile, another, more important rebellion was going on. North Carolina and South Carolina were among the 17 states that required public schools to be segregated by race. Beginning in the late 1940s, African-American families in several communities, encouraged and assisted by the National Association for the Advancement of Colored People and its Legal Defense Fund, challenged school segregation and the idea that schools could be "separate but equal." A number of those cases, including one initiated in Clarendon County, South Carolina, were combined by the courts in the case known as *Brown v. Board of Education* of Topeka, Kansas. On May 17, 1954, the U.S. Supreme Court ruled in that case that racially segregated schools were inherently unequal and therefore that racial segregation in public education was unconstitutional.

It would take years, and a number of other lawsuits and court rulings, for the decision to be fully implemented in Southern school districts. But the ruling had obvious implications that reached far beyond public school pupil assignments. Since the Civil War and the abolition of slavery, the mostly unspoken and even largely disavowed notion of white supremacy had remained a decisive element in Southern social, cultural, and economic life and in law, politics, and public policy. Suddenly, in that spring of 1954, it was clear, at least to thoughtful people, that the walls that divided the races and defined much of the Southern way of life were going to be torn down. How quickly, how fully – and whether peacefully or violently – were troubling, unanswered questions that most white Southerners had never believed they would have to confront.

Seven weeks after the Supreme Court outlawed school segregation, 19-year-old Elvis Presley went into the Sun Records studio in Memphis for what amounted to an audition. He had been there before, paying for studio time to record a couple of tunes to give to his mother – and perhaps hoping he would be discovered.

He'd been born in a two-room house in Tupelo, Mississippi, a few minutes after a twin who was stillborn. He had grown up poor and now, a high school graduate, he was driving a truck to make a living. Since moving to Memphis with his parents six years earlier, he had often visited Beale Street to hear the blues. He loved the sound of the black blues singers. He also loved country music. Although he had been a shy boy into his early teens, he had started slicking back his long dark hair into a ducktail and learned to play guitar a bit, and he liked to sing. But his efforts to join up with a band or singing group performing locally had met with little success. Several times he had been told simply that he couldn't sing.

Sam Phillips, the owner of Sun Records, had invited the young man back to the studio that summer evening because he was looking for something – or, more accurately, listening for something. He knew white kids were listening to black rhythm and blues artists on records and on the radio. He also understood that while white kids were becoming color-deaf in that sense, they were not color-blind. Skin color was still a barrier, not only in the South, but across the country.

In the summer of 1954, Sam Phillips was looking for someone with white skin and a black voice to perform rhythm and blues, or something like it. So he invited Presley in to record more songs, with guitarist Scotty Moore and bassist Bill Black to accompany him.

Song after song failed to make much of an impression. Presley was still an essentially shy white boy trying to sing pretty. But late that night he tackled something written by a Delta blues singer named

Arthur "Big Boy" Crudup, "That's All Right." He began to move with the beat, to jump around, and so did Moore and Black. Phillips told them to hold up, start over, and he turned on the tape. What he was hearing was what he had been trying to find.

A few days later, a Memphis disc jockey played "That's All Right," and listeners began calling in asking who the singer was. Presley began cranking out the records on the Sun label. Some fit comfortably in the country music category. Others, like "That's All Right," were clearly based on the blues. Some people called it "rockabilly." Some called it rock and roll. It was a fusion of the music of blue-collar white Southerners and the music of the black victims of segregation and white supremacy.

There was no connection, of course, between the Supreme Court's school desegregation ruling and that night in the Sun Records studio seven weeks later, but the confluence had a kind of social and cultural symmetry. Certainly they were parallel developments in a recalibration of race relations and racial assumptions that would trouble and transform the nation, and particularly the South, for the rest of the century and beyond.

In 1955, RCA Records bought Presley's contract from Sun, and in 1956 he had five records that hit Number One on the pop music charts.

To the extent that Charles Crutchfield was paying any attention to Elvis Presley, he probably disapproved. But he and WBT were not particularly interested in the musical tastes of teenagers. The parents were the ones with the money to spend on sponsors' products. Advertisers were most interested in reaching adult listeners, who controlled the checkbooks. But their kids were quickly taking control of all the radios.

Some old-line broadcasters ignored the hybrid music that was becoming known as rock and roll, or simply rock, but the recording industry quickly began paying attention. Companies such as Atlantic and Federal continued to find a growing white teen market for recordings by Ray Charles, Ruth Brown, Billy Ward, the Clovers, and other rhythm and blues artists. Other labels, old and new, began turning up young white singers with long, slick, upswept hair and creating overnight teenage idols, backed by heavy promotion and, in some cases, illegal payments to radio programmers and disc jockeys.

It was more about popularity and profits than about taste or talent, and many adults, probably including Charles Crutchfield, assumed it was an aberration that would pass as that generation of teenagers outgrew it.

Pee Wee Crutchfield was perhaps a bit more liberal and open-minded than her husband and throughout her life had been known for her enthusiasm for popular music and dance. She loved Elvis.

Chapter Twenty-Six
New Sounds, New Voices, New Building

TRENDS IN MUSIC weren't a major concern for Jefferson Standard Broadcasting executives in the early and mid-1950s. Crutchfield faced the challenge of directing, managing, and manipulating a series of rapid developments tied to television's coming-of-age. One was to equip and staff WBTV to produce local programs.

Norman Prevatte was an announcer at WIST radio in Charlotte when WBTV went on the air. He was young, creative, and ambitious, and when he saw a test pattern in a furniture store window he realized television was where he wanted to be. He got a job at WFMY-TV in Greensboro, which had signed on shortly after WBTV. While WFMY-TV was second in the state to sign on, it was first to have a television camera, and Prevatte became interested in production. In the early spring of 1951 he was hired as a producer and director at WBTV.

Without a camera to work behind, Prevatte spent most of his early months at WBTV in a van carrying film back and forth between the Wilder Building and the transmitter on Spencer Mountain. It was six months before he produced his first local program, in a converted radio studio in the Wilder Building. It aired on September 30, 1951, with Jim Patterson as master of ceremonies. On air guests included Jefferson Standard Broadcasting President Joseph Bryan, Charlotte

Mayor Victor Shaw, and Dr. George Heaton, pastor of Myers Park Baptist Church. Patterson also introduced the station's announcing staff, and viewers could finally see some of the faces that went with the voices they had heard on WBT radio.

In March 1953, WBTV increased its signal power to 50,000 watts, and three months later to 100,000 watts, the maximum allowed for its channel. The station aired its first live remote telecast on May 20, 1953, sending three cameras to Charlotte's Freedom Park to cover a speech by newly inaugurated President Dwight D. Eisenhower in celebration of the 179th anniversary of the signing of the Mecklenburg Declaration of Independence.

The following January, Jefferson Standard Broadcasting held a groundbreaking for a new building on a site just off West Morehead Street on the western edge of downtown Charlotte. In May WBTV became the first station in the southeast to transmit a color test pattern.

Meanwhile, the Federal Communications Commission lifted its freeze on the granting of new television licenses in 1952, and Crutchfield and Joseph Bryan began making plans to expand Jefferson Standard Broadcasting's television operations into other markets. One target was the northern coastal plain of South Carolina, where a signal would reach the resort communities in the Myrtle Beach area. Another was the Raleigh-Durham-Chapel Hill area, home of the state capital and two major state institutions, the University of North Carolina and NC State College.

They acquired a license to operate a station on channel 8 in Florence, South Carolina, and station WBTW signed on there in October of 1954. They had completed the paperwork for an application for channel 4 in the Raleigh-Durham-Chapel Hill market and were looking for land for a tower there.

When the FCC freeze was lifted, one of the best-known alumni of the University of North Carolina, bandleader Kay Kyser, went to his friend William C. "Billy" Carmichael, Jr., the university's vice president for finance, and proposed that UNC establish a public, or "educational," television station. Carmichael and Kyser took the idea to William C. Friday, assistant to consolidated university President Gordon Gray. University trustees approved the proposal in May of 1953. Kyser, Carmichael, and Friday raised almost $2 million from foundations, individuals, and corporations, and persuaded the legislature to appropriate $217,000 for the proposed station. Joseph Bryan, arguably the state's most important commercial radio and television executive, was an enthusiastic supporter of the effort.

The channel UNC officials and Kyser assumed would be available to the university was channel 4. Then they learned that Jefferson Standard Broadcasting had its license application ready to file for the same channel. Carmichael and Kyser drove to Charlotte and asked Charles Crutchfield for advice on how to proceed.

Crutchfield, along with Bryan, had encouraged the university's pursuit of a public television station. While Carmichael and Kyser sat in his office, he immediately telephoned Bryan in Greensboro. He later recalled that when he informed Bryan that the university was seeking the same channel Jefferson Standard wanted, Bryan's first response was "Ugh," but he soon told Crutchfield that Jefferson Standard would give its application to the university and direct the corporation's lawyers in Washington to assist the university in getting FCC approval of its license. He also asked Crutchfield to make himself available to assist in planning the new station.

Crutchfield had the pleasure of delivering the good news to his guests. He later called it "the biggest decision and most important decision Joe ever made…a great and wise decision…one of the greatest things he ever did for the people of this state." Bryan's decision cost his company a television station in one of the two or three most important markets in North Carolina, and his gift of the license paperwork and legal assistance saved the university many thousands of dollars.

WUNC-TV in Chapel Hill signed on the air January 8, 1955, with a telecast of the basketball game between the North Carolina Tar Heels and the Wake Forest Demon Deacons in Woolen Gymnasium on the UNC campus. The new station's production crew had to cut a hole in the second story of the building to get its camera inside. The Tar Heels won, 95-78. From that beginning, a statewide public television network would grow and prosper.

A major advantage for a radio station in having a television affiliate under the same roof was the ability to attract outstanding talent. Most ambitious young radio announcers wanted a shot at television. At WBT, they would have that opportunity. One who tried but somehow couldn't transfer his radio personality to television was Kurt Webster. He moved on to a radio announcing job in another market.

The cramped quarters in the Wilder Building were bursting with enthusiasm and creativity. Although the studio space was inadequate and increasingly out of date, downtown Charlotte was an exciting place to be. In a few years, sprawling suburbs, shopping centers, and malls would begin to drain the life out of the central business district, but in the 1950s it was the commercial heart of the region, with several "five and ten cent" or "dime" stores, three large department stores, elegant small shops, good hotels and restaurants, drugstores, sandwich shops, the train station and bus station, and people hawking hot-off-the-press issues of the *Charlotte News* along the sidewalks every afternoon.

While Jefferson Standard Broadcasting's new building in Charlotte was under construction, there were several important additions to the staff. None turned out to be more important to Crutchfield than Alan Newcomb, a slender Ohio native who had flown B-17s over Europe in World War II, been shot down twice, and spent eight months in a German prisoner of war camp. With Crutchfield's support and encouragement, Newcomb would create nationally known patriotic and anti-communist programming on WBT and WBTV.

Bob Raiford also joined WBT in the early 1950s as nighttime disc jockey. Still in his twenties, Raiford had grown up in nearby Concord, but he brought a more urbane, contemporary musical taste and announcing style to the after-hours air time formerly occupied by Kurt Webster.

One applicant who wasn't hired in 1953 was a 24-year-old actor and singer named Andy Griffith, from Mount Airy by way of the University of North Carolina. Griffith wanted $75 per week for an announcing job. Crutchfield refused to pay that much. Although Crutchfield would take a lot of kidding over the years for his failure to hire Griffith, it is hard to imagine now how Griffith's considerable talents could have been put to good use as a radio or television announcer. So it probably was the right decision for WBT. And it was absolutely the right decision for Andy Griffith.

Without a daily radio or television gig to perform, Griffith was free to pursue other career options. Within a year, his comedy monologue "What It Was, Was Football" was among the Top Ten recordings in the nation. In March of 1955, he starred in a teleplay of *No Time for Sergeants*. In October, the play, with Griffith in the starring role and another young actor named Don Knotts as Corporal Manual Dexterity, moved to Broadway, where it ran for 796 performances. Griffith was nominated for a Tony award. He then went to Hollywood and delivered a stunning dramatic performance in the 1957 film, *A Face in the Crowd*. Warner Brothers brought *No Time for Sergeants* with Griffith and Knotts to the screen in 1958. A couple of years later Mayberry became America's favorite small town. Years later came the seersucker-clad lawyer, Matlock. Andy Griffith became one of the most widely known and beloved performers in the history of American entertainment.

More radio stations were devoting almost all their air time to recorded music, and many were aiming for the teenage market with rock and roll records. Others were enjoying success with country and western formats. WBT and a number of old-line, big-signal stations stuck with their traditional pattern of different kinds of programs for different times of day. Grady Cole remained firmly entrenched as the "morning man." The April 1952 issue of *Colliers* magazine included a long feature story about Cole, labeling him "Mr. Dixie" in his 23rd year on the air at WBT and reporting that he made $100,000 a year.

Cole continued to sandwich news reports, farm reports, opinionated comments, and earnest personal endorsements of his sponsors' products between phonograph records. The musical selections probably appealed more to the older listeners in his audience than to young adults or teenagers. Neither he nor anyone else on the air at WBT acknowledged the existence of rhythm and blues and the increasing popularity of rock and roll.

But Bob Raiford, the new nighttime voice of WBT with his show *Raiford at Random*, attracted a more hip young adult audience than his predecessors. Raiford also made WBT one of the few stations outside the major metropolitan markets to program modern or "progressive" jazz, which was enjoying a few years of popularity with college students and young business and professional people. On weeknights Raiford played songs from Broadway, Hollywood, and "Tin Pan Alley," performed by artists such as Frank Sinatra, Nat "King" Cole, Ella Fitzgerald, the Four Freshmen, Peggy Lee, and Jeri Southern. On Saturday nights he played jazz.

Raiford had an assured, relaxed style and a pleasant baritone voice with just a hint of Southern accent. With the benefit of a signal reaching the entire east coast, he was quickly recognized by a New York media critic as one of the top disc jockeys in the nation. His identification with jazz and jazz-influenced popular music also won him a spot on some of WBTV's live local musical programs.

Another musical influence on WBT and WBTV was Loonis McGlohon, even before he was part of the staff. McGlohon was from Ayden, a small town in eastern North Carolina and home of the annual Collard Festival. He was recognized as a child prodigy on piano, and when he enrolled at nearby East Carolina Teachers College (now East Carolina University) in Greenville, he quickly became known as a top pianist and began working with student musical groups. After serving in an Army Air Corps band in Florida during World War II, he and his wife, Nan, headed for New York City, where he was supposed to join a popular touring dance band. But they stopped along the way in Charlotte to visit a college friend, bandleader Billy Knauff, and they never left.

McGlohon decided life on the road in a band wasn't the future he wanted. Knauff offered him a spot in his band, which had regular dates for school and country club dances. Despite state law forbidding the sale of liquor by the drink, Charlotte had a number of supper clubs providing opportunities for a jazz pianist or a piano trio. All McGlohon needed was a day job to pay the bills, and he found one at the Southern Railway freight office.

He quickly built a strong reputation as a musician, which brought him in contact with a number of people on the WBT staff. He was impressed with their enthusiasm for their jobs and their company. Their boss, Charles Crutchfield, had a reputation as someone who hired good people and then stepped back and encouraged them to take initiatives, and even risks. McGlohon decided that Jefferson Standard Broadcasting was where he wanted to work. It would be a few years before he was hired for a full-time position there, but he began to be a part-time presence behind the scenes and occasionally on television, at the piano.

Another important addition to the staff was 23-year-old James G. Babb. A Charlotte native, Babb was ready to accept a job as a sportswriter at the *Charlotte Observer* in 1955 when he changed his mind and took a job as writer in the Jefferson Standard Broadcasting promotional department. Babb's early duties involved writing press releases and delivering them in person to the *Observer*'s radio-television editor, Dick Banks. Over the next three decades Jim Babb worked in almost every department and subsidiary of the company, including radio sales, television sales, and Jefferson Productions, and ended up as manager of each one – eventually becoming head of the company in 1988.

On April 13, 1955, Jefferson Standard Broadcasting dedicated its new building, a $1.25 million contemporary structure that provided up-to-date radio and television studios, offices for administrative and sales staff, and a cafeteria. It was the first facility in the nation designed specifically for color telecasts.

For the staff, morale already was high, but the opportunity to spread out in a fine new building with the latest technology only made it higher.

For Crutchfield, it meant an office appropriate to his status, and presiding over a workplace of a quality and scale appropriate to his company's status.

For all of them, it meant more opportunities to create better programming, entertain and inform the audience, serve and influence the community and the region, and shape the future.

The short cul-de-sac leading from West Morehead Street to the new building was named for the late former president of Jefferson Standard Life Insurance. The new address of Jefferson Standard Broadcasting in Charlotte was One Julian Price Place.

Celebrities from the worlds of entertainment, broadcasting, business, and politics arrived to help Crutchfield & Co. celebrate the move to the new building. Other news and advertising media put aside competitive instincts and covered the speeches and other special events. Jefferson Standard Broadcasting announced that each Wednesday and Saturday would be "Visitors Days" at One Julian Price Place, with staff available to provide guided tours of the new radio and television studios. Many people took advantage of the opportunities. The new headquarters was a sort of museum in reverse. Instead of artifacts of the past, it gave visitors a look at the new tools and techniques shaping the future of communications.

WBTV still had no competition in its market and was progressing nicely after a shaky start. On the radio side, however, WBT, despite its wonderful new studios, Canada-to-Cuba audience, and national reputation, was losing market share to smaller local radio stations with lower advertising and production rates. Jefferson Standard's radio profits, once taken for granted, were disappearing. One reason may have been the attention being paid to television within the company. Another may have been that, with people increasingly turning to television for other kinds of entertainment, what they wanted from radio was simply music. A small radio station with programming consisting of a succession of disc jockeys playing records had minimal overhead and could sell its advertising time for less. WBT's big signal was a great benefit in selling time to national advertisers, but it represented a lot of unnecessary capacity for local advertisers.

Whatever the reasons, Crutchfield had barely settled into his new office when he had to find ways to cut costs at the radio station. He asked the station's announcers to accept a cut in talent fees for recording spot announcements in which two or more voices were used. Instead of complaining, the announcers seemed willing to agree to the cuts. Crutchfield formalized the request and laid out the terms and his reasons in a letter to Doug Mayes, who represented the WBT staff with the Charlotte local of the American Federation of Radio Artists.

"WBT's business has been constantly dropping for the past 18 months," Crutchfield wrote, adding that the station's new advertising rate card represented "drastic reductions" in local advertising rates in order to remain competitive. "All we are asking is that the announcers – as well as all the others interested in the future of WBT – pitch in and help."

Mayes' response, in a memorandum October 9, reflected the extraordinary respect Crutchfield commanded among the announcers: "Thanks a million! The memo from you states the conditions of the agreement as we understood it. We are happy that we are able to contribute to help in putting WBT Radio back in good shape.... If there is anything further that the announcers can do, either individually or collectively, let's get together and talk it over."

CHAPTER TWENTY-SEVEN
The Blue Glow

THE FACES OF CHANNEL THREE 's young announcers quickly became as familiar to the people of Charlotte and the surrounding region as Grady Cole's voice – and even more familiar than Cole to a new generation of adult listeners and viewers. Many of the names and voices already were familiar from their work on WBT radio.

Now Doug Mayes became a nightly visitor in the region's homes as the Esso Reporter, sitting at a desk in front of a calendar and reading the national and international news from Associated Press reports, his owlish face looking wise beyond his years and his voice reassuringly warm and confident. Soon the station's own reporters and cameras would be providing Mayes with local and state news to pass along.

With Mayes on the early news was Clyde McLean, who could have passed for a skinny, bespectacled teenager as he stared into the camera and drew swoops and squiggles with a marker across an outline of the United States. He was not a trained meteorologist, but for much of his audience, McLean provided the first encounter with anything resembling meteorology – cold fronts, warm fronts, storm systems sweeping across the country and eventually affecting the weather in the Carolinas. It was on-the-job training in weather forecasting for McLean, and as he learned, he taught his viewers. He soon became

Doug Mayes on the air

known among colleagues and to his audience as "Cloudy" McLean.

When a late news report was added, Bob Bean was the anchor – a term that hadn't been invented – with Alan Newcomb as the Atlantic (for the sponsoring oil company) Weatherman.

Both early and late news soon would feature sports reports by "Big Bill" Ward, who also announced professional wrestling matches broadcast on Channel Three. Ward urged his viewers to "be good sports wherever you go," and reminded them that "you don't have to play a sport to be one."

Those same announcers and others, including Gil Stamper, Jim Patterson, and Phil Agresta, worked with Norman Prevatte to create local live programs. Television for them was like a new toy. They played with it and were fascinated and challenged by it. Prevatte later recalled that they worked 80 hours a week and loved it. One attraction of television work was the $2.50 clothing allowance an announcer got for each appearance.

Their early efforts were pretty basic, but people who just a few years earlier had never heard of television were happy to watch, and there was no competition. On one regular program, called *The Pipe and the Book*, Stamper sat in a chair, smoking his pipe and holding a book in his hand as he introduced documentary and educational films. On another, he provided a lead-in to old Hollywood movies. On December 21, 1955, WBTV aired its first live color telecast, which featured Dr. George Heaton of Myers Park Baptist Church, simply talking.

As their experience grew and equipment improved, their projects became more sophisticated. Arthur Smith and his Crackerjacks started the day with an early morning country music show from the new WBTV studios. On an afternoon show, singing cowboy Fred Kirby, who had been a WBT radio favorite years before, showed off his horse, Calico, played his guitar, and sang songs, bantered with "Uncle Jim" (Jim Patterson), and showed old *Our Gang* and *Little Rascals* comedy films, with a live audience of children. Kids loved it. Parents at the time observed that in the annual Thanksgiving parade in downtown Charlotte, Fred Kirby was a bigger attraction for their children than Santa Claus.

One of the better early live local programs, and one in which Prevatte took special pride, was called *Nocturne*. It probably was the first controversial program ever shown on WBTV, although the controversy may have been manufactured. In 1955 Prevatte asked Loonis McGlohon, not yet on the staff, to help him put together a 15-minute jazz music show. McGlohon assembled a quartet with some of the musicians who played with him on nightclub gigs: Jim Stack on vibraphone, Creighton Spivey on bass, and Earl Blankenship on drums. The combination provided a very listenable "cool jazz" sound similar to George Shearing's quintet. McGlohon also recruited some of the better local dance band and jazz singers in the area, and sometimes added a saxophone to the mix. There was even an occasional dancer.

Bob Raiford was the natural choice for master of ceremonies. In addition to the voice, suave delivery, and knowledgeable commentary that made him popular with jazz fans on the radio, Raiford was tall, slim, good-looking, and dressed in the "natural shoulder" style favored on college campuses.

Prevatte and McGlohon came up with a theme for each show, and staff designer Mark Rascovich created appropriate sets. For songs about Paris, for example, there would be travel posters, a sidewalk café, with the Eiffel Tower in the background. Some of the sets suggested a nightclub ambience. It was all somewhat sophisticated, thematically and technically, for its time and place. Most important, the music was as good as a fan of "modern" jazz could find anywhere.

But someone wrote to the "letters to the editor" column of the *Charlotte Observer* complaining that *Nocturne* was too risque:

> A couple of weeks ago they had some sort of dancers on there that I sure wouldn't want my children to see. Nearly every time it's got some kind of drinking going on....
>
> I can't see any reason for the program at all, and all my friends can't, either....
>
> After all, TV is mighty important in our lives. We ought to at least keep it as decent as possible.

The letter was signed Jessie May. A few days later the newspaper published letters from fans of *Nocturne*, defending the program. One called it "one of the best produced local TV programs." Another said, "It's wonderful!"

"It has achieved a rare combination of atmosphere, intelligence and subtleness," said another writer. "In fact, out-of-town associates of mine have often commented about the 'network quality' of the show."

It is doubtful that WBTV could have bought that much publicity for *Nocturne* at any price, which, in long retrospect, raises the question of Jessie May's true identity. Loonis McGlohon loved to play practical jokes and was very much capable of writing the letter signed Jessie May. And then there was Charlie Briarhopper himself. There was no love lost between him and the *Charlotte Observer*. He would have loved to put something over on the newspaper. Was there a real Jessie May? Or did her letter emanate from One Julian Price Place? It's an unsolved mystery.

In an interview some 30 years later, Norman Prevatte said *Nocturne* was "the best ongoing show I was ever a part of." It marked the beginning of WBTV's national reputation for quality local programming and Prevatte's national reputation as a television producer. It also was the first of McGlohon's many creative, high quality, and highly praised contributions to WBT and WBTV programming.

WBTV's first competition in its market was WAYS-TV, which signed on channel 36 in 1954, but it went off the air the following year, and WBTV was again the only television station in Charlotte. Raiford recalled, many years later, the creative freedom that came with that distinction, with no competition to worry about or respond to. He remembered driving to work after dark and seeing "that blue glow" from television sets through the windows of houses as he passed, and knowing if the sets were on, they were tuned to Channel 3.

Nocturne made Raiford, already a popular disc jockey, even more of a local celebrity. That, and his national reputation, helped him keep his job despite a sometimes irreverent attitude toward management.

The staff was well aware that Crutchfield was particularly fond of the sundial that Dorothy Baker Billings, a prominent interior decorator, had installed as part of the décor of the new headquarters at One Julian Price Place. When the sundial mysteriously disappeared one night, Crutchfield immediately suspected Raiford of taking it, simply to irritate the boss. Some people recalling the incident say Raiford was not the only culprit, but was assisted by Norman Prevatte and perhaps one other co-conspirator, all possibly under the influence of some after-hours libation at the studio.

Crutchfield fired off a memorandum warning, in effect, that heads would roll if the sundial did not reappear at its proper place by the following day. The thieves put the sundial back in place that night and the crisis appeared to have passed. But the next night Raiford, according to legend, removed it again and stashed it in a closet in another employee's office. With Crutchfield once again fuming, that employee happened to open his closet door and almost went into shock when he saw the sundial.

At some point the sundial was returned to its proper place, and Raiford survived the incident, despite the boss's suspicions. He did not, however, survive another instance of insurrection.

On April 10, 1956, Nat "King" Cole appeared in concert in the Birmingham Municipal Auditorium in Birmingham, Alabama, backed by England's top big band, the Ted Heath Orchestra. Ku Klux Klan groups and White Citizens Councils had been organizing across the South in response to the Supreme Court's 1954 school desegregation ruling. The White Citizens Council in Alabama was dedicated to, among other things, the elimination of rhythm and blues music, which it considered a threat to the morals of white teenagers. Cole was a jazz musician and pop singer who didn't play rhythm and blues, but he was black, so council members planned to charge the stage during his performance, apparently hoping to chase him out of town. Only three of them actually responded to the signal and attacked Cole. Police quickly stepped in, and Cole suffered only minor injuries.

News of the attack spread across the country. On April 12, Bob Raiford took a tape recorder downtown and interviewed Charlotte Chief of Police Frank Littlejohn, asking him if he thought such an incident could occur in Charlotte. He also went a few blocks east and taped interviews with students at Central High School. He planned to play the tapes on his radio show that night. He thought the interviews might even win WBT some kind of award.

When station management learned of his plan, Raiford was ordered not to play the tapes. During his program that night he told his listeners about the tapes, said he had been ordered not to play them, criticized station management for its position, and then played the tapes. A few minutes later he got a phone call telling him to sign off. He was fired.

Some people believe Raiford lost his job because he stood up for a principle. Others believe he was a self-destructively stubborn and arrogant young man with no respect for proper authority. Some believed Crutchfield and his management team were ducking controversy and intimidated by racists. Others said management understandably didn't want disc jockeys editorializing about volatile events in the news. There probably were elements of truth in all those views.

The incident attracted enough national attention in the broadcasting industry to prompt Crutchfield to issue a press release defending the decision. A story in *Billboard* magazine reported his explanation. Raiford was fired, Crutchfield said, because he disobeyed explicit instructions by airing taped material which was improperly gathered, and because he criticized the station on the station's own facilities.

After he got the call telling him he was fired, Raiford put on a recording of "For All We Know (we may never meet again)" and told his audience good night for the last time. A few hours later, on a sunny spring morning, he drove his MG, top down, to Chapel Hill, where he was master of ceremonies for a student jazz competition at the university.

Raiford later had news announcing jobs in other markets and then returned to Charlotte as a daytime disc jockey on another radio station. Along the way he jumped out of airplanes, rode a motorcycle, and had roles in several movies. Eventually he created a new persona for himself as Robert D. Raiford, curmudgeonly commentator on the syndicated *John Boy and Billy* radio show, which originated in Charlotte.

WSOC-TV, Channel 9 in Charlotte, signed on in April 1957. It was the television affiliate of the city's second radio station, WSOC, which had been broadcasting since 1929. The new station, affiliated with the NBC network, brought a fresh set of national entertainment programs, news programs, and sports events to viewers in the region. But by the time the new station appeared, TV sets throughout the market were, as a metaphor of the time expressed it, "rusted on Channel Three."

With WBTV's eight-year head start and with CBS as the nation's most popular network, it would be years before another television station seriously challenged Channel Three for dominance in the Charlotte market.

Chapter Twenty-Eight
The First March Madness

B Y THE LAST QUARTER of the 20th century, college basketball
was a popular and familiar spectacle on television from late fall
until early spring, and one of the most prized franchises in network
television was the National Collegiate Athletic Association (NCAA)
men's basketball championship tournament. Known as "March
Madness," the tournament culminates in the Final Four, with two semifinal games sending winners into the championship game – an event
that ranks with the Super Bowl and the World Series atop the annual
sports calendar in America.

There was no such madness in March of 1957, but there was a
basketball team completing a historic season at the University of
North Carolina, and it occurred to an entrepreneurial graduate of that
institution that people around the state might want to watch the
climax on television.

In the 1950s, people in North Carolina, as in the rest of the South,
were a lot more interested in college football than in basketball. But
from 1946 through 1955, the NC State Wolfpack had won nine con-
secutive conference basketball championships – six in the old
Southern Conference and the first three in the new Atlantic Coast
Conference (ACC). Nearby rivals – at UNC, Duke, and Wake Forest,

which was then located in the town of the same name, just outside Raleigh – quickly got tired of NC State's dominance and were working to beef up their own basketball programs.

UNC had lured Frank McGuire from a successful career as baseball and basketball coach at his alma mater, St. John's University in New York City. McGuire, dapper, immaculately groomed, and oozing Irish charm, arrived in Chapel Hill in 1952 and immediately began using his contacts to recruit players from New York neighborhoods and high schools where basketball was taken very seriously. By the start of the 1956-57 season he had assembled a team of extraordinary and complementary talent, led by the high-scoring senior forward, Lennie Rosenbluth.

That team completed its regular season undefeated, with 27 victories and the ACC championship, and on March 12, 1957, it entered the playoffs for the national Division 1 NCAA championship. After beating Yale, Canisius, and Syracuse, UNC headed for Kansas City, Missouri, for a national semifinal date with Michigan State University as one of the Final Four teams. That's when a former UNC football player, Castleman D. Chesley, did something as remarkable in its own way as the Tar Heels' unbeaten season.

Televised basketball in North Carolina had been limited to a few games on the UNC public television station, most without audio. Just as football coaches had been concerned about attendance some 30 years earlier when Crutchfield wanted to broadcast games on radio, basketball coaches feared that televised games would hurt ticket sales. But that was not an issue when a North Carolina team was playing for the national championship in faraway Kansas City.

Chesley was familiar with the technology and logistics of putting sports on television through his college football work with ABC, NBC, and the old Dumont network. That March, in the barely six days between UNC's March 16 victory over Syracuse and its March 22 semifinal against Michigan State, he acquired television rights from the NCAA, signed up commercial sponsors, and put together a statewide network of stations and the staffing and equipment to telecast the Tar Heels' Kansas City games across North Carolina.

From the earliest days of radio, Charles Crutchfield had known that live sports should and would become one of the more important parts of broadcast programming. In the old Wilder Building studio he had improvised broadcasts of major league baseball games from inning-by-inning teletype reports, slapping a baseball bat with a screw driver for sound effects whenever anyone got a hit. He had persuaded Southern Conference officials to allow live radio coverage of football games and had been the first play-by-play announcer on Duke football broadcasts. WBTV was part of George Preston Marshall's pioneering Washington Redskins network. So there was no doubt that Crutchfield would sign on with Chesley's network for an experimental but ultimately historic weekend of television.

It's difficult to imagine what the significance of Chesley's hastily arranged telecasts would have been if UNC had lost to Michigan State, or even if the Tar Heels had won the semifinal but lost the final. But Chesley himself could not have devised a scenario more certain to guarantee the success of his efforts.

It took three overtime periods for UNC to defeat Michigan State, 74-70, in one of the most exciting games in NCAA playoff history. Then it had to face the Kansas University Jayhawks for the championship.

Although the Tar Heels were unbeaten and ranked Number One in national polls, they went into the final game as underdogs, primarily because of the Kansas center, Wilt "the Stilt" Chamberlain. In an era when the tallest basketball players stood about six and a half feet, give or take a couple of inches (UNC's tallest player, center Joe Quigg, was 6'9"), Chamberlain was over seven feet tall, towering over opponents. On defense he was a fearsome shot-blocker. On offense, if he had the ball anywhere near the basket, he was all but unstoppable. In addition to Chamberlain, Kansas also had most of the crowd in that Kansas City arena.

The Tar Heels reflected their coach's personality: cool, relaxed, confident almost to the point of being cocky. They had survived a number of very close games through the season and seemed to believe they could not lose. In a bit of psychological one-upmanships, McGuire sent 5'11" guard Tommy Kearns to contest the opening tipoff with Chamberlain. He was conceding the tip to Kansas, but he also was serving notice that his team wasn't intimidated by Wilt the Stilt.

Again, the game went into one, two, and finally three overtimes, stretching late into the night after many Tar Heel fans lost hope when their star, Rosenbluth, fouled out. But UNC won, 54-53.

There was no reliable measure of how many people in the Carolinas watched the game that night, but judging from conversations across the two states the following week, everybody had seen it. Many homes at the time did not have television sets. People who didn't have a set went to neighbors' homes to watch, or to appliance stores that stayed open late so potential customers could see the game. There were reports of heart attacks among viewers across the state. It was, at least in North Carolina, the beginning of March Madness.

Two months later Chesley established the C.D. Chesley Network and arranged to televise Atlantic Coast Conference games on Saturday afternoons the following season, with Pilot Life Insurance, a Jefferson Standard subsidiary, as primary sponsor. In later seasons the schedule expanded to include weeknight contests, and ACC basketball on television became a colorful and exciting part of life in the Carolinas.

Chapter Twenty-Nine
Behind the Iron Curtain

T HE YEAR 1950 BROUGHT the beginning of the Korean War, and Edward R. Murrow traveled there to report the events on CBS. Over the next few years the legendary radio reporter would make a highly successful transition to television. With his lean, dark good looks, crisp articulation, and the atmospheric smoke curling up from his ever-present cigarette, Murrow was as much a natural for television news as Humphrey Bogart was for noir motion pictures.

Murrow's weekly radio digest of news, called *Hear It Now*, was based on the format of an earlier project, *I Can Hear It Now*. The earlier program presented history through recorded speeches and old news broadcasts of the featured event and was produced by Murrow and Fred W. Friendly. *I Can Hear It Now* adopted the same format to current events. Murrow's *See It Now* later transferred the format to television, and took viewers into such previously unfilmed areas as a submerged submarine, a fighter plane during air defense exercises, and a session of the Arkansas General Assembly.

During the creation and rise of *See It Now*, Murrow continued to report the news from Korea – not just the major events of the day but also stories about the individual American soldiers risking their lives on the other side of the globe in what for a time appeared to be a losing cause. One of his *See It Now* broadcasts, "This Is Korea... Christmas 1952," was praised by a writer in the *New Yorker* magazine as "one of the most impressive presentations in television's short life."

When World War II hero, Gen. Dwight D. Eisenhower, was elected president in 1952, he was determined to extricate the United States from the Korean War. Either surrendering or abandoning the South Koreans was out of the question, but United Nations forces, primarily American, and North Koreans, aided by Communist China, were locked in a prolonged stalemate. Eisenhower went to Korea as president-elect in the fall of 1952 and apparently accelerated negotiations that resulted in an armistice agreement signed on July 27, 1953. There was no peace treaty and no official end to the war, but the fighting was over.

Americans were no longer engaged in combat against communist forces, but fear of the spread of communism was undiminished, as was fear of subversive communist influence within the United States – a fear encouraged and exploited by a number of politicians, most notably Sen. Joseph McCarthy, Republican of Wisconsin. McCarthy's critics called his tactics "witch hunts," as he raised questions about the loyalty and patriotism of dozens of thoroughly loyal and patriotic Americans, some of whom had embraced socialism and criticized the excesses of capitalism in the past.

Murrow's *See It Now* program on March 9, 1954, broadcast on CBS and WBTV, examined the McCarthy phenomenon. Murrow calmly and methodically detailed the inaccuracies and inconsistencies in McCarthy's indiscriminate charges against innocent people. The program won a Peabody Award for Excellence in Broadcasting and probably accelerated the erosion of support for McCarthy in Washington and around the nation. Murrow, however, did not place all of the blame for McCarthyism on McCarthy.

"We will not walk in fear, one of another," said Murrow. "We will not be driven by fear into an age of unreason if we dig deep in our history and remember we are not descended from fearful men.... The actions of the junior senator from Wisconsin have caused alarm and dismay...and whose fault is that? Not really his; he didn't create this situation of fear; he merely exploited it, and rather successfully. Cassius was right: 'The fault, dear Brutus, is not in our stars, but in ourselves.'"

Murrow was one of Crutchfield's heroes, but if Murrow's broadcast marked the decline of McCarthyism, it did not end Crutchfield's fear of communism, or the nation's determination to block the spread of that ideology – with military force if necessary.

The Soviet Union, which had spied on U.S. development of the atomic bomb even as the two countries were allies in World War II, tested its first nuclear weapon in 1949, and in 1955 it exploded its first hydrogen bomb. The nuclear standoff was now firmly in place, with the fate of the human race hanging on a sturdy but scary peg called Mutually Assured Destruction, or MAD.

At three p.m. on October 4, 1956, a Scandinavian Air System DC-7C airliner took off from Idlewild Airport in New York City and headed across the Atlantic toward Denmark. The age of jet airliners was about to begin, but that autumn the DC-7C, the last piston-engine airliner built by the Douglas Aircraft Company, was state-of-the-art in passenger comfort. Introduced just four months earlier, it had a longer body than its predecessors, and longer wings to position the engines farther from the body, for a quieter ride in the passenger cabin.

On board the SAS flight were 48 American business executives chosen by the U.S. State Department to visit the Soviet Union for the purpose of improving understanding and relations between the two countries. The group included the vice president and general manager of the United States Rubber Company, the chairman of the Executive Committee of the A.B. Dick Company, a director of A.G. Spalding and Brothers, Inc., a director of the Empire Trust Company, the executive vice president of Burroughs Corporation, the director of development of E.I. DuPont de Nemours and Company, a director of Burlington Mills, the president of Midland Steel Products Company, the president of Vanadium Corporation of America, the president of Montreal Locomotive Works, Ltd., the president of the United States Tobacco Company, the chairman of the board of the Emerson Electric

Manufacturing Company, and the president of the Mead Corporation. And Charles H. Crutchfield, executive vice president of Jefferson Standard Broadcasting Company. Crutchfield's boss, Joseph Bryan, had been invited, but had a conflicting obligation, and Crutchfield was happy to take his place.

In Copenhagen, they would leave the DC-7C and board planes provided by the Soviet Union to take them on to Moscow.

In quiet moments in the plush comfort of that stretch limo of an aircraft, as it hummed above the clouds over the ocean and into the night, Crutchfield, now 44 years old, must have mused a bit about the arc of his life and career: his boyhood in a very middle-class family in Spartanburg, his failure to complete even a year of college, his early skipping from job to job, sometimes unable to pay the rent, his first claim to fame as the wisecracking announcer for a hillbilly band. And now....

As one of 48 business executives chosen to represent the United States of American behind the Iron Curtain, he did seem to take himself a bit more seriously than he had before the trip.

Crutchfield in Moscow, 1956

He returned home knowing that he had gotten a closer look at a system that was toxic to the human spirit, and a regime with nuclear weapons that was interested in peace only on its own belligerent and intransigent terms.

The best way to describe the trip and its impact on Crutchfield is from a letter he wrote to his children shortly after his return. The letter is a fascinating example of his informal writing style, his understandable cynicism about the Soviet leadership, and his sardonic sense of humor. It is also an interesting glimpse, by a keen observer, of the Soviet Union in the early years of the Cold War:

> *…When we landed in Moscow, it was 12 midnight there. And much to my surprise, the customs officials simply welcomed our group and ushered us to long black automobiles, which were exact duplicates of our Cadillacs. There was a car, a driver, and an interpreter for each two of us – 24 cars in all. They took us to the hotel (the Metropole). We didn't have to register, but went directly to our rooms, where we saw our baggage for the first time since we left New York.… They didn't examine us in customs at the airport, but they did go through everything we had at least once a day, while we were away from the hotel. I checked this very carefully once by placing certain items in my bag at exact angles and positions, to find them almost, but not quite, correctly placed upon my return. They didn't steal anything, so I guess they were after confidential papers or something they could photograph. We were very careful though not to have anything in writing which they weren't welcome to examine.*

> *The Commies really rolled out the red carpet, and they were very careful to see that nothing happened to any of our group. They showed us the things they wanted to impress us with – but fortunately we were able to see a lot they didn't intend us to get a peek at. They allowed us to take as many pictures in color and black and white as we wanted. We got pictures of scenic stuff in cities, railway stations, airports, subways and general landscapes in certain areas.*

> *Our first trip out of Moscow was to Leningrad, on the Gulf of Finland. Leningrad has a population of 1,200,000. And this is a trip, Dick, that I wish you could have been on. As you and Les may recall from your history books, this was a Russian fort in the old days. In 1703 though, they decided to redo the place, so they imported a lot of French architects who built it in typical French fashion. It has since become highly industrialized,*

*though, and they took us to many factories – automobiles, fur-
niture, television sets, etc. The thing I believe you'd have liked
most was the Hermitage Museum in the Winter Palace. This
place contains literally acres of originals by Rembrandt and all
the great European artists. Our interpreters denied emphatically
these had been "borrowed" from the countries they had taken
over – but of course we knew better. In addition, there is a perfectly magnificent cemetery in Leningrad where all the Russians
czars are buried – Peter the Great and Ivan the Terrible are
planted there.*

*Our next trip was by Russian plane to Kharkov, in the east of
the Ukraine, and Kiev in the west-central part.... Kharkov's
population is 3,000,000. It is dirty and drab – smoky because
of many factories (shoes, tractors, machine tools, electric gener-
ators, etc.) I did notice, however, that whereas the terrain
between Leningrad and Moscow was mostly agricultural...the
Ukraine area – much to my surprise -- was mostly industrial-
ized, with many more villages and fewer and smaller farms,
although it is generally believed...that the land in the Ukraine
is far more productive or more fertile than the land to the north.*

*Kiev, with a population of 1,500,000, is the most modern city
we saw; and for some reason, the people there are better dressed,
would smile occasionally, and seemed almost happy. The reason
the town looks better is that it was completely destroyed by the
Germans during the war and has since been completely rebuilt.
It looks more like Cairo than any place I've seen.*

*We got back to Moscow and the temperature had dropped to
15 degrees above zero, which they told us was quite unusual
for this time of year. Be that as it may, it went on down to 10 –
and by the time we got back to the hotel, we were in the middle
of the damndest snowstorm I've seen.*

*Russian people, by the way, have a very grim look on their faces
– they never smile – they apparently never bathe or wash their
clothes – they wear dark gray and black – and they are about*

six inches shorter in height than the average American.

…(W)e went through every nook and cranny of the Kremlin, including the building that the Supreme Soviet big-shots operate in. The old part of the Kremlin is absolutely magnificent and is chock-full of the finest antique stuff I've ever seen – was built in 1491. The newer addition, including the diamond- and ruby-studded palace, was built in 1848.

After this three-hour session, we went through the tomb of Lenin and Stalin, which is a part of the Kremlin but is actually built in the center, outside the Kremlin wall, on Red Square. Lenin, you remember, died in 1924, and his body looked a little waxy after 32 years. In looking at him, I figured in my own mind that after all this time they had replaced the actual body with a wax figure. Stalin's body, since he has been dead only four years, looked like the real McCoy.…

I was told later by one of the Russian officials that the son and daughter of Stalin had been begging the government to allow them to remove the body to the family burial place, but that the government had refused.… The truth of the matter is that the Communists – now that Stalin has become a bum rather than a god – are forcing the family to make this request. They want to remove the body away from Lenin's, but they are a little touchy about it until they are absolutely sure that the people are convinced that Stalin was a "meany." In my opinion, they are far from convinced at this point.

In the Kremlin museum, we saw many interesting and histori-cal things – the solid ivory throne of Ivan the Terrible – the ruby-studded gold throne of Peter the Great's father.… We saw the 16th century coach which was given to Russia by Elizabeth the First of Britain – and the 17th century coach-sled (runners, no wheels) which Elizabeth slid around Russia in.… Also…we saw the crown jewels of all the czars – also the gowns and other apparel worn by the ladyfolks in those days.… While browsing around, I couldn't help but wonder what the purpose of such a display of extravagance really was! After seeing hundreds and hundreds of drably dressed Russians gazing upon the splendor, though, it finally dawned on me that the Commies are showing them glaring evidence of how the old czars (before the Revolution) threw away the people's money. It is pretty small propaganda in my opinion. But I know also that the so-called Supreme Soviet Presidium is stealing from the population now to an extent which makes the czars' thievery seem like peanuts!

...Another thing I couldn't get over were the wide streets and tremendous squares in Moscow – and the kids, from 12 to 16, in black full-length sweat pants and black shirts, doing cross-country up and down the middle of the highways and streets. I understand all kids this age in Russia are required to run 15 miles a day, as a part of their educational training. Since there is no particular traffic pattern in Moscow for pedestrians or for cars, and there are very few stoplights, I am wondering if maybe this practice...isn't actually designed to kill off the kids! One would certainly get that impression!

The streets and sidewalks in Moscow are clean as a whistle – the reason being that literally thousands of women are constantly sweeping them with homemade brooms.... The women in Russia seem to do all the hard work – truck driving, carpentry, brick laying, ditch digging, about everything you can imagine.

We spent a whole day going through the agricultural and industrial exhibits outside of Moscow.... It's like our World's Fair, except it covers 550 acres and all the buildings are permanent.... And here again, with the thousands and thousands of people looking through it, I wondered how the average Russian (making 700 rubles a month, about $160) felt about all this food and silk and wool and expensive Persian gowns being available when he personally could afford very little of it. I mean by this that a pair of shoes – cheap shoes – cost about $150 in Russia. A suit that I wouldn't put on costs approximately $500. Overcoats are from $600 to $700 and up. Honestly, I have never seen such prices and such poor materials.

...Of particular interest was the accuracy with which they have copied American automobiles, American tractors, cranes, fire trucks, ambulances and machine tools. One of the men in our group, who is executive vice president of U.S. Steel, observed however that the tensile strength of their steel for non-military purposes must be pretty sorry. He explained this by the fact that they use approximately four nuts and bolts to hold their steel together where we use only one....

It was interesting too that during our entire trip we saw only one jet plane, and that was parked at the airport in Riga. In discussing this with the Minister of Foreign Commerce, who was very anxious for us to do some business with Russia, he explained that unlike America, the USSR was not planning for war! He said that they are only interested in peace and prosperity. This is the kind of bull we were fed constantly....

The subways in Moscow are amazing – they have 80 miles of it under the town.... And the reason they take such good care of it is pretty obvious. They whole system is 200 feet underground – and you go up and down on very modern escalators. The point is, there's enough room down there 200 feet underground to house Moscow's entire 6,500,000 population during an air raid....

It is against the law to ride a bus or subway in Russia on Sunday. That is one of the ways they have of keeping people away from church, except the State churches which are found everywhere.

...All the stores, all the farms, all businesses are controlled by the state. They tell the factories how much to make and where to send what they make. The State hires the people for farming and industrial work, of course giving the best jobs to the best Communists and the lousy jobs with lousy pay to those who have not yet "seen the light." The Russian works 46 hours a week; and he must buy government bonds, at no interest, with one month's salary each year. He pays 5 percent of his salary

for housing. The government owns all the houses and all the apartments and all the hotels.

Impressions, not conclusions: The Russian people I met were I think basically friendly. They were badly hurt during the war, and I think the main thing the man in the street does not want is war. They talk about peace constantly. The boys at the Kremlin I think have entirely different ideas on the subject. I think most Russians, whether peasant or diplomat, have an inferiority complex. They want to be noticed – they want to be important. I think this is why they claim they invent everything. They steal stuff from us and everybody else, copy it perfectly and then claim they originated it.

… I would say that the Supreme Soviet…would have to be completely nuts to start a war in the foreseeable future. I do believe, however, that quite a few of them, not excluding Khrushchev the big boss and Bulganin the stooge, are two-thirds batty. How in the world 3 ½ percent of the nation's population can completely dominate and control this tremendous majority is beyond me! …there are over 200 million people in the USSR and only 7 ½ million of them are members of the Communist Party.

Well, that's the story…and since I thought you kids would be interested, I am having a copy made for each of you.

Love to you both,
Dad

Crutchfield, getting ready to board the plane for his return to the United States, carried a bottle of Russian vodka to take home as a souvenir. A Soviet official told him he could not take the bottle onto the plane. Rather than argue or have a confrontation over the vodka, Crutchfield simply dropped it, and it shattered on the runway.

The trip clearly reinforced Crutchfield's distrust and dislike of the Soviet Union and its oppressive government, and his conviction that the spread of that system constituted a threat to Western democracies. In the years just ahead, with the resources of a 50,000-watt radio station and one of the dominant television stations in America, he would launch his own war against communism.

Chapter Thirty
Radio Moscow

WHILE THE GROWING NUCLEAR arsenals on both sides of the Iron Curtain remained dormant, deterring a third world war through a "balance of terror," the weapon actually employed in the early years of the Cold War was propaganda, and perhaps the most effective delivery system was short-wave radio. Although Americans were engaged in armed combat against communist forces in Korea and later in Vietnam, the battle between the United States and the Soviet Union was not for territory, but for ears, and through them, for hearts and minds.

The United States government had launched the Voice of America in 1942 to broadcast truthful and objective news of the war in Europe to European listeners. In the 1950s it continued a policy of careful accuracy and objectivity, but one of its aims was to counter Soviet propaganda, and the Soviets jammed the broadcasts whenever and wherever they could.

Radio Free Europe, controlled by a bipartisan board and funded by Congress, went on the air in 1949 specifically to broadcast anti-communist propaganda – truthful, but designed not just to inform, but also to persuade.

From the other side, Radio Moscow beamed an English-language program to short-wave sets in the United States and Canada at 6 p.m. Eastern Standard Time every day. Its news reports and commentary were obviously intended to discredit the United States and other western democracies and extol the benign intentions and other virtues of Soviet communism.

In the late 1950s a listener familiar with the Soviet propaganda broadcasts wrote to WBT to ask why no American radio station was rebutting the misinformation and misinterpretations Moscow was transmitting to U.S. citizens. Crutchfield, whose trip to Moscow had reinforced his distrust of Soviet posturing and rhetoric and his sense that communism was inherently evil, decided that his station should take up that challenge.

In Alan Newcomb, he had a valuable lieutenant in launching WBT's broadcast war on communism. Newcomb's World War II experience, which included his liberation from a German prisoner-of-war camp by Russian forces, had made him a serious student of foreign affairs, communism, and Soviet Cold War strategies. He and Crutchfield shared a deep concern about the effectiveness of Soviet propaganda

Alan Newcomb

and the spread of communist influence in Western Europe and the Americas. They knew there was extensive espionage on both sides, of course, but they worried even more about the number of American citizens – particularly those in academia, the arts, and entertainment and perhaps even in high government positions – who were either clandestine communists or "communist sympathizers."

Newcomb was an extremely talented and versatile announcer. Before the war he had graduated from Ohio Wesleyan University with a degree in speech and dramatics. Now in his late 30s, he had polished his skills at stations in Asheville and Columbia and at WFBC in Greenville, South Carolina, where he also became active in the civic life of the community. Since coming to Jefferson Standard Broadcasting, he had been an afternoon disc jockey on WBT, host of a morning variety show on WBTV, creator and master of ceremonies of a quiz show on WBTV, the weatherman on WBTV's evening news, and a frequent speaker to civic clubs, church groups, and other organizations. While encouraging him to take on yet another assignment in rebutting communist propaganda, Crutchfield apparently wasn't willing to go without his services in those other radio and television roles. He was willing, however, to get Newcomb some help with the new challenge. For that, he hired a veteran newspaper journalist, Rupert Gillett.

Gillett held undergraduate and masters degrees from the University of Texas and had studied international relations in Paris at the Sorbonne. He had spent 28 years at the *Charlotte Observer*, the last 10 as associate editor and editorial writer. At the *Observer* he was considered something of an intellectual, serious-minded, more interested in international affairs than in local or state politics or federal domestic issues. He was politically conservative and perhaps became more so as the perceived linkage of political conservatism and anti-communism grew stronger.

Those views made him increasingly uncomfortable at the *Observer* after brothers James and John S. Knight added the newspaper to their growing chain in 1954 and a few months later hired C.A. "Pete" McKnight as editor. McKnight wanted to avoid having the *Observer* labeled "liberal" by its generally conservative readership. (Tom Wicker, a Hamlet, North Carolina native who later joined the *New York Times* and became one of the brightest stars in American journalism, was turned down for an editorial writing job by McKnight, who thought he was too liberal for the *Observer*.) But McKnight himself was about as liberal as an *Observer* editor in 1955 could afford to be. Gillett's somber anti-communist commentaries were not a good fit with the new editor's view of the world and his newspaper's role in it.

The veteran editorialist resigned in 1957, and a short while later, Crutchfield realized that Gillett might be the right person to bring a measure of gravitas and intellectual respectability to WBT's new venture into anti-communist programming. Intellectual respectability was of serious concern to the Wofford dropout as he steered his radio station into the sometimes murky rhetorical waters where Marxist political and economic theories became indistinguishable from the brutal reality of Soviet communism.

In a March 1954 CBS telecast, Edward R. Murrow had used Joseph McCarthy's own irresponsible rantings and contradictions to discredit the senator from Wisconsin. Crutchfield was wary of having any anti-communist programming on WBT perceived as a revival of McCarthyism. Whatever his station aired would have to be scrupulously factual, with evidence on hand to back it up if anyone challenged it. It would not engage in name-calling or guilt by association. It would be fair-minded, carefully reasoned, and dispassionately presented.

What Crutchfield, Gillett, and Newcomb came up with was an innovative program they called *Radio Moscow* – the same name as the Soviet propaganda broadcasts they intended to refute. With new equipment acquired for that purpose, WBT's engineers were able to tape the English-language Soviet short-wave broadcasts. Each week, Gillett listened to the tapes, chose excerpts that he considered good examples of the rhetorical techniques with which Soviet propagandists attempted to persuade and proselytize American listeners. Gillett would then write brief commentaries pointing out the factual omissions, distortions, and logical flaws in the Soviet presentation.

Gillett was the writer and researcher, obviously devoting many hours to documenting the points he wanted to make, using material from his own extensive files, from the public library, and sometimes with help from the Voice of America, Radio Free Europe, and the U.S. Information Service. Newcomb was the producer and the announcer, reading what Gillett wrote. Thus Newcomb became the voice of

WBT's anti-communist crusade, and increasingly he wanted to do more of that kind of work and less, if any, of playing records and reading weather forecasts. He surely had to believe that those on-air chores tended to compromise the seriousness of his *Radio Moscow* role and image.

After months of preparation, *Radio Moscow* went on the air in January of 1959. A promotional brochure about the new program cited its virtues. It was factual, fair, objective, researched and written by a respected and scholarly journalist. The station's seriousness of purpose was underscored by its decision not to air commercials during the 30-minute program. But the brochure also revealed a somewhat condescending attitude toward a segment of the audience identified as "the intellectuals:"

> ....bearing in mind that Radio Moscow beams its North American broadcasts to the intellectuals, we have carefully respected the intelligence of those whom the Soviet agency is trying to reach. A Communist, once convinced, is usually irredeemable. We waste no time on him. But we believe the almost-persuaded can be dissuaded if the facile plausibilities of Radio Moscow are subjected to the unemotional rules of both logic and evidence.
>
> For this reason we have refrained from name-calling in all its forms and have been cautious not to resort to wisecracks and retorts as substitutes for argument....

Half a century later there is no credible information regarding the number of listeners who tuned in to WBT's *Radio Moscow*, but the program was an immediate critical success. It won the Sigma Delta Chi Distinguished Service Award for Public Service in Radio Journalism, the George Washington Honor Medal from the Freedoms Foundation at Valley Forge, and the Gold Medal Award for the most original radio program in the Southern states from *Radio-TV Mirror* magazine.

Radio Moscow was in tune with its time, and it quickly attracted the attention of other broadcasters as well as politicians and others concerned about national security, including J. Edgar Hoover of the FBI, who wrote to congratulate WBT on the awards and added, "Your continued interest in seeking to alert our citizenry to the menace of atheistic communism is indeed encouraging."

Among many other congratulatory and appreciative comments were these:

It is gratifying to see the management of a powerful radio station devoting so much of their special talents and valuable time to this public service...."
—Lt. Gen. Herbert Powell
Continental Army Commander

It is gratifying to learn that Radio Station WBT is devoting time and effort to inform its listeners on a subject so essential to our nation's survival. The strength and welfare of our country demand responsible and educated citizens who are aware of the true character of communism and its danger to the free world.... I hope the other media through the country will follow the lead and support the vital service of keeping the American public informed and alert to the Communist threat...."
—Gen. Bruce Clark
Commander, U.S. European forces

I feel that WBT is doing this nation a great service by using its facilities to expose the distortions and half-truths that characterize communist propaganda techniques...."
—Gen. Hugh P. Harris
Commander, U.S. Army Infantry Center
Headquarters, Fort Benning, Georgia

I found the programs most interesting and congratulate you on a most worthwhile and professional show. I thought your technique of breaking in and giving the counter-argument was most effective...."
—Henry Loomis
director, Voice of America

Rep. Robert Hemphill of South Carolina commended WBT in the Congressional Record: "I salute this magnificent effort. For the people of my district and for the people of the nation, I thank this station."

CBS declined an offer to put the program on the network, but WBT made it available to other stations outside its primary market area, and a number of them carried it. Within three years *Radio Moscow* could be heard on 15 radio stations in the states of Maryland, Virginia, Connecticut, New York, Washington, Florida, and California, and on public stations based at the University of North Carolina at Chapel Hill, Northwestern University in Chicago, Clemson College in South Carolina, and the University of South Dakota. With that coverage, WBT estimated that 90 percent of the people of the United States were within earshot of *Radio Moscow*.

Here are a couple of examples of what *Radio Moscow* listeners heard in 1961.

Radio Moscow (taped from a Soviet broadcast): The Asian, African and Latin American countries are dissatisfied first of all because United States assistance does not further their economic and cultural growth. The lion's share goes for direct and indirect military expenditures. Sixty percent of the total is channeled to Asia and Africa. Just about ten percent is allocated to the economic development of eastern countries. At the same time, recipients are required to commit themselves to support the so-called mutual security program.

Alan Newcomb: Let us call your attention to some very tricky language used by this Radio Moscow observer. First he says the lion's share of all American aid goes for military expenditures in the countries receiving it. There is no basis for this statement, because in a majority of the countries very little of the aid goes for military purposes. Now notice the trick. The man says, "The lion's share goes for direct and indirect military expenditures." Then his very next words are, "Sixty percent of the total is channeled to Asia." He is putting phrases that have different meanings close together so that his hearers will get the impression that they mean the same thing. He hopes you will understand him to mean that sixty percent of the aid goes for military expenditures, though he does not say that. His next words are that "about ten percent is allocated to the economic development of eastern countries. He means ten percent of total American aid, not ten percent of the aid to eastern countries. Moreover, he does not tell what eastern countries he is talking about; hence, there is no way of checking up on his figures.

Radio Moscow: On the following day, Dean Rusk, Secretary of State, backed up Gilpatrick's statement and added himself that all future talks with the Soviet Union will be conducted only from a position of strength. At the same time in the charged atmosphere of Berlin, American personnel began traveling from West Berlin to Democratic Berlin without any reason at all, just to test nerves, as they are so fond of saying. These are nothing but provocations. American tanks were standing before the Democratic Berlin border. American soldiers were fixing bayonets, and they were alerted every day.

Alan Newcomb: These defensive measures by the western authorities in Berlin were a reaction to Soviet provocation. Under Soviet direction the East Berlin authorities built the now famous wall surmounted by barbed wire to keep their own people from fleeing out of the Communist paradise. This wall is a clear violation of the New York agreement of May 14, 1945, confirmed a month later by the Foreign Ministers of the four allied powers in Paris, confirmed again by the Foreign Ministers in Paris May 4, 1949, in the agreement that ended the Berlin Blockade.

Radio Moscow opened up a new career for Alan Newcomb as an expert on communism, which made him increasingly frustrated with his inability to shed his old career as multipurpose radio-television announcer. Newcomb wanted Crutchfield to create a new position –

public affairs director for Jefferson Standard Broadcasting – which Newcomb would be the logical person to fill. But Crutchfield wasn't ready to deprive the radio and television stations of Newcomb's announcing talents.

In correspondence with someone who had offered suggestions for other public affairs programming Newcomb might undertake, Newcomb replied that he didn't have time for any new projects. He was doing a television weather program, was a radio disc jockey in the afternoons, and produced and served as announcer for *Radio Moscow*.

Despite that busy schedule, Newcomb took advantage of other opportunities to establish himself as an authority on the communist menace. In a speech to the Junior Woman's Club of Charlotte in early 1961, he declared, "We in the western world are pitifully ignorant of the long range plans of communism for world domination.... Time after time we persist in believing they don't mean what they say or that they are going to change. They will not."

To the Mecklenburg Christian Ministers Association, he said, "You may not feel yourself at war with them, but they are at war with you. Not only do they mean to win that war, but they are fanatically certain that they cannot lose it, that history is on their side, not yours...."

He had plenty of ideas, but not enough time to pursue them. *Readers Digest* magazine published frequent articles on communism, and Newcomb thought they should collect some of them in a book, along with material that he would contribute. In the spring of 1961 he presented the idea to Crutchfield, who liked it and said he would contact the magazine on Newcomb's behalf. Crutchfield wrote to Editor Dewitt Wallace at *Readers Digest* about Newcomb's proposal, and told him that Newcomb was "imminently qualified on the subject of communism generally and communist objectives in particular." He offered to send Newcomb to the *Readers Digest*'s offices in New York City at no cost to the magazine for as long as he could be useful in implementing the idea.

While he waited for Wallace's reply, Crutchfield wrote to Radio Free Europe about the proposal, and to Secretary of State Dean Rusk, suggesting that the State Department might want to review the proposal book prior to publication. In his letter to Rusk, he added: "Incidentally, my 26-year-old son, Richard D. Crutchfield, is going to work for the State Department there in Washington as soon as his security checks are completed. I am delighted."

When Wallace replied, he said the magazine was interested in the idea but that he wanted it reviewed by a senior editor, Eugene Lyons, who was "better informed on the subject of how to fight communism than most other people." Lyons, said Wallace, was in Hong Kong and wouldn't return for several weeks. When Lyons got back to his office and considered the proposal, he wrote Crutchfield to say that *Readers Digest* didn't produce books containing anything but articles published in *Readers Digest*. Crutchfield apparently suggested that the magazine could publish some articles by Newcomb and then put them into the book. He was then informed that *Readers Digest* had all the articles on communism it could handle at the moment.

Newcomb's concerns about communism – and Crutchfield's – were not at all out of the American mainstream. But while Newcomb seemed to believe the American people were not sufficiently informed or alarmed about communism, it would be hard to imagine them being more informed or alarmed than they were. Communism was very much on the public mind. A popular saying among patriotic Americans at the time was that they would rather be "dead than Red." The nation lived with the fear of having to make a choice between nuclear war and surrender to communist aggression, and defending the nation and the free world against communism was a major topic in the political dialogues and debates of the time.

The 1960 presidential election was a good example. Vice President Richard Nixon was the Republican nominee, while the Democratic nomination went to Sen. John F. Kennedy. Kennedy was a decorated hero for his service in combat in the Navy in World War II, but he knew that as a Democrat, he might be perceived by some voters as liberal, and therefore perhaps not as vigilantly anti-communist as his opponent. He also knew that Nixon, as a successful candidate for the U.S. Senate in 1950, had suggested that his opponent, Helen Gahagan Douglas, an advocate of world disarmament, was soft on communism. So Kennedy ran a hawkish campaign, charging that the nation's military might had eroded during the Eisenhower-Nixon administration, and that a "missile gap" had developed between the United States and the Soviet Union. It was a term apparently coined by the Kennedy campaign, and after the election, which Kennedy won, there was no more talk of a "missile gap."

Radio Moscow put WBT on the radar of anti-communist organizations seeking the station's help in sponsoring and promoting forums, seminars, and other programs. For all his anti-communist zeal, Crutchfield remained wary of the potential for demagoguery and exploitation by people and organizations more interested in profit than in patriotism. In July of 1961 he wrote to J. Edgar Hoover, listing some of the groups that had solicited WBT's support and asking Hoover's opinion of them. Hoover replied that the FBI, "being strictly an investigative agency of the federal government, does not make evaluations nor draw conclusions as to the character or integrity of any individual, organization or publication...."

While he was wary of anyone trying to exploit Americans' fear of communism, Crutchfield could be quick to suspect communist sympathies when someone suggested that the United States and the Soviet Union could peacefully coexist. In the spring of 1961, WBT Sports Director Phil Agresta received a letter from Cyrus S. Eaton, chairman of the board of the Chesapeake and Ohio railroad:

> American sports editors deserve full credit for their contribution to better international understanding, through their objective coverage of Soviet-American athletic contests. Is there some way this same spirit of sportsmanship can be transmitted to the other departments of most newspapers, and particularly to the editorial page...?
>
> I have sat in the mammoth stadium in Moscow on a sunny afternoon and seen a hundred thousand happy young Russians enjoying a spirited soccer game. I have visited the public li-

braries in Moscow and watched hundreds of eager Russians, young and old, pursuing their studies with zest.

Spectacular Soviet strides in science, the arts and industry, as well as sports, attest to Russian enthusiasm and determination to excel. If we ungrudgingly acknowledged Soviet successes in whatever field, and redoubled our own efforts to hold the leadership in some spheres and recapture it in others, in the sporting spirit of friendly rivalry, wouldn't this world be big enough for both our system and theirs?

Needless to add, I am going to go on working my head off for the capitalist system, as I have been for more than three quarters of a century."

Agresta showed the letter to Crutchfield, who promptly mailed a copy to J. Edgar Hoover. In a cover letter to Hoover, Crutchfield wrote:

....This obviously is a form letter sent to all radio and television stations and probably to all sports editors in the country. I am not personally acquainted with Mr. Eaton; but I imagine your bureau is familiar with his general reputation.

I would like to call your attention to two basic errors in Mr. Eaton's remarkable statements. First of all, the happy young Russians disporting themselves in the Moscow stadium are the favorite few in a system which holds twenty million others in slave labor camps in Siberia....

Secondly, while the world may be considered big enough for both systems to exist, it has been the consistent policy and practice of every communist leader to fanatically maintain that the world is not big enough for both of us."

He also sent a copy of both letters to Secretary of State Dean Rusk.

Hoover replied, saying: "I feel certain most Americans, armed with the true facts presented by our news media, will not be fooled by attempts to glorify the Soviet Union."

In the early 1960s Crutchfield and Newcomb added television to their arsenal in the war on communism with a WBTV program called *Land of the Free*. A statement of the objective of the program said:

> In presenting a patriotic series of programs, WBTV is well aware of the fact that love of country is expressed in many different ways, and it is difficult to find a universal touchstone through which all Americans can be moved through patriotic response to be more active citizens.
>
> The sophisticated intellectual may have an abiding love of country, but look with disdain on the flag-waving patriot; while the man filled with nationalistic fervor may look with suspicion on his quieter countryman.
>
> Using the mass medium of television, we have attempted to strike a compromise which will identify land of the free with both types.

An introduction to the program described it this way:

> *Land of the Free!* A new series of programs designed to place 20th century America in perspective, to help you better understand the forces at work in America and in the world; to analyze the place you have in the history of tomorrow!
>
> This analysis is expected to cover many contrasts in modern philosophy and cultures: between communism and democracy; between socialism and private enterprise; between totalitarianism and freedom; between religion and atheism; and between the varieties of opinion which lie within the current framework of American society.

The pilot program for the series, scheduled for 30 minutes at 6:30 every Sunday evening, was titled *The Religion of Communism*. Future programs would feature William Sullivan of the FBI discussing "communism in the Carolinas" and John Noble, author of *I Was a Slave in Russia*.

A promotional flyer on the new program, mailed to prospective sponsors, said:

> America and all of the free world are facing a threat more powerful and more frightening than that of a mere nuclear war. This menace is COMMUNISM...and it is only vaguely understood by most people.
>
> To promote greater understanding, to rekindle the feeling of pride in our own system of government and to emphasize the danger of communism, WBTV has initiated the series *Land of the Free*.
>
> Alan Newcomb, commentator on the award-winning *Radio Moscow* series, which is syndicated throughout the country, is host-moderator for the half-hour program. His views and opinions on communism will be fortified by dramatic presentations, special guests and dynamic films...."

Crutchfield came across an article in the February 1961 issue of *Presbyterian Survey* magazine that reinforced his concerns about communist's intransigence in pursuit of their goals. Titled "Letter from a Young Communist," it was written, according to the magazine's editor, by a young man who had grown up in the southern United States, in a Presbyterian family, and was sent to a friend back home. Here are some excerpts:

> I have already been in jail because of my ideas, and if necessary I am ready to go before a firing squad.... We constantly look for places where the class struggle is the hardest, exploiting those situations to the limit of their possibilities. We lead strikes. We organize demonstrations.... We've been described as fanatics. We are. Our lives are dominated by one great, overshadowing factor—the struggle for socialism.... And if our personal lives seem hard or our egos appear to suffer through subordination to the party, then we are adequately compensated by the thought that each of us is in his small way helping to contribute something new and true, something better to mankind.

Crutchfield sent copies of the article to friends and acquaintances around the country and arranged for its republication in other periodicals.

In 1962 he granted Alan Newcomb's wish and named him public affairs director for WBT and WBTV. Newcomb continued to produce and narrate *Radio Moscow* on radio and *Land of the Free* on television, and to write and speak about the threat of communism. He traveled to Chicago in October of 1966 to address a trade convention. While there he had emergency surgery for a ruptured appendix and died of respiratory failure following the operation. He was 45 years old.

Chapter Thirty-One
A More Sophisticated Sound

WHILE *RADIO MOSCOW* BROUGHT a new dimension to WBT's public service programming, Loonis McGlohon was giving the musical programs a more contemporary edge. After working part-time at the station for several years, McGlohon was hired full-time in 1957. When Clarence Etters retired in January of 1960 after many years as WBT's music director, McGlohon was chosen as his successor, putting him in charge of the station's huge library of recordings, classical, jazz, country, and popular, on old 78 rpm discs, 45 rpm "extended play" discs, and 33 1/3 rpm long playing discs. Within his grasp and control were the great musical heritage of western civilization and the best artists' recordings of what would become known as the Great American Songbook – the songs written in the first half of the 20th century on Tin Pan Alley and for Broadway and Hollywood musicals.

From that library McGlohon chose the records to be played by the announcers on WBT, including the venerable Grady Cole. His choices reflected his own musical tastes – jazz-influenced versions of great standards as well as new songs in that same traditional genre. A talented jazz pianist and songwriter himself, he had excellent taste based on a sophisticated understanding and almost encyclopedic knowledge of the music. But his selections did not always reflect the tastes of the announcers who had to play them, particularly Grady Cole, who preferred music by Guy Lombardo's orchestra, and Wayne King (the "Waltz King") and others from an earlier generation.

On the air, Cole disparagingly referred to McGlohon's choices as "Looney Tunes." Apparently Crutchfield found some of those choices inappropriate for Cole's style and sound. He complained to McGlohon that he was hearing too many records by Stan Kenton and the Four Freshmen on the Grady Cole show. Crutchfield believed in putting talented people in place and letting them do their jobs, and he respected McGlohon's musicianship and his musical judgment. But he also wanted to keep his iconic morning man happy.

Crutchfield also understood that Cole represented the station's musical past, and McGlohon, by Crutchfield's choice, was in control of its musical future – at least briefly. Elvis Presley was the most popular recording artist in the country, and when he returned from military service in 1960 he began turning out more hit records. His popularity had spawned numerous other "rockabilly" and rock and roll artists with similar hairdos and musical styles. Black rhythm and blues music continued to grow in popularity among young people, white and black. Record producers, with the help of some under-the-table money paid to popular disc jockeys and program directors at rock and roll radio stations, were making rock stars out of clean-cut white kids who had minimal ability but whose appearance would not offend the parents of young white girls. Rock music in its various manifestations, all growing initially out of the American black experience, with a bit of indigenous country music thrown in, was the big story in the recording industry by the late 1950s.

But anyone over 30 years of age had grown up, dated, fallen in love, gotten married, perhaps gone off to war and come back, to the soundtrack of the great songbook standards, and for a few more years those songs would remain America's popular music. Crutchfield believed, correctly, that his advertisers were more interested in reaching adult listeners than teenagers, so McGlohon's musical selections were the right ones for WBT.

While Crutchfield's musical tastes were a bit more old-fashioned than McGlohon's, they shared an aversion to rock music that bordered on alarm. With the boss's blessing, McGlohon wrote and produced, with announcer Clyde McLean, a program called *Ninety-eight Cents Worth of Trash*. Ninety-eight cents referenced the retail price of a 33 1/3 rpm recording, and "trash" expressed McGlohon's, and McLean's – and presumably Crutchfield's – opinion of rock music.

The program condemned the music as tasteless, crude, lacking melodic and harmonic quality. It complained that many of the performers demonstrated little or no talent, while genuinely talented musicians and singers were having more and more trouble finding work. The lyrics, it said, were usually inane and often vulgar. Much of it, McLean said, was simply not fit to put on the air. In his script, McGlohon asserted that of the hundreds of records WBT received every week, he could find only a few that met the station's standards for decent programming.

The *Charlotte Observer* took note of the program in an editorial, giving it a favorable review and adding the newspaper's own opinion of rock music:

> Rock and roll is carefully calculated garbage…. The disturbing thing is not that it came upon the scene; it is that it has stayed so long.

In addition to his musical taste and talent, McGlohon quickly learned something about radio production and programming and took full advantage of the creative freedom Crutchfield encouraged. "Crutch would let you do what you thought you did best," McGlohon later recalled. "If you came to him with an idea, he'd say 'Go for it!'"

In addition to *Radio Moscow*, Crutchfield's youthful staff created a number of network-quality programs, including a documentary series called *Project 60*. McGlohon used the *Project 60* format to produce special programs for holidays and to interview other musicians – well-known as well as obscure – about their work. One *Project 60* show featured a telephone interview by McGlohon with the legendary jazz singer Billie Holiday. Sadly, it was one of her last interviews; she died a week later.

Paul Marion, WBT's program director in the 1950s, became general manager and in 1960 initiated a new, more contemporary format. Despite the growing popularity of rock music, WBT's music remained middle-of-the-road, but there was more of it, interspersed with briefer informative or humorous comments by the announcers. The epitome of the new style was Bill Curry, a native of nearby York, South Carolina. Curry, a jazz enthusiast, moved into the afternoon time period, where he offered knowledgeable commentary about some of the music he played, and displayed an understated but quick sense of humor.

One afternoon during a report on traffic conditions on area streets and highways, he noted that traffic was moving smoothly through the Belmont Tunnel. There was no Belmont Tunnel, but some listeners probably assumed there was, maybe connecting Charlotte to the small textile town of Belmont across the Catawba River. Over the next few weeks the myth of the Belmont Tunnel took on a life of its own on Curry's show. With the help of some of the other sometimes zany people in and around the WBT studios, Curry created a cast of characters involved with the tunnel, including the man who owned it, and his family. It was a funny routine, delivered in straight-faced style, and for a while it was part of the talk of Charlotte.

WBT's transformation to a more urbane, up-to-date sound was completed in the spring of 1961 when Grady Cole retired after 32 years as the station's morning man and Marion hired Ty Boyd to replace him.

Boyd was not quite 30 years of age. He had gotten his first radio job as a teenager in his home town of Statesville. In the mid-1950s he became the afternoon deejay on WCHL in Chapel Hill, where he developed and sharpened his wry wit and youthful but polished delivery to appeal to a university community audience.

By 1962 there were more radios that could be tuned to FM signals than there had been when the first WBT-FM went on the air in 1947,

Crutcheild at his desk at One Julian Price Place

and Jefferson Standard Broadcasting decided to give FM another try. The new WBT-FM was at 107.9 on the FM dial and featured classical and "easy-listening" music.

With so many creative people scrambling to explore the possibilities of the still-new medium of television and responding to the challenges of changing musical tastes and formats in radio, One Julian Price Place was by most accounts an exciting place to work in the early 1960s. It was an environment shaped by the personality, experience, and management style of Charles Crutchfield, who had once been a creative and occasionally zany young broadcaster himself.

But he had long since shed that early image of Charlie Briarhopper, and although he gave creative people room to grow and freedom to innovate, his style and manner left no room to doubt that he was in charge, and serious about it. He dressed and acted the part of the traditional, conservative executive. While close friends knew him as witty and fun-loving, mid-level and lower level employees at Jefferson Standard Broadcasting saw him passing stern-faced along the hall or through the lobby, always in a well-tailored suit, tie knotted snugly under his collar, dark hair perfectly groomed, and some of them found his presence intimidating. Indeed, he could be a demanding boss, but not at all times or in every situation.

Tom Camp recalls one afternoon shortly after he had left a newspaper sportswriting job to join the WBT-WBTV public relations staff under another former sportswriter, Larry Harding. Camp was still a very young man. Crutchfield called him "boy" and Camp called Crutchfield "boss," and apparently they hit it off from the start. That afternoon "boy" was helping "boss" carry some material to Crutchfield's car, parked behind the building. It was shortly before 4 p.m. and, as Camp recalled, Crutchfield said, "Boy, if you'll look around at the building, in the windows of the second floor you will see (so and so, and so and so, I forget the names) looking out the windows to be sure I am leaving. As soon as I leave, they will, an hour early. They think I don't know."

PART
5

TRANSITIONS

Chapter Thirty-Two
New Generations

JUST AS WORLD WAR II, with Edward R. Murrow's reports from London and subsequent accounts of land, air, and sea battles and the climactic nuclear bombing of Japan, elevated radio from an entertainment medium to serious institutional status, so the political and social triumphs and tragedies of the 1960s made television an essential component of American life.

In the 1950s, in-home television sets had begun replacing small-town and neighborhood movie theaters as providers of easily accessible, inexpensive, middle-brow drama and entertainment. Then came what was arguably the most traumatic American decade in a century, and it was no longer a matter of replacing existing media. Television provided something unprecedented: a window through which Americans in almost every home became witnesses to the historic events of their time – often live, as they happened, or at least within the next few hours.

The decade began optimistically, with the nation at peace and experiencing a refreshing generational change of leadership. Americans could watch, for the first time, live televised debates between the two presidential candidates, Democratic Sen. John F. Kennedy, age 43, of Massachusetts and Republican Vice President Richard M. Nixon, 47, of California. Kennedy seemed to benefit most from the debates, based less on content, perhaps, than on the image of brisk, cool confidence he projected.

The 1960 election also involved the first generation of American voters whose political and social views were significantly influenced by television. Its black and white, sometimes grainy images of candidates making speeches and shaking hands and riding in motorcades were like newspaper photographs set in motion, with sound. Its reporters, news anchors, and commentators not only described the events of the day in well chosen words; they also provided motion pictures, so we could see for ourselves what was going on. It had a sort of visual and visceral credibility that no older medium could achieve.

Over the next three years television brought the young President Kennedy into American homes – delivering a soaring inaugural address in his crisp New England cadences on a bright winter afternoon ("… the torch has been passed to a new generation of Americans – born in this century, tempered by war, disciplined by a hard and bitter peace…."), displaying flashes of wit in live press conferences, enjoying family life with his lovely wife and two small children, and somberly announcing evidence of Soviet missiles being installed in Cuba, less than a hundred miles from American shores.

Early in the decade the torch was also passed to a new generation at Jefferson Standard Broadcasting. In 1963, Crutchfield was named president of the company.

There were also generational changes in the Crutchfield family. When Dick graduated from Washington & Lee in 1957, his father helped him get a summer job at a broadcasting station in Tulsa, Oklahoma. But Dick had no interest in the radio and television business or, for that matter, any business. Unable to decide what kind of career to pursue, he joined the Army, where he studied Russian and was involved in security activities in Germany. As a new decade began, he spent some time in Charlotte with his parents and then, with the help of some of his father's Washington connections, got a job with the U.S. State Department under the Bureau of Intelligence Research,

Office of Current Indications.

Leslie got her degree at the University of North Carolina at Chapel Hill in 1959 and by the end of the following year was married to Charles Tompkins of Alexandria, Virginia, who was getting his law degree at Harvard. Crutchfield had sometimes called Leslie "Lillie;" now he referred to her and her husband, Charlie, as "Lillie and Chilly." The new son-in-law called the Crutchfields by the same affectionate names Leslie used: "Maw" and "Paw." Two years later the Crutchfields would have their first grandchild, Charles Tompkins, Jr., called Bo.

They sold the Mecklenburg Avenue house in 1959 and moved to a handsome brick home on Sedgewood Circle. The new residence included a swimming pool in a garden setting. Pee Wee decorated the rooms in French Provincial style, with unusual antiques, including a glazed, blue-green porcelain stove in the living room and a rosewood piano, circa 1830, embellished with Oriental art. The grounds were beautifully planted and landscaped, with much of it done by Crutchfield himself, who had developed a love for yard work as he earlier had for carpentry. In the fall of 1961, less than two years after they moved to their new address, the home was one of eight featured and opened to the public in the annual Mint Museum Home Tour.

Dick Crutchfield left the State Department to teach Spanish at Mercersburg Academy in Pennsylvania. In March of 1966 he married Malinda Lobdell, daughter of Charlotte attorney Hugh Venable Lobdell. Malinda encouraged Dick to pursue a graduate degree, a path that led through the Indiana University masters program in Spanish to the doctoral program at the University of Texas, where he studied Spanish literature. The couple's two children, John Randolph and Lilian Anne, were born in Texas.

Pee Wee had always made time for volunteer activities. As a member of the Charlotte Memorial Hospital Auxiliary, she was a co-founder of the hospital's Cheer Corner gift shop, and she represented the hospital as a speaker at a symposium in Chapel Hill on hospital auxiliary fundraising.

She used her talents, whether sewing, decorating, or producing special-occasion parties for friends, often with hilarious skits or verses.

Now, as an empty-nest housewife, she took her community spirit, creativity, and sense of style even further. She served on the board of trustees at the Mint Museum of Art, and her great love was the Mint's puppet theater, which she started as a workshop in 1960 for anyone interested in learning about puppetry, an art she had been exploring for several years at Puppets of America festivals.

Puppetry experts from around the country and Canada were invited to lead Mint workshops in script writing, sound, manipulation, staging, scenery, costuming, and production. Some members of her evolving puppetry group in the Mint traveled with her to other puppet theaters and festivals around the nation and abroad to learn more and share ideas. The Crutchfield garage became the group's workshop and storage area.

The puppet theater, known as the Queen's Mintkins, became a popular attraction at the Mint, particularly for children, and took shows and demonstrations to schools and other venues, including veterans' hospitals. She directed the program until it ended in 1974. Charlotte Mayor John Belk and long-time Mint benefactor Harry Dalton spoke at a dinner in her honor, and she responded from behind a screen through two hand puppets.

In 1985 she presented the Mint with a check for $24,527.24, which represented all proceeds from ticket sales and the sale of shows and sets from the puppet theater.

Crutchfield was proud of his wife's achievements and recognized that they also contributed to his own continuing success. He and several other prominent men were interviewed for a *Charlotte News* feature story in the early 1960s about how women could help their husbands succeed. For the reporter, Crutchfield listed some of the things a smart woman does.

> First, she knows how far to go in her conversation; second, she dresses properly, but conservatively; third, she makes it a business of having a nice hairdo and careful make-up; fourth, she knows how to listen; fifth, she indicates interest in a conversa-

tion; and sixth, she doesn't try to be entertaining.

If she tries to be entertaining, she's sure to be a failure. It's the gal who can entertain naturally who makes a success.

That air of naturalness is easily detected, he says. 'It relaxes people.'

Any intelligent woman can be of great help to a man.

That description fell far short of acknowledging the nature and importance of the help one particular intelligent woman – his wife – had been to his own career. He counted on her emotional and social support, of course. But she also understood him and the environment in which he worked, in and out of the office, and he recognized that her advice and counsel – solicited, as it often was, or otherwise – was honest, realistic, and invaluable, and a major reason for his success.

A few years later some of the points he made in the interview would be considered sexist and anachronistic, but they were very much in line with the order of things at that time. In the Piedmont Carolinas, women had worked in the textile mills and sewing plants for generations to help support blue-collar families, but the idealized version of a woman's role was as homemaker and housewife. WBTV's *Betty Feezor Show*, offering tips on cooking and housekeeping, was the third most-watched "women's show" in the nation at that time. But, in another of the revolutions just beginning, a new generation of women would soon begin moving into the workplace in unprecedented numbers and in an unprecedented variety of roles.

The Crutchfields had always been a sociable couple. She loved parties, whether as host or guest. Now, with no children in the home, they became even more socially active and socially prominent, hosting and co-hosting debutante parties and parties raising money for community cultural programs and facilities.

In 1959 the Quail Hollow Country Club, immediately as prestigious and exclusive as Charlotte Country Club, was established just south of the city. A few years later, Crutchfield received an invitation from the Board of Governors of Quail Hollow Country Club to become a member. He accepted. A newspaper account of a 1967 Christmas party at the new club announced that Crutchfield would read "The Night Before Christmas" to the children attending. The children were probably as awed by the deep resonance of the reader's voice as they were by the images of flying reindeer and a jolly old elf coming down the chimney.

Theirs was a very good life, but not immune to the inevitable shocks and sadness that are part of the human experience. The sudden death of Crutchfield's close – perhaps closest – friend, Dr. Elias Faison, age 66, in 1968 left Crutchfield sick with grief for days afterward.

Chapter Thirty-Three
Madison Avenue at Morehead Street

I N THE EARLY 1960s Crutchfield once again recognized, as he had so many times in his career, a next big thing, and seized it. Early television commercials were essentially radio commercials with pictures. The advertising genius David Ogilvie, in an introduction to a new edition of his 1962 classic, *Confessions of an Advertising Man*, acknowledged that the chapter on television advertising in the original book was "inadequate. I can only plead," he added, "that, in 1962, very little was known about what works and what doesn't work on television."

But advertisers were quickly learning how to make more effective use of the new medium. Their efforts involved a different kind of copy writing and directing, actors instead of announcers, and increasingly sophisticated and expensive equipment. Production of national television commercials was centered in New York City, but with the WBTV staff becoming more adept at producing local and regional spots, Crutchfield was persuaded that they could compete for national business.

In 1963 he created a subsidiary called Jefferson Productions to produce videotape programs and commercials. The staff, under Managing Director Fred Gibson, consisted of John Dillon, sales manager; Norman Prevatte, producer-director; Frank Bateman, technical operations manager; Jim Rogers, production manager; Reg Dunlap, production assistant; and Barbara Wilson, administrative assistant (also known as Secretary and Boss of the Office). Brothers Don and Doug McDaniel were also on the staff, along with engineer Bob Dycus. The new production company initially operated out of a mail room on the second floor of the new building at One Julian Price Place. Based on its early success, Crutchfield, in the face of skepticism from the executive offices in Greensboro and among his own staff, won the company's approval for construction of a two-story, 7,5000 square-foot, $500,000 wing to house Jefferson Productions. He believed it was going to be a successful enterprise and, as he had been so often in the past, he was right.

Shortly after the new subsidiary was up and running, Fred Gibson died. John Dillon went to Crutchfield and asked to be named managing director of Jefferson Productions. It was not a clear choice. Crutchfield and his top subordinates such as Wallace Jorgenson, Paul Marion, and Tom Cookerly, epitomized the executive style and manner of the time – handsomely but conservatively tailored and guarding their dignity. Dillon was more a down-to-earth type – unpretentious, unpolished, and plain-spoken. To the surprise of some of the staff, Crutchfield put Dillon in charge and, again, he was right.

National advertising agencies such as Dancer Fitzgerald Sample and N.W. Ayers quickly recognized the creativity and quality available at Jefferson Productions, and at lower cost. A steady parade of creative and executive talent from Madison Avenue was soon flowing to Charlotte. The sale of liquor by the drink was still illegal in North Carolina, but Barbara Wilson kept a large liquor cabinet stocked in the Jefferson Production studios. "Oh, was I popular," she recalled, years later.

Swain's Steak House was just across Morehead Street from Jefferson Standard, and a short distance around the corner, on Wilkinson Boulevard, were several "gentlemen's clubs" that featured topless dancers. So the Madison Avenue people found a trip to Charlotte entertaining as well as productive.

Among the more memorable commercials created at Jefferson Productions were comedian Bill Cosby's spots for Jello, Euell Gibbons' comparison of Grape-Nuts cereal to the taste of wild hickory nuts, Noxema's "take it off, take it all off" series, Ford Motor Company's 75th anniversary ads, actor Robert Wagner's first television commercial, and spots for Jif peanut butter.

The new subsidiary produced telecasts of Atlantic Coast Conference basketball games on Saturdays for a regional network of stations. WBTV Sports Director Jim Thacker was the play-by-play announcer, with analysis and commentary by former Wake Forest basketball star Billy Packer.

Jefferson Productions also videotaped the syndicated Arthur Smith television program, in the studio and on location, duplicating and sending tapes by bus, mail, and hand-delivered to as many as 38 television stations. It also produced, taped, and delivered syndicated gospel music shows.

One important early addition to the staff was Jan Thompson, who worked for several months under contract and was later an employee. She developed a talent agency supplying local and regional actors and models for television productions and was also directly involved in production. The involvement of women in the sometimes physically demanding business of television production led to a revision of the corporate dress code at One Julian Price Place. When Barbara Wilson came to work in a pants suit, the higher-ups across the way called a management meeting to decide whether her attire was acceptable. Then Jan Thompson showed up in blue jeans. Their tasks included climbing under and over cables and sets and maneuvering equipment, and the standard dress or skirt uniform for office work was not practical. Management reluctantly decided slacks and jeans were okay, at least at Jefferson Productions.

The sometimes unpredictable schedules and scenarios of a busy television production studio also raised eyebrows among their 9-to-5 colleagues. With others in the Jefferson Productions crew, Barbara Wilson often worked late into the night and sometimes came in late the next morning. When someone in another part of the building complained about her late arrivals, it was occasion for another management meeting, with Crutchfield himself presiding. After the complaints were aired, John Dillon addressed his fellow department heads, telling them about the late hours his staff worked.

"How many of your broads leave at five o'clock?" Dillon asked. "She never leaves at 5 o'clock."

Crutchfield said, "I think this meeting is over."

The boss did not spend a lot of time at Jefferson Productions, but he kept in touch through weekly meetings, and it was a somewhat open secret that engineer Bryan Yandle was Crutchfield's "spy" at the production subsidiary, keeping him informed of everything that was going on there.

CHAPTER THIRTY-FOUR
Assassinations and Other Traumas

WHILE SOCIAL LIFE and cultural and creative activities occupied Mrs. Crutchfield's time, and Mr. Crutchfield launched a successful production company, the nation was on the verge of cumulative chaos. A new generation of black leadership was losing patience with continuing racial discrimination and the halting pace of desegregation. An even newer generation, mostly white, was about to assert itself against what it perceived as the catastrophic mistakes of its elders.

In 1954 the U.S. Supreme Court had ruled racial segregation in public schools unconstitutional. In 1956, it ruled the Alabama laws requiring racial segregation on public buses unconstitutional. In 1962, some students and segregationist outsiders rioted when an African American, James Meredith, was admitted to the University of Mississippi under court order. (That year the Washington Redskins hired their first black player.) The following year Gov. George Wallace of Alabama stood in a doorway at that state's university in a symbolic effort to block the admission of two African-American students, and police in Birmingham, Alabama, used attack dogs and fire hoses to disperse a crowd of civil rights demonstrators.

People across America saw all of that, in their homes, on television.

They also saw, a few weeks later, in August, a crowd estimated at 250,000 people march in the nation's capital in support of civil rights, and heard the most charismatic and transformational leader of his time, Martin Luther King, Jr., tell the throng that he had a dream.

Then in the early afternoon of Friday, November 22, CBS television interrupted its regular programming and newsman Walter Cronkite reported that President Kennedy had been shot during a motorcade in Dallas, Texas. People who saw and heard that called their neighbors and relatives, and television sets that had been blank and silent were quickly turned on. A short while later, Cronkite, barely able to control his emotions, announced that the president was dead.

Over the next three days, television, with the three networks cooperating to maintain constant, comprehensive coverage, brought the American people together for the first truly national funeral in their history, transmitting the sounds and black-and-white images of a capital in mourning: muffled drumbeats accompanying the clip-clop of horses pulling a caisson and its flag-draped casket; the Capitol, the White House, and Arlington National Cemetery, its bone-white headstones aligned as precisely as soldiers on parade; the veiled widow and her small children, a brother gaunt with grief, the visiting heads of state and other foreign dignitaries, and the thousands of ordinary Americans standing silent under the bare branches of late November. Millions of people saw and heard it, live or on subsequent newscasts.

As the slain president lay in state in the Capitol and thousands filed by to pay their respects, Dallas police were escorting the man suspected of the assassination through a corridor when a local night club owner jumped into their path and shot the suspect dead. Millions of Americans saw that, too, on television, and continued in the days ahead to watch and listen and wait for each new bit of information that might give them a clearer idea of what was happening to their country, of what terrible and bizarre conspiracy might be playing out, and where it might lead.

Television was no longer a novelty or just a source of entertainment. It was as essential as a stove or refrigerator or running water. It changed the way people perceived the world and their places in it, and it changed the way public opinion was shaped and manipulated.

Vice President Lyndon Johnson of Texas, a very effective arm-twister over many years in the House and Senate, had been put on the ticket in 1960 in an effort to provide some balance to Kennedy's New England background and Catholic faith, and to help secure Southern and Southwestern votes. But he had never had a close personal relationship with Jack Kennedy, and by some reports Kennedy and his top campaign aides, including his brother Robert, were holding their noses when they invited the drawling Texan to be JFK's running mate.

But Johnson, quickly sworn in as president before boarding a plane carrying him from Dallas back to Washington, completed and expanded Kennedy's legislative agenda. Almost a year later, riding a national wave of emotion following the assassination, Johnson won 61 percent of the popular vote against Republican Barry Goldwater in the presidential election and Democrats took overwhelming control of both houses of Congress. Taking advantage of that momentum, Johnson pushed through Congress the most ambitious program of social legislation since the New Deal, including massive anti-poverty programs, Medicare for older citizens, and Medicaid for the indigent. He also proposed, and Congress enacted, legislation making the most fundamental changes in the status of African Americans since the Emancipation Proclamation: the Civil Rights Act of 1964, the Voting Rights Act of 1964, and the Civil Rights Act of 1968.

While those achievements overcame much of the lingering liberal distrust of Johnson, events on the other side of the world were undermining his domestic political successes and causing even more turmoil in America. Kennedy had begun sending military advisers to help the government of South Vietnam resist the encroachment of communist North Vietnam. In an interview shortly before his death he emphasized that the conflict in Vietnam ultimately would have to be settled by the Vietnamese, not by the United States. That has led historians to wonder if sending advisers would have been the extent of U.S. involvement had Kennedy lived. But Johnson inherited a Vietnam War in which Americans were at least marginally involved, and he was reported to have said that he refused to be the first U.S. president to lose a war. As South Vietnam seemed more and more at risk of being overwhelmed, Johnson committed combat troops with air support and over the next few years made it very much America's war.

Johnson's decisions were consistent with the nation's unlegislated Cold War policy of resisting communist expansion wherever it threatened to occur, using force if necessary. Indeed, an affirmation of such a policy still resonated from Kennedy's inaugural promise that America would "pay any price, bear any burden, meet any hardship, support any friend, oppose any foe, in order to assure the survival and the success of liberty." But as the cost in lives and money kept rising, along with frustration with the results, many Americans were wondering what the Vietnam War had to do with their own nation's security or best interests, or even with "the survival and the success of liberty."

America's ally in Vietnam was a widely distrusted government that was by no means an example of democracy in action, and even with more and more American military support, the South was making no headway against the North. The war was being fought primarily on the ground in areas populated by citizens whose loyalties were mixed and sometimes unknown and unreliable. Young Americans began demonstrating against the war, demanding that the United States withdraw. Others of draft age left the country, many to Canada, to avoid service. Some of them simply didn't want to fight in any war, but others were acting, at the risk of prosecution, on principled opposition to what their nation was doing. In either case, many Americans on the older side of what was becoming known as the Generation Gap viewed the protesters and draft-dodgers as cowardly or unpatriotic or both, and believed their actions were evidence of the nation's moral and spiritual decay.

Charles Crutchfield identified more with that view than with the young people demonstrating for civil rights or against the Vietnam War. The defining events of the 1960s were pulling him further to the right politically, but his published and publicly spoken words revealed a struggle for balance. He knew he was not just some ordinary citizen who could spout knee-jerk opinions without consequences. He was in command of some of the most powerful means of communication in the nation, and with that came the responsibility to respect and give fair consideration to opinions he did not share.

He was publicly critical of the *Charlotte Observer*'s editorial opinions, which he thought were far more liberal than its readership. That prompted the *Observer*'s editor, C.A. "Pete" McKnight, to comment that he didn't intend to let "a former Briarhoppers announcer tell me how to run my newspaper."

Crutchfield decided that his radio and television stations should have their own editorial voice. He was wise and wary enough not to implement that decision as a personal crusade, but as an expression of an institutional point of view. In 1962 he appointed an editorial board, including representation from various departments of WBT and WBTV. If there was disagreement on the board, he would argue his positions vigorously, but he declined to have the last word. He insisted that the editorials reflect a consensus on the board, although his relationship to the other participants surely affected their opinions. He did not deliver the editorials himself, but turned that over to several different announcers over the years, beginning with Alan Newcomb. While he participated in the writing and editing, primary responsibility for those tasks was also delegated to others. The best of the broadcast editorials – clear, concise, tightly and elegantly reasoned – were written by Larry Harding, a former journalist in charge of the stations' public relations, who was becoming Crutchfield's intellectual, public-policy, and literary alter-ego.

On local issues, the stations' editorials did not contrast significantly with those of the local newspapers – supportive of business and industry, economic growth, good schools and infrastructure, peaceful accommodation of the legitimate demands of civil rights advocates. On national and foreign policy issues, WBT and WBTV offered a more conservative voice that generally reflected Crutchfield's views.

While he wisely yielded control of his stations' editorial positions to the consensus of his editorial board, Crutchfield did not hesitate to express his own views in articles, letters, and speeches. He was uncomfortable and even alarmed by the extent to which Johnson's legislative successes were moving the nation in the direction of socialism and expanding the role of the federal government in American life. He was not opposed to the demands of African Americans for civil rights, but when their demonstrations turned confrontational and even violent, he opposed their tactics. He also suspected that subversive influences were manipulating them in an effort to divide and weaken the country. Those feelings were reflected in carefully modulated editorials on WBT and WBTV, but articulated more forcefully in his own words, as in this speech in 1964, as Johnson's "Great Society" programs were being launched:

> ...Time was when we as a nation bowed our heads at the mere thought of accepting charity, when we dared those whom we had elected to govern us to coddle and pet us, when we charted our own course – falteringly sometimes, slowly often, but always in our own way, at our own speed, in our own time.

> But now, it is no longer stylish to be independent. A softness has wrapped its downy arms around us, sapping the vital fiber that made us what we are – pillowing us with promises of a Great New Society stretching off on the horizon, where care and strife and want and need do not exist. Just leave it to us, the social liberals say, and we'll give you a world where poverty does not exist, where all men will be swaddled in a blanket of security. We'll give you that utopia surpassing anything Thomas More dreamed about.

> And the price for this heaven on earth? There is a price, and it must be costly to promise so much. It is a quickening loss of our individual liberty as it is subordinated to the Great Dream. It is a corralling of our masses into the stall of sweeping socialism as our elected knights leap to their white charger and set off in hot pursuit of the Holy Grail – vintage 1964. It is all these

things, and more.

And if this Great New Society succeeds, where is he left who prefers to command his own fate, and not be herded along toward Utopia by a beneficent central government?

He is left – and let me be deliberately blunt here – where he should be, where he will be (if he acquiesces) a serf of the state. He will be 180 degrees removed from the concept that founded this nation and which guided our forefathers to draft the greatest document ever devised – the Constitution. He will be, sooner or later, subordinate to the state. His worth and dignity as an individual will be diminished – to the extent, I believe, that power is centralized.

The advocates of centralized government will tell you that this isn't so. Don't you buy it! The greatest teacher of all history, and history across the ages, has borne out the wise words of Lord Acton, "All power corrupts; absolute power corrupts absolutely."

Although Crutchfield had never been particularly demonstrative about his religious beliefs, and was frequently and good-naturedly irreverent, he worried about what he described in one speech as "the rapidly diminishing role of religion in our lives." Along with other conservatives, he also was critical of some of the decisions coming out of the U.S. Supreme Court, where America's 200-year-old Constitution and Bill of Rights were being interpreted in light of the realities of an increasingly diverse society.

Religion was once part and parcel of our national makeup, and as such was both a stimulant and a sedative," he wrote. "It was not then one of the social graces, but a vital and vigorous way of life interwoven into the national fabric...

For almost two centuries the role of religion in our government was unquestioned. And then...our structure began to crumble."

To illustrate, he cited the example of "an atheistic mother" who, appalled that her small son was exposed to prayer and Bible reading in school, appealed to the Supreme Court that this was unconstitutional.

> The court, in a decision without precedent, upheld her plea and set into motion events which I predict will affect our civilization far beyond the life span of any of us now occupying the planet....

> We have, with surgical certainty, amputated the living limb of faith from a key part of our society – our schools...not with the blessings of the majority, but at the whim of a single individual....

> There is irony here. The court's decision has succeeded in accomplishing exactly what our forefathers feared when they penned the "separation of church and state" doctrine. Because of a fancied infringement on somebody's rights, the mass of America has been denied the right to have daily Bible reading and prayer in the schools.

With another presidential election just months away, the drama in the streets, which television brought into American homes each evening, became ever more chaotic. It was also becoming more difficult for the Johnson administration and commanders in the field to maintain any credibility for their claims that North Vietnam was losing a war of attrition that would soon be over. On January 31 of 1968, the first day of the Lunar New Year, a Vietnamese holiday known as Tet, the North Vietnamese launched a series of massive surprise attacks across South Vietnam. Although it fell short of its military objective, the Tet offensive demonstrated that the war was far from over, and it had a shattering impact on American opinion.

In February the *CBS Evening News* anchor, Walter Cronkite, and the program's executive producer, Ernest Leiser, went to Vietnam to try to see for themselves how the war was going. In his six years as anchor, Cronkite, then 52 years of age, had demonstrated an image of maturity and integrity that a few years later would establish him in public opinion polls as "the most trusted man in America." He was a fine writer and editor, and he delivered the news with what the *New York Times*, in his obituary in 2009, called "plain-spoken grace." His colleague Eric Sevareid's brief editorials, which followed the newscast, sometimes drew political fire. (As early as 1966 Sevareid had suggested that the United States negotiate an end to the war.) But Cronkite somehow remained above and immune to partisan politics.

When he and Leiser returned from Vietnam they drafted an editorial statement, which Cronkite read on the February 27 *Evening News* on WBTV and other stations carrying CBS television:

> We have been too often disappointed by the optimism of the American leaders, both in Vietnam and Washington, to have faith any longer in the silver linings they find in the darkest clouds. They may be right, that Hanoi's winter-spring offensive has been forced by the Communist realization that they could not win the longer war of attrition, and that the Communists hope that any success in the offensive will improve their position for eventual negotiations. It would improve their position, and it would also require our realization, that we should have had all along, that any negotiations must be that – negotiations, not the dictation of peace terms. For it seems now more certain than ever that the bloody experience of Vietnam is to end in a stalemate.

> This summer's almost certain standoff will either end in real give-and-take negotiations or terrible escalation; and for every means we have to escalate, the enemy can match us, and that applies to invasion of the North, the use of nuclear weapons, or the mere commitment of one hundred, or two hundred, or three hundred thousand more American troops to the battle. And with each escalation, the world comes closer to the brink of cosmic disaster. To say that we are closer to victory today is to believe, in the face of the evidence, the optimists who have been wrong in the past. To suggest we are on the edge of defeat is to yield to unreasonable pessimism. To say that we are mired in stalemate seems the only realistic, yet unsatisfactory, conclusion.

On the off chance that military and political analysts are right, in the next few months we must test the enemy's intentions, in case this is indeed his last big gasp before negotiations. But it is increasingly clear to this reporter that the only rational way out then will be to negotiate, not as victors, but as an honorable people who lived up to their pledge to defend democracy, and did the best they could.

It was widely reported that President Johnson, after hearing the editorial, said if he had lost Cronkite, he had lost middle America. Such was the impact of television generally, CBS News more particularly, and even more particularly, Walter Cronkite. The President could also have added that he was losing his party. More and more politicians, including Robert F. Kennedy and a number of other Democratic Party leaders, were questioning the war and the administration's conduct of it. On March 31, 1968, Johnson, in failing health and with his political base falling apart, surprised the nation by announcing that he would not seek reelection.

Two weeks later, on April 14, Martin Luther King, Jr., was shot and killed while standing on a motel balcony in Memphis, Tennessee. Less than two months after that, on June 5, Robert F. Kennedy, campaigning for the Democratic nomination for president, was assassinated in a Los Angeles hotel hallway a few hours after winning the California primary.

The murder of Robert Kennedy sent waves of despair through the antiwar movement and the younger elements of the Democratic Party. The murder of Martin Luther King had already sent waves of African Americans into the streets of their own inner-city neighborhoods and business districts in New York City, Los Angeles, and other urban centers. The rioters overturned passing vehicles, shattered store windows, attacked bystanders, and in their wake came the looters. Police moved in and met violence with violence. Young black men eschewed King's philosophy of passive resistance and called instead for "black power." Television brought all of it into American homes, and the responses of viewers depended to some extent on their race, political affiliation and age. But for many the reaction was anger and confusion, along with gratitude that it was all happening somewhere other than their own city, town, or neighborhood – but also bewilderment and even disbelief that it could be happening anywhere in the United States of America.

Television also took everyone to the battlefields of Vietnam, where young Americans were still dying in a war that increasingly seemed futile. Just 20 years ago it had been morning in America. Now what people were seeing on television each night looked more like the twilight of the republic.

Chapter Thirty-Five
Nixon

POLITICIANS OF BOTH PARTIES stumbled toward the November national elections, but one politician, Richard M. Nixon, moved forward with confidence.

After losing the 1960 presidential election to Kennedy, Nixon reportedly believed the narrow margin was accounted for by fraudulent vote counts in Chicago, but he declined to challenge the outcome. He returned to California and two years later made a run for governor. He was crushed by incumbent Democrat Pat Brown and in a post-election news conference said, "You won't have Nixon to kick around anymore." It seemed his political career was over. But in 1968 he saw, in the chaotic national landscape, an opportunity. While Democrats fought with each other over the war and civil rights, Nixon was lining up convention delegates. Many Republicans, as well as some Democrats, saw him as a mature, experienced candidate who represented the normalcy of the recent past. When Republicans met for their national convention in Miami Beach in early August, they nominated the former vice president on the first ballot.

Americans who watched the convention, which was an assembly of mostly white, mostly well-to-do, mostly middle-aged, mostly well-dressed and well-behaved delegates, had to be struck by the contrast

With President Nixon at the White House

with the youthful rioting and violence swirling around the country. To some it may have seemed that the Republican delegates were out of touch with the terrible realities of the time. But for many, the convention was a welcome reminder of how they believed American life and politics should be. To those Americans whom Nixon would later call "the silent majority," his nomination offered hope that with new leadership that harkened back to a calmer time, their country could once again find its way. Nixon encouraged that hope in his acceptance speech, with references to the Eisenhower years, the not-so-long-ago good old days. (Eisenhower himself, in failing health, did not attend.)

Nixon had the support of Sen. Strom Thurmond of South Carolina, who had abandoned the Democratic Party some years earlier over the issue of civil rights. No longer a fire-breathing segregationist but still a powerful symbol of Southern resistance to civil rights legislation, Thurmond helped Nixon develop a "Southern strategy," aimed at attracting the votes of conservative Southern Democrats and bringing the Republican Party out of its century-old minority status in the former Confederate states. While never expressing opposition to civil rights and desegregation, Nixon generally avoided the subject and counted on the support of Thurmond and like-minded Southern Republicans to reassure white Southern voters that he was a better choice for president in 1968 than any Democrat.

If the Republican convention in balmy Miami provided a welcome contrast to the usual disturbing national news, its contrast with the Democratic National Convention almost three weeks later was even more dramatic and, possibly, decisive. As Democratic delegates headed for Chicago, so did thousands of antiwar protesters and civil rights demonstrators. Delegates met in the International Amphitheatre behind bullet-proof doors and fencing topped with barbed wire, while throngs of angry, disillusioned, and mostly young Americans gathered outside. The Chicago police were ready with clubs and teargas, and the Illinois National Guard was on alert, with orders to shoot if necessary. Over the next three days the televised teargas-fogged spectacle of demonstrators' violence and police brutality overshadowed what was happening inside the convention, where Vice President Hubert Humphrey was nominated for president.

Humphrey's candidacy was crippled from the start by the extraordinary political cross-currents of the time. He had been one of the most passionate and consistent liberal voices in the U.S. Senate. But as Johnson's vice president, he had been loyal to the administration and defended its conduct of the war, and many liberal Democrats refused to forgive him for that.

Humphrey's dilemma was just one of the realities of 1968 converging in ironic and paradoxical patterns to impel what may have been the most remarkable comeback in American political history.

Just four years after the Johnson-Humphrey ticket had carried 44 states and the District of Columbia, Humphrey carried only 13 states and the district. Nixon's "Southern Strategy" was preempted to some extent by the candidacy of former Alabama Governor George Wallace, who won five Deep South states. But Nixon carried Virginia, Tennessee, the Carolinas, and Florida, which were once part of the Democrats' Solid South, and won, in all, 32 states, representing almost

56 percent of the nation's electoral votes.

En route to that victory, Nixon's campaign passed through Charlotte where, waiting to tape a television program at WBTV, he visited a delighted Charles Crutchfield in his office. The two men seemed to have an instant rapport, despite some obvious differences in background and circumstances. Crutchfield was an entertainer turned broadcast executive and outspoken political conservative. Nixon had a law degree from Duke but was essentially a career politician who had already spent eight years, as the cliché puts it, a heartbeat from the presidency. He was considered conservative, but he was more pragmatic than ideological or principled.

Crutchfield was more confident – more manly, perhaps – than Nixon, whose evasive manner and sometimes ambiguous rhetoric made it impossible for him to shed the sobriquet "Tricky Dick." But a stern anti-communism was part of Nixon's political persona, and that appealed to Crutchfield. And, given the crushing defeat of Barry Goldwater four years earlier, perhaps Crutchfield recognized that Nixon's views were as close to his own as any successful presidential candidate was likely to have.

They were about the same age. Nixon was younger, but by less than six months. They were dressed and groomed in the same conservative executive style, and their public behavior reflected proper regard for good manners. Some of Nixon's detractors believed that his public, political face masked a disturbingly paranoid inner self. Meeting him in person, however, Crutchfield liked what he saw and sensed, and he was confident in his judgment about people. Nixon made himself comfortable that day, putting his feet up on Crutchfield's coffee table as they talked. Crutchfield became a Nixon supporter and remained fiercely loyal until he and other Nixon supporters were finally betrayed. His friendship with Nixon, along with his status as an important broadcasting executive, gave him access to the White House and the upper levels of the Nixon administration over the next few years. He was proud of that access and took advantage of it to offer opinions and encouragement to the President and his top advisors.

On an April evening in 1970, the Crutchfields were among the guests in the East Room of the White House for a musical presentation featuring the country singer Johnny Cash. It would not be their last visit to the Nixon White House.

In 1971, as Chamber of Commerce president, Crutchfield took the lead in organizing Billy Graham Day to honor the Charlotte native who had become the world's foremost evangelist. It was a labor of love for Crutchfield. He and Graham had become friends over the years, and it was Crutchfield's advice that led Graham to start televising his crusades. Other civic leaders were involved in the planning, and the event was scheduled for October at the Charlotte Coliseum.

Charlotteans generally were proud of Billy Graham, and there normally would have been no cause for controversy over such an event. But Graham had made a few publicized visits to the Nixon White House, and President Nixon accepted an invitation to attend Billy Graham Day and even make a few remarks. It was a little over a year until the next presidential election, but some local Democrats complained that Nixon's presence would make the Graham tribute a political event promoting the President's coming reelection bid. Also, Nixon had said more than once that he had a secret plan to end the war in Vietnam, but the war raged on and the protests against it were as robust as ever. Protesters showed up in large numbers outside the Coliseum that day, as did local police, with the Secret Service on alert inside.

The controversy became personal for Crutchfield. It was no secret that he supported Nixon, and his television station promoted Billy Graham Day heavily, with public service announcements and news stories. An assistant professor of political science at Davidson College, William E. Jackson, Jr., wrote a long letter to the *Charlotte Observer* asserting that Crutchfield had misused his influence as Chamber president and as head of Jefferson Standard Broadcasting for Nixon's political benefit.

He began: "It is a joke, of course, to refer to the Richard Nixon-Billy Graham affair as a 'non-political' event…. There was heavy political con-

Crutchfield and Billy Graham on the golf course

tents to the speeches at the Coliseum, especially Graham's...."

The harangue continued with numerous examples of what Jackson considered inappropriate activity by Crutchfield, with little distinction implied between the trivial and the serious. Jackson cited Crutchfield's closeness to the President and called him "in effect, a White House agent in the local area.

"There is nothing wrong with this activity in itself," he wrote. "But when the same man sits on the editorial board of a television station, the public must be alert to conflicts of interest."

He concluded:

Mr. Crutchfield is only human. He uses his influential position to get across his point of view, without much interest in others' points of view. He is acting on the basis of what he believes is good for the public.

Like the federal regulators he has often warned us about, however, he has enormous power while not being directly responsible to the people in his use of the public air waves. As license renewal time comes along, the public must be on guard – and not rely solely upon congressional and FCC investigation – lest we allow ourselves to be subjected over the air to the propagation of the political ideas of one man. "Big Brother" comes in many guises.

The *Observer*'s editorial page editor sent a copy of the letter to Crutchfield, inviting him to respond, which he did, writing: "It is true that the idea of honoring Dr. Graham was mine. It is also true that I invited the President to participate, and I do not intend to apologize to Jackson or anyone else for my part in this historic occasion. I'm proud of it."

He then offered a point-by-point rebuttal to Jackson's charges, noting that some of them were not factual. Regarding the WBTV editorial board, Crutchfield wrote: "Even were Jackson's charges true, however, there would be no 'conflict of interest' with WBT-WBTV editorials. Here's why. I am only one of nine voices on the Editorial Board. I have one vote...no more, no less.... I have never prohibited an editorial from airing because it did not reflect my own thinking, nor do I ever plan to."

The two letters were published on the same day, Nov. 1, 1971, two weeks after the Billy Graham event had taken place.

The controversy over Nixon's presence at Billy Graham Day did nothing to diminish Crutchfield's loyalty to the President. Nixon obviously appreciated that loyalty and rewarded it accordingly. For example, on July 26, 1972, the day before his 60th birthday, Crutchfield received this message via Western Union wire from the White House:

JULY 27 BRINGS US A WELCOME OPPORTUNITY TO SEND GREETINGS YOUR WAY. THE THOUGHTS OF ALL THE NIXONS ARE WITH YOU AS ARE OUR FONDEST WISHES FOR THE HAPPIEST OF BIRTHDAYS.
RICHARD NIXON

Earlier that month, police had arrested five men breaking into Democratic National Committee headquarters at the Watergate office complex in Washington. The burglars, who were attempting to wiretap the offices and steal information from files, were soon linked by the FBI to an organization called the Committee to Re-elect the President, also known by the prophetic acronym CREEP. It was briefly a big story, but most news organizations soon turned their attention back to the usual political give and take of a presidential election year – except for two young reporters at the *Washington Post*, Carl Bernstein and Bob Woodward.

Nixon won a second term that fall, and on February 1, 1973, a few days after the inauguration, the Crutchfields were among the guests at a White House dinner honoring Prime Minister Edward Heath and a number of high-ranking British officials.

By that time, reporting by Woodward and Bernstein and official investigations were linking the Watergate crime – and subsequent cover-up efforts – to some of the President's top advisors. That spring the United States Senate appointed a special committee to investigate the connections between CREEP, the White House, and the Watergate burglary. The committee, chaired by Sen. Sam Ervin of North Carolina, a conservative Democrat who already had a deep distrust of Richard Nixon, began hearings on May 17.

Once again, television brought history into American homes. The televised hearings, with Ervin and his colleagues grilling the President's closest aides, were devastating to the administration. But Crutchfield remained loyal and refused to believe Nixon had done anything wrong. In fact, he was critical of the news media, including CBS, for their coverage of the Watergate investigation. He was convinced, with good reason, that many reporters, editors, and commentators were politically liberal and instinctively disliked Nixon; now, he believed, they were out to destroy the Nixon presidency.

Meanwhile, in October, an unrelated scandal rattled the White House. Vice President Spiro Agnew, a former governor of Maryland, was charged in his home state with tax fraud, bribery, extortion and accepting bribes. He pleaded no contest to one of the lesser tax charges and the other charges were dropped on the condition that he resign as vice president, which he did on October 10. President Nixon chose a popular congressman, Gerald Ford of Michigan, to replace Agnew. Later that month the President requested network television time to address the nation regarding the Watergate investigation on October 24. That morning, Crutchfield sent a telegram to Rose Mary Woods, the President's executive assistant:

> WITH THE LIBERALS OF THE PRESS AND OTHERS, EVEN INCLUD-ING THE CHANCELLOR AT DUKE UNIVERSITY, THE PRESIDENT'S ALMA MATER, STILL YAPPING FOR IMPEACHMENT, I RESPECT-FULLY RECOMMEND THAT THE PRESIDENT RECONSIDER HIS DECISION TO ADDRESS THE PUBLIC FORMALLY TONIGHT. AS A PROFESSIONAL BROADCASTER, I CANNOT EMPHASIZE TOO STRONGLY HOW MUCH MORE EFFECTIVE AND CONVINCING HE WOULD BE STANDING UP TOE-TO-TOE AGAINST HIS ADVERSARIES IN AN OPEN PRESS CONFERENCE PRECEDED BY A STATEMENT OF POSITION. THE PRESIDENT HAS BEEN MASTER OF EVERY PRESS CONFERENCE HE HAS EVER HELD. SINCE TONIGHT IS PROBABLY HIS MOST IMPORTANT ONE, PLEASE, FOR HIS SAKE, AND FOR THAT OF THE GREAT MAJORITY OF AMERICANS WHO BELIEVE IN HIM, URGE HIM TO USE HIS MOST EFFECTIVE WEAPON TONIGHT.

Less than a week later, Crutchfield received a letter from the President:

> Dear Charlie:
>
> Rose Mary Woods has given me your telegram of October 24, in which you urged that I reconsider my decision to make a formal address to the Nation and, instead, hold a Press Conference. As you know, I did decide in favor of a Press Conference on Friday night. Judging from the comments which have been received thus far, many of our fellow citizens share your views about the effectiveness of such a forum.

Many thanks for your interest in passing along this suggestion – and I hope you will continue to give me the benefit of your views on such matters in the future.

With kind personal regards,
Sincerely,
(signed) RN

The following month, Nixon spoke at a meeting of Associated Press managing editors in Washington, where he made a declaration that would resonate over the following months as more and more evidence to the contrary was piling up: "I am not a crook."

The Ervin committee issued its report on June 27, 1974. The death blow to the Nixon presidency came from the tape recording system in the Oval Office. The courts ordered the release of taped conversations between the President and members of his staff concerning the Watergate burglary and how to conceal the administration's involvement. It was clear that the President himself was a party to the cover-up. The tapes also revealed Nixon as an unabashedly dishonest person, and his comments, laced with profanity, must have shocked many supporters who had been impressed by his relationship with the Rev. Billy Graham.

Crutchfield was devastated by the betrayal of the trust he and so many others had placed in the President. Facing certain impeachment and likely conviction, Nixon resigned on August 9, 1974.

Gerald Ford, who had never won an election outside his district in Michigan, became president. He promptly issued a full pardon of his predecessor, indicating that he did not want the nation distracted by the prosecution of a former president. It was time to close the curtain on Watergate. Ford's decision was almost certainly in the best interests of the country, but it probably was a factor in the election two years later, which he lost to Jimmy Carter of Georgia.

A few weeks after Nixon's resignation, Crutchfield's brother, Ralph, died in Spartanburg at age 67. Ralph Crutchfield had been as successful in his field, retail sporting goods, as his younger brother was in broadcasting. *Spartanburg Journal* Sports Editor Ed McGrath had written a column about him several years earlier, noting that Crutchfield had "had dealings with all of the great and near great in South Carolina sports for the past four decades." McGrath wrote that in addition to the fine sporting goods store on Pine Street in Spartanburg, the "bread and butter" of Crutchfield's business was selling uniforms and equipment to high school and college teams, church teams, and athletic clubs across a market that stretched from North Carolina into Georgia.

Ralph's soft-spoken, gentle strength had always been there for his younger brother, Chock. Now it was gone.

In 1972, the Crutchfields' residence was once again featured in the Mint Museum Home Tour. This time, one of the visitors was William Pahlmann, perhaps the most celebrated and influential interior designer of the mid-20th century. After his visit to Charlotte, Pahlmann wrote a column published in newspapers across the nation about the house that Pee Wee decorated.

One of my favorite American cities is Charlotte, N.C., where fortunately my work and enthusiasms occasionally take me....

I have never believed that set rules should be followed in planning the interiors of a home, but that people should express their own tastes and interests in their surroundings and, when I find a house that is a positive assertion on the part of the people who live there, I applaud. Such a house is the home of Mr. and Mrs. Charles H. Crutchfield of Charlotte.... They are both sturdy individualists and their house reflects them – full of imagination and warmth....

The Crutchfield house has fine and beautiful treasures, many of them worthy of a museum, but the atmosphere of the house is one of good living and casual comfort, an inviting ambience.... The house reflects the many interests of its busy and gregarious owners, and provides a setting for entertainment that is always warm and hospitable. Real conversation transpires in its rooms and there is lots of laughter. It was difficult to persuade me to leave!

—*William Pahlmann*

CHAPTER THIRTY-SIX
Dissonance

NIXON'S RESIGNATION was one of several dissonant events that marred the final decade of a career that had generally been as harmonious as an old Briarhoppers' ballad.

A serious challenge to WBT's historic dominance of the Charlotte radio market began in 1965 with the purchase of WAYS by Stan Kaplan and his wife, Harriet "Sis" Kaplan. Crutchfield, who knew Sis Kaplan's father, Chicago broadcasting pioneer H. Leslie Atlass, gave the couple a personal tour of the impressive WBT-WBTV headquarters. Stan Kaplan found Crutchfield's attitude that day somewhat condescending. WAYS was a run-down operation located in a house trailer in a rural community on the western edge of Charlotte – an unlikely threat to the deeply entrenched and lavishly housed WBT. But the Kaplans' audacious vision was much grander than the station they had bought.

They turned the call letters into a word, christening the station Big WAYS, installed a fast-moving Top 40 format with young, talented disc jockeys, and launched a treasure hunt. On the air and on billboards across the city was the news that Big WAYS had buried $10,000 somewhere in Charlotte. People could get clues to the location of the treasure by tuning to 610 on the AM radio dial. As clues dribbled out on the radio day after day, the hunt created traffic jams, and suddenly unwelcome crowds of people were trampling across other people's property. Other stations' news departments ignored the commotion, but the newspapers took notice. Big WAYS was off and running.

The treasure hunt was only the first of a continuing stream of creative and high-powered promotions. By the late 1960s, American Research Bureau (ARB) audience measurements showed WAYS as the top station in the market, not only with teenagers but also in the young adult category that was so important to advertisers. When the spring ARB numbers in 1970 showed WBT in ninth place, the station's national advertising representative, Blair Radio, sent word to Charlotte that something had to be done. It could not successfully sell time to national accounts on a station with such poor audience numbers.

WBT's general manager Harold Hinson got the message. Despite its powerful signal, fine facilities, and long history of success, WBT was no longer competitive. By the standards of contemporary AM radio, its audience was getting old. Its programming had to change. But Hinson knew change would not be easy. WBT was an institution, with traditions, owned by a large, conservative insurance company. Its image, and Charles Crutchfield's personal tastes, seemed incompatible with raucous rock and roll and teenage "bubble-gum" music, but that was what most listeners under 40 years of age wanted to hear.

Hinson decided it would take more research than an ARB book could provide, and a clear presentation of the facts and a detailed plan of action, to persuade his bosses, including Crutchfield, to bring WBT up to date in a world where the "American songbook" from Broadway shows and old movies was no longer the nation's most popular music. That would mean playing the kind of music WBT had condemned on the air just a few years earlier as "ninety-eight cents worth of trash."

In the summer of 1970 he commissioned a respected research firm and a hot young programming consultant named Tom McMurray to measure radio listening habits, musical tastes, and programming preferences, as well as economic and demographic information, to create a deep and extensive portrait of the AM radio market in the WBT coverage area. Hinson took the research reports to the top executives under Crutchfield at Jefferson Standard Broadcasting. They arranged for a presentation for Crutchfield, who reluctantly agreed to a format change.

No doubt a happier change for Crutchfield at the time came on the television side, where Bob Inman joined the station as a news anchor. Inman, an Alabama native and a Phi Beta Kappa graduate of his home state university, had a handsome face, a wide smile, and an accent pleasantly poised between well-educated Southern and broadcaster generic. If as a young television journalist he was at all intimidated by going to work at the dominant powerhouse that was WBTV, it was not obvious. His on-screen presence was amiable and at ease, and he soon became one of the most popular news anchors in the history of the station. With a break for some post-graduate education, Inman remained with WBTV for more than 25 years.

Meanwhile, Harold Hinson put his plans for WBT-AM into action. He hired McMurray as program director. The station spent $200,000 for studio and other renovations, new equipment, and new station identification jingles. The first two of what eventually would be an entirely new team of disc jockeys, H.A. Thompson and Rob Hunter, were hired in early 1971. Based on the summer research, McMurray developed an "adult contemporary" playlist of recordings that featured current hits, plus rock and pop music "standards" by artists such as Diana Ross, the Platters, Fats Domino, Neil Diamond, Tom Jones, Elvis Presley, the Beatles, the Beach Boys, and others – eclectic, but all post-1940s. CBS programs and some locally produced features were cancelled.

Before any changes were on air, everything was polished and put in place during late 1970 and early 1971. On Monday, March 8, 1971, listeners heard an announcement that at 7 p.m. on Sunday WBT would become a thing of the past – hinting that it might be going out of business. That Sunday evening the new WBT started rocking and rolling with what would become a staple for years – the *Original Sunday Night Hall of Fame.*

If the transition was slick in terms of the product, it was not smooth internally at One Julian Price Place. Some employees took early retirement and others were let go or bought out to make room for new people. Some long-time listeners and local advertisers expressed their displeasure with the new format. Some employees still on the staff didn't like the change or the music. Recalling that spring, H.A. Thompson said, "We were the bad boys."

Among the people most unhappy with the music was Charles Crutchfield, who still thought it was "trash" and occasionally tried to get a particular record taken off the air. He succeeded in the case of a Conway Twitty song called "We've Never Gone This Far Before," but in most cases he was persuaded to withdraw his objections.

Cullie Tarleton, sales manager at the time of the change, remembers being summoned into the boss's office on several occasions for essentially the same conversation. Crutchfield, returning from lunch, would say that "the boys at the club" had complained about some song they had heard on his station. "Do you have to play that song?" he would ask.

Tarleton said his answer was always something like this: "No, sir, the easiest thing in the world would be to call Andy and tell him to pull that song. But if we're going to be the kind of radio station you want us to be and make the kind of money you want us to make, I have to play that song."

At that point, Crutchfield would simply say, "Get out of here."

While Crutchfield continued to argue about the music, he could not argue with the results. Over the next two years WBT regained its traditional position of number one in the market. McMurray later wrote that by 1973 the station had the highest ARB audience numbers ever achieved by any station in the market and was number one in every time period and every demographic category.

There's little evidence that Crutchfield felt personally challenged by, or was seriously engaged in, the battle for radio audience ratings. The fundamental nature of the medium and its audience had changed radically since his formative years as a radio announcer and station manager. Radio was no longer the family fireside or the primary source of in-home entertainment, cultural features, or comprehensive news programs. That was more descriptive now of television.

Congress passed, and President Johnson signed, the Public Broadcasting Act in 1967, creating the Corporation for Public Broadcasting to support non-commercial radio. Public stations such as the one Crutchfield had helped create at the University of North Carolina at Chapel Hill increasingly provided the classical music, jazz, and extended news programs no longer available on commercial stations.

Crutchfield understood the generational change in the music business, which now provided almost all of commercial radio programming. Years later he told an interviewer that "the big change came about when the Beatles came. This was very obvious to me that they changed the beat, they changed the rhythm, they changed the type program that the public went for. They also changed the hairstyle. I think that is attributable directly to the Beatles."

Another difficult moment for Crutchfield that year was Arthur Smith's decision to move the home of his syndicated country music television show from WBTV to rival WSOC-TV. Tom Cookerly, vice president and general manager of WBTV, said the split was amicable. Cookerly himself left a short while later to manage a television station in Washington, D.C.

Crutchfield served that year as president of the Charlotte Chamber of Commerce, a prestigious position in the fast-growing, business-oriented city. Racial sensitivities were acute at the time. School districts across North Carolina were trying to comply with court orders to not only end racial segregation, but to implement plans to achieve racial proportions in individual schools that reflected the proportion in the overall student population. In Charlotte and Mecklenburg County, Judge James B. McMillan had ordered the school district to bus students as needed to achieve that goal, although a final busing plan had not yet been approved. The school board was bitterly divided over what to do. Many white parents were upset at the prospect of their children being carried across town to a formerly

Editorial cartoon by Gene Payne lampooning Crutchfield

black school, and some educators feared the result would be "white flight" from the public schools.

Generally recognized as an advocate for good race relations, Crutchfield was very much aware of the tension and the potential even for violence. Although he personally believed McMillan's decision was extreme, WBTV created special public service announcements, including one featuring Billy Graham, urging the community to be calm, keep the peace, and obey the law.

It is worth noting that Crutchfield had not always exhibited finesse when handling racial issues, and had made what could be considered a serious misstep in 1967. That May, as Chamber president, while attending an informal meeting with members of the Mecklenburg County legislative delegation in Raleigh, Crutchfield expressed the opinion that many African Americans were not "mentally qualified" to run a city. An aide immediately suggested to him that he had misspoken, and Crutchfield quickly explained that he had meant to say "educationally," not "mentally." But there were reporters present, including Paul Jones of WBTV, and the statement became a big story.

Crutchfield, stung by the media coverage, including stories on his own stations, went on with a planned weekend trip to the beach, where he fumed. He did not expect any special treatment from WBTV's news department, but he did expect fair treatment, which he did not believe he received. While he was away, the rest of WBTV's top management held a private meeting to discuss the uproar over their boss's choice of words. After his return, on Tuesday, June 1, Crutchfield called a management meeting, which he began by saying, "I'm going to read my remarks so that they can be referred back to. This has to do with the situation in Raleigh last week." He continued:

> The reason I didn't cancel my trip to the beach last weekend and call this meeting immediately was because I wanted to sleep on it and, above all, have a chance to study my Raleigh error and cool off. I have slept on it, studied all the reports, but, frankly, my cool is slow in coming.

> The other day, the 64 clubs from Asheville to Winston-Salem which make up the Civitan West District presented me their Distinguished Citizenship Award for what they termed "service to my fellowman." During that same occasion they presented a special international award to a young black student here for outstanding contributions to his school, his fellow students and to the community. This happened right here in Charlotte where we are experiencing an enormous amount of tension currently in our public schools. Not one single reporter from our Company was there.

> Four nights later, in a spontaneous and informal discussion with our delegation in Raleigh, I unfortunately used a word, "mentally" qualified rather than "educationally" qualified, and our news department made a federal case out of it, despite the fact that I corrected and explained the intent of my remark... in less than two minutes after the error was called to my attention – and despite the fact that immediately after the meeting I explained the error again to Paul Jones and other reporters that were standing with him, and suggested that he not use the word "mentally" since I had corrected it publicly at the time of the same meeting and since it could cause misunderstanding

and resentment among the blacks. You know the rest of the story.

What I want to do this morning is find out why this irresponsible journalism hit our air before it hit any other media, and figure out ways of correcting the problem. Certainly, I emphatically do not expect any personal favors or protection personally by our news people. I do, however, demand that they conduct themselves in a fair and objective manner, whether the story concerns me or anyone else, especially when the issues are racially explosive.

If we in the Company are going to start publicly beheading each other for one admitted and corrected error, I want to know about this new game because whether you and they know it or not, I still hold the trump card....

It would be nice, of course, if all the people in our Company tried to help me during the difficult year as head of the Chamber of Commerce – and many are doing this. If some are determined to create unnecessary problems and embarrassment for me and my family, and for my Company, so be it. And these problems include telephone threats, obscenities from automobiles and people I meet on the street, black people, and you name it, which also created [the need for] a guard out at the house – the threats had become so bad.

In this connection, however, there are only two things I expect of our people, including you people in management. One is reasonable performance in productivity; the other is complete loyalty – and on this latter requirement there is no compromise. I hope that I'm understood....

This report on *The Early Scene* on May 27, 1971, led with a statement that the president of the Chamber of Commerce "sought to clarify statements he made last night that brought strong reaction from black leaders." The implication here is that it was not until a day later that I clarified the statements when, in fact, the statement was clarified publicly at the meeting with the legislators less than two minutes after the original statement was made. The implication that I "sought to clarify" is also misleading, in that I not only completely cleared the matter or the intent of the statement, but the whole group present at that time was also, as stated, advised, as was Paul Jones, that I thought the word "mentally" was inflammable in this context....

Ben Waters, the reporter, also found it desirable to pour fuel on the fire by contacting several of the leading liberals and blacks in town for comments. By giving their comments immediately after my statement, the implication was that these critical comments were reaction to my clarification, when they were, in fact, reaction to...the completely irresponsible journalism created by Paul Jones in our own news department the night before.

...it's now Tuesday morning and the news department has yet to call me on the subject....

Now, the next thing I want to say – and then I'll be through – there seems to be some misunderstanding as to who's in charge here. I am. And I intend to be until I decide to retire or until I'm retired at age 65. Following this episode, I would like to announce here and now that I have no intentions of retiring early.

In closing, I want you to be aware of this new policy – and this has to do with meetings. There are to be no further meetings or discussions involving me personally, directly or indirectly, unless I am in attendance or without my knowledge and consent.

I'd like to repeat that. There are to be no further meetings or discussions involving me as president of this company, directly or indirectly, unless I am in attendance at those meetings or without my knowledge and consent....

Now, the meeting is over.
Thank you.

Several years later, continuing concern about race relations quite likely influenced his tentative decision in January of 1971 to refuse to carry a new CBS prime-time situation comedy *All in the Family*. The show's main character, Archie Bunker, brilliantly portrayed by Carroll O'Connor, was the epitome of political incorrectness – racist, sexist, anti-Semitic, and an admirer of President Nixon – who verbally abused his wife and constantly harangued his live-in, liberal son-in-law. It was hilarious satire and, paradoxically, deeply humane. But Crutchfield worried about how it might play in a market potentially on the verge of serious racial strife.

The network and his management team persuaded him to accept the program, which became one of the most popular in television history, with no apparent effect on Charlotte's problems.

CHAPTER THIRTY-SEVEN
Speaking of Freedom and the Future

THE CRITICAL CHANGES and controversies of 1970 and 1971 surely left Crutchfield's psyche damaged, but it also may have left him a bit wiser and mellower. He understood that politics was, at any given moment, temporal and temporary. His political views did not shape his personality or define his character. People who knew him well may have thought his increasingly conservative politics had narrowed his mind, but they knew it had never constricted his abundant good will and compassion. Jim Babb, whose political opinions were well to the left of Crutchfield's, said, "He was a bleeding heart." Babb never attempted to conceal his loyalty to the Democratic Party and his political activism, to which the boss responded tolerantly with some occasional good-natured needling.

Crutchfield had no problem looking beyond the day's political conflicts to focus on matters of more profound and lasting importance. He continued to complain about what he saw as the liberal bias of the news media, particularly as it involved coverage of President Nixon. But in a speech to the National Association of Broadcasters convention in 1972 he made it clear that media bias, in one direction or another, was not as important an issue as the media freedom guaranteed in the Bill of Rights:

I suspect that, when the perspective of time has drawn the social revolution of the 1960s into sharper focus, historians will marvel at the maturity which characterized the movement. I further suspect that they will conclude that this comparatively bloodless revolution was made possible, in large part, by the free press and the free broadcaster.

I say this, realizing fully that – as is always the case when two opposing sides are presented – much of what has been said and written has been shaded by the reporters' own personal preferences and opinions.

Nonetheless, the fact that reporters were able to report and interpret events and actions as they saw them – instead of being bound by the "official line" in what they wrote and said – lent credibility and a certain dignity to reports emanating from scenes of crises. In short, readers and viewers received a cross-section of fact and opinion – a composite picture as it were, and – by application of their own intelligence and reasoning to the varied reports – were able to get as clear and as truthful a picture of what was happening as was possible.

Obviously, had citizens been exposed only to the "official line," a completely one-sided account would have been forthcoming.

It is therefore alarming – and somewhat ironic – that there now are in our midst those who would diminish the rights and duties of the media to gather and report the facts.

The most blatant example occurred earlier this year when the Massachusetts legislature enacted into law a bill limiting the activities of newspapers and broadcasters in reporting courts and criminal news. This legislation empowered the attorney general to "set up an adequate staff to check the publication of all news media operating throughout the commonwealth, day by day, week by week, thoroughly and methodically, and cite for contempt those news media breaking the existing laws of the commonwealth regarding the reporting of court and criminal news...."

Let us be thankful that this exercise in arrogance has not gone unchallenged. "Editor and Publisher," that staid old Bible of the newspaper industry, barked its disapproval in its usual succinct manner, saying "...to give such a code the sanction of law is to make every newspaper responsible to the government and to the attorney general's office for what it prints. In this instance, the reference is to court and criminal news. The next time...it might concern news of the legislature or the governor's office. This is the very thing the First Amendment was designed to guard against...."

William L. Shirer...outlined in *The Rise and Fall of the Third Reich* how easy it was for Hitler to control public thinking, once he controlled Germany's newspapers and radio stations....

When the Federal Communications Commission recently attempted to dictate to broadcasters the length and frequency of commercials they could air, newspapers rose almost as one to denounce such tactics. The *Dallas Morning News*...said: "If the American people are to be told – by official government regulation – what advertising they can hear or see, won't they be told what advertising they can read in the newspapers, and how much? If they can be told that, can't they be told what they are to read in the news columns and on the editorial page? Is this free enterprise? Is it even America?"

The *St. Louis Globe-Democrat*...said: "Let us hear no more of men in Washington telling the broadcaster in Walla Walla just how much time he is to allot for commercials, or we shall one day hear the same men tell him just what he is to put on the air."

The *Seattle Post-Intelligencer* said: "...FCC dictatorship must inevitably mean programming control by the government."....

In 1950, a board established by presidential order to study overall communications policy said: "One of the bulwarks of a free society is freedom of communications. Its commerce, its education, its politics, its spiritual integrity and its security depend upon an unimpeded and unsubservient exchange of information and ideas."

But still the fight continues....

And in August of 1973, in a commencement address at Appalachian State University in Boone, where he received an Honorary Degree of Doctor of Humane Letters, he did not look back nostalgically at the age of miracles he had known, or despair about the turbulence of the present. Instead, he preached a bit, and he looked with hope and perhaps an excess of optimism at the miracles to come, which he knew he would not likely live to see:

> I don't know of anything that can revitalize a person more quickly, or renew his perspective more completely, than to come back to this beautiful campus and these magnificent mountains.... As I was driving up yesterday morning, I was very conscious of this. And I experienced, as I always do up here, a sense of stability and permanence. And yet I realized that this feeling was illusory, for there is little that is permanent in our world today.

> Change is converging on us at unbelievable speed.... This change is a relatively new phenomenon – occurring basically within our own lifetime.

> For example, the world into which I was born did not differ greatly from the one into which my father was born, and his world differed even less from the one into which his father was born.

> But shortly after the turn of this century, all this began to change. Technology engulfed us almost overnight, and began to feed on itself. In little more than a half-century, we conquered the skies, split the atom, built enough highways to reach to the moon and back, plumbed – and polluted – the oceans, elevated the standard of living to undreamed-of heights and, in the process, thoroughly confused ourselves.

> Too much had happened too quickly to us. We couldn't com-

prehend and we couldn't cope. We were suddenly strangers in a strange new world.

Economist Kenneth Boulding explains why when he summarized the change this way: "The world of today is as different from the world into which I was born as that world was from Julius Caesar's. I was born in the middle of human history . Almost as much has happened since I was born as happened before...."

But, in comparison with the speed of change that is to come, we have only begun to crawl....

For just a moment...let's peer into your generation's crystal ball and see what is in store for you:

– Your generation will conquer cancer and heart disease.
– You will harness to sun to supply all your power and fuel needs.
– You will wipe out pollution.
– You, or your children, will vacation on the moon.
– You will work a four-day, a three-day, perhaps a two-day week.
– You will master the weather to make it rain at your command.
– ...you will conquer your planet's final frontier, the oceans, and in doing so you will tap an inexhaustible food supply.
– You will make contact with extra-terrestrial life, assuming it exists – as a growing number of scientists believe it does.
– Nobel laureate Joshua Lederberg even predicts that your capacity to make biological carbon copies of yourself, a process called "cloning," will have been reached within 15 years – or before you graduates are 40 years old!
– Experiments will be conducted to modify the brain and certain of its sensory qualities, bringing these mental processes under direct environmental control – also within 15 years.
– A woman will be able to buy a frozen embryo, have it implanted in her body, and give birth to it nine months later. She will be told, in advance, the baby's sex, its eye and hair

color, its approximate size at maturity, and its probable I.Q.

Aren't these fascinating — and frightening prospects?

...You, if you are to function, will have to find ways to cope with tremendous, unprecedented change....

You will have to become more adaptable than any other generation...in history....

How, then, can you meet and cope with the world you are about to enter? What inner resources can you draw upon to retain your balance and your perspective?

I believe...that you will have to return to the past to find those things which you simply must have to sustain yourself – those enduring values which have led men from the darkness of the caves into the sunlight of civilization.

First among these values is faith – simple, childlike faith – faith in a Supreme Being.

Since he began to walk upright, man has felt a compulsion to identify with his God; he has found it essential that he believe in a Power greater than himself.

This need is as great now as it ever has been, and – at the risk of preaching this morning – I don't believe any of us can find meaning and purpose in our life until we establish a personal relationship with our Maker....

Another enduring value is integrity – plain, old-fashioned personal integrity....

In addition...you will need something else – something the great thinkers and the great religions have advocated over the centuries.

It is tolerance – tolerance to other men, their point of view and their way of life.

And here, your generation is far ahead of mine.

Not only are you less racially prejudiced, but also less class conscious. You are more prone to judge people on their merits than (I regret to admit) some of us have been....

...when you commit yourselves to these values... you will have gained the inner strength to cope with whatever comes.

I hope that your generation understands this. I believe that, by and large, it does.

And this, more than any other single thing, kindles my confidence in your future and the future of our nation....

Chapter Thirty-Eight
Looking Back, Moving On

I N 1973 JEFFERSON STANDARD Broadcasting Company changed its name to Jefferson-Pilot Broadcasting Company, reflecting another corporate merger. WBT's new format had rapidly gained traction. WBTV remained the top television station in the market, with CBS the top network. Crutchfield, now age 61, had been named general manager of WBT in 1945 and president of Jefferson Standard Broadcasting in 1963. During those 28 years he had hired and trained good people and given them room to grow, freedom to innovate, and responsibility for the results. With good people now in place, he was less and less a hands-on executive. In part that meant more time for long lunches and card games with friends at the country club. It also meant time to take on more civic responsibilities and to advocate for things in which he believed.

Although he had begun his career as an entertainer on radio, his primary concerns as a broadcasting executive were informing and educating the public, and his own responsibilities to his community, state, and nation. Evidence of this were his term as head of the Chamber of Commerce and his early and persistent advocacy on behalf of a CBS experiment called *60 Minutes*. The network described it as a news magazine for television. It was launched in September of

1968, airing every other week, on Tuesdays. Despite outstanding work by reporters Mike Wallace and Harry Reasoner, ratings were low. In early 1972, the network moved it to Sundays, and then back and forth among various times and days over the next three years, without great success.

Crutchfield liked the concept and the objective investigative reporting. He believed it exemplified what television at its best was supposed to be, and he urged the network not to abandon it. When the program settled into early prime time on Sunday nights in 1975, he advised CBS to keep it there. In that spot, *60 Minutes* became one of the most successful programs in television history.

Even as retirement loomed, Crutchfield continued to offer frequent advice and counsel, usually unsolicited, to CBS, and particularly its news department. When Richard Salant became president of CBS News in 1961, Crutchfield had begun a regular correspondence with him that continued for years and became legendary at the network and among its affiliates. Occasionally Crutchfield would write to applaud some program or piece of reporting that he liked. But more often his letters pointed to examples of what he considered biased reporting, or segments that blurred the line between objective reporting, analysis, and commentary. Some of his letters produced results. Most did not. Crutchfield was a good debater, keeping his points tightly focused and often anticipating the direction of the rebuttal to come. Salant respected his integrity and intelligence, but generally disagreed with him. He did not, however – could not – ignore him.

In October, 1977, at the Grove Park Inn in Asheville, where the autumn colors across the mountains were at their peak, Crutchfield and Salant attended an annual meeting of the North Carolina Associated Press Broadcasters. Crutchfield spoke at a luncheon. Salant, down from New York City, was the dinner speaker that evening. His subject was Charles Crutchfield:

> ...I'm not here because this is a lovely place – it is indeed; nor

am I here because the company is exceedingly good – although it certainly is; I'm not even here because I'm especially fond of Jim and Mary Lou Babb – as I surely am. I am here for one reason only – one overwhelming, surpassing reason... Charles Crutchfield. Charles is, and has been for all these many years, a truly great broadcaster – a man who knows what broadcasting, and its special responsibilities, are all about, and has dedicated his life to realizing his, and his stations', ideals. He has been, and I trust will continue to be, good for all of us in broadcasting and particularly good for us at CBS News and for me.

As all CBS affiliates know, Charles and I have had a running dialogue – as neutral a word as I can find – since the day I became president of the CBS News Division more than 16 years ago.... I had my first letter from him on February 10, 1961– less than a week after I became president.... In that letter Charles suggested that we do a closed circuit 5 o'clock newsfeed for affiliates' use in their local news. That suggestion was adopted and implemented. And it wasn't the last time that we adopted a Crutchfield suggestion....

The last – or rather most recent – one I had from Charles was dated exactly a month ago – September 29, 1977 – a generous letter praising one of our news stories....

In preparing for this evening, I reread all the correspondence between Charles and me that remained in our files during that entire period. And so I relived the period and the terrible traumas through which the country went and the awesome problems and responsibilities that the events of those years placed on all in journalism, particularly on us at CBS News. In our correspondence, Charles and I managed to touch on a great part of that history and those problems and that responsibility. And, the letters and wires dealt with the raw-nerved issues – Vietnam and Watergate. It covered so many things – ... Martin Luther King; political, student and civil rights demonstrations; the Voice of America; the use of the word "goddam" by some of the interviewees in news broadcasts; nudity – more or less; byssinosis; ...the difference between news reporting and editorializing; whether it is proper ever to include background, interpretation and analysis in hard news – I think yes; Charles knows no; and so on, and so on.... Fundamental issues of the time and fundamental issues relating to good journalism – all were covered by that correspondence – sometimes quietly and sometimes violently, sometimes philosophically and in good humor, sometimes emotionally and in ill humor, considerably more often than not. Charles and I disagreed – vigorously.

What surprised me...is how often Charles took the time to write letters of praise about some of the things we did. That reminded me again...that Charles is not a knee-jerk, but however passionate in his beliefs, a thoughtful, perceptive and selective man.... In our continuous game of one-upmanship, we even on rare occasions admitted that we were wrong.... There was that wonderful letter in 1970 in which Charles wrote me: "For heaven sake, don't apologize about any foul-ups – as a matter of fact, I made an error once myself."

But most of the time, it was not sweetness and light or sunshine and blue skies. There were letters from me and letters from Charles which, to understate it very considerable – were testy....

But no matter how tense and testy our correspondence became, a sense of humor never totally fled us. There was the time in June of 1968 when Charles wrote me, dropping a very important name in the world of business – but then he added, "I am not trying to impress you with my name-calling proclivities. I have some real bums for friends also."

...There was serious discussion and extended debate. There was the time in 1975 when Charles and I argued at great length about a piece Dan Rather had done for the *Morning News* – Charles hated it; I thought it was OK; each of us iterated and reiterated our points three or four times; and neither of us would budge an inch....

But what is important is that beside all the argumentation and the occasional excesses – usually mine – there emerges from the letters...a deep respect which grew into genuine affection, and a commonality of objective in reaching for the best in journalistic practice and policy....

And then in a letter on May 13, 1976, Charles wrote me this:

"While in Miami several weeks ago, I ran across a little paragraph in one of the papers which I clipped and saved, which goes this way: 'He has lived long enough to get his temper pretty well under control, and to understand that the world stage is not peopled only by villains and heroes, but mostly by well-intentioned persons doing the best they can. In such a maturing process, one's jugular instincts tend to dry up. A man sees efforts one way by the blazing light of the noon day sun; in twilight, the shadows are softer."

And then Charles went on to write:

"I am now in twilight, and find this to be so true and yet, I have never viewed our differences as personal ones – only professional. I like to think that we have done battle in the sense that Walt Whitman had in mind when he wrote: 'Have you learned lessons only of those who admired you and were tender with you and stood aside for you? Have you not learned great lessons from those who braced themselves against you and disputed the passage with you?"

Indeed, I have learned great lessons from you, who have braced yourself against me and disputed the passage with me....

At the end of his speech, Salant presented Crutchfield two bound volumes of their long correspondence, and said, "Read it in good health, and God bless you and Pee Wee."

That evening, Crutchfield was less than a year from his 65th birthday, which would mean retirement. When retirement came, on May 1, 1978, it came with an outpouring of tributes, praise, roasts, admiration, and affection. The Board of Directors of Jefferson-Pilot Corporation adopted a resolution in his honor, briefly sketching his career and adding:

> His services, awards, honors, and recognitions are too numer-
> ous to list, but notable among them is charter membership in
> the North Carolina Broadcasting Hall of Fame, the first recip-
> ient of the Abe Lincoln Railsplitter Award, membership on the
> Board of the Corporation for Public Broadcasting, and
> member of the Board of Directors of the United States
> Chamber of Commerce. Also, in 1951, the United States
> Department of State screened the nation's 18 top radio exec-
> utives to find an advisor to assist in the establishment of a radio
> network in Greece.... Charles Crutchfield was selected for the
> job. He spent four months touring Greece in establishing a
> powerful Voice for Freedom. Later he was sent to Rome, Paris
> and London to investigate and assist in the operation of the
> Voice of America. His latest and most notable award was the
> receipt in 1977 of the North Carolina Distinguished Citizen
> Award, the State's highest service recognition to a citizen and
> presented for the first time since 1972.
>
> Charles Crutchfield has carried two character traits into his work
> and life – these being purposeful energy and creative ability....

None of those tributes spoke more powerfully and truthfully
about Charles Crutchfield, his character and his career than his old
friend and adversary Richard Salant had done that October night in
Asheville.

Crutchfield's "purposeful energy and creative ability," cited by the
Jefferson-Pilot board resolution, remained intact, and retirement did
not mean an end to constructive activity and advocacy. Instead, it
brought new challenges, honors and responsibilities.

In 1975 the Crutchfields had moved from their celebrated house
on Sedgewood Circle and into a condominium in a new high-rise building in south Charlotte. There they joined a number of friends and
acquaintances who were also retired and increasingly security conscious.

He set up a company called Media Communications, Inc., with
an office on East Boulevard. There he coached business executives and

civic leaders on dealing with the broadcast media and how to handle radio and television interviews and press conferences.

He took a greater interest in Pee Wee's genealogical research. Since the 1960s he had corresponded with faraway relatives, following links from close to distant, from the east coast to Texas and Arkansas, and now he continued to fill in the gaps in his knowledge of his ancestry.

In 1979 the state legislature established the North Carolina Agency for Public Telecommunications, to guide departments of state government in the use of radio and television to inform and communicate with the people of the state. Gov. Jim Hunt appointed Crutchfield as the agency's chairman of the board. Because the agency would from time to time solicit bids from commercial radio and television production companies, Crutchfield resigned from the board of Jefferson-Pilot Broadcasting to avoid possible conflicts of interest. Although he remained loyal to the company he had helped to build, he was moving on, giving priority to his new responsibilities. Along with Executive Director Lee Wing, Crutchfield built an agency that continues to provide valuable service to state government and the people it serves well into the next century.

He also donated equipment to help Appalachian State University establish a student-operated public radio station, and on October 26, 1979, the university named and dedicated the Charles H. Crutchfield Radio and Television Center. The program for that occasion declared: "When the history of the twentieth century in North Carolina is written, one man will stand at the front in the story of the beginnings and growth of the state's broadcasting industry. That man is Charles H. Crutchfield...."

John Thomas, Appalachian State's vice chancellor for academic affairs, delivered the dedication address. He and Crutchfield became good friends. Thomas eventually became chancellor of the university and later served with Crutchfield on the board of the Agency for Public Telecommunications.

Crutchfield maintained an active correspondence on behalf of his political convictions and other advocacy. In exchanges of letters, he and retired CBS head Richard Salant bemoaned the state of television programming in the 1980s. Salant, responding to a letter from Crutchfield in August of 1985, wrote: "I tend to be depressed by what's happening in journalism today – and at CBS News. But sometimes I have to stop myself and wonder whether it is just the nostalgia of an old fogey whom time has passed by....

"Maybe the old days were the good old days after all. They were for me...."

Crutchfield's sister, Marietta Crutchfield Davis, 70, died in 1980, leaving her younger brother, Charles, as the last of the Crutchfield siblings.

The following year, more sad news came when their daughter Leslie told her parents that her 20-year marriage to Charles Tompkins, which had produced three sons, was ending in divorce. Leslie found her parents, particularly her father, supportive at that difficult moment in her life.

He and Pee Wee were also unfailingly supportive as Dick went through a period of crippling stress and health problems and lost the teaching position his father had helped him secure at Appalachian State in the late 1970s. Their emotional support continued when Dick and Malinda divorced.

It had to be deeply disappointing for a couple continuing an almost 60-year love affair to witness both their children's marriages fail. They continued to cherish relations with their grandchildren, inviting them for Easter egg hunts, picnics at the pool, beach trips, and skiing in the mountains.

In the late summer of 1988 the Crutchfields bought a house in the high foothills just outside Saluda, North Carolina. It was a rather plain, sturdy house on a country road, with a view of the Blue Ridge Mountains to the northwest. There was enough room to accommodate six people overnight (seven if someone slept in the storage room). Saluda is in what is called an "isothermal belt," where summers are generally a bit cooler than in Charlotte, and winters usually mild. They spent long weekends there year-round, often joined by children and grandchildren. The house also gave Crutchfield an opportunity to resume some of the activities he had always enjoyed. He built a deck and a tool shed and planted and pruned in the yard.

In Charlotte, the Crutchfields organized a study club with other couples for discussions of current events and other subjects. The couples took turns hosting the meetings and planning the programs. Some shared their particular knowledge of a subject, some used slide presentations or brought in outside speakers. After Pee Wee returned from a trip to Russia sponsored by Appalachian State University, she gave a thoroughly researched program on Genghis Khan. She wanted to keep learning, and she worked at keeping her husband active and engaged in retirement.

Crutchfield's conservative Republican political views did not interfere with his dedication to public broadcasting, which he had helped to establish in North Carolina. In 1995 a newly elected Republican majority in the U.S. House of Representatives put federal subsidies for public radio and television on the budget chopping block. After a long career in commercial broadcasting, Crutchfield understood that commercial radio and television would never again provide in-depth newscasts and a rich diversity of cultural programming. That would depend on public broadcasting, supported by individual and foundation philanthropy, but also in need of government subsidy.

Thus in early 1995 he wrote to the new speaker of the U.S. House of Representatives, Newt Gingrich, urging him not to eliminate funding for public broadcasting. He followed with a letter to U.S. Representative Sue Myrick, a Republican whose district included Charlotte and Mecklenburg County:

> I couldn't agree more with your determination to eliminate all these massive subsidies on everything from farm conglomerates to snails. But you are dead wrong to include the one and only means we have for massive education of our children and untold numbers of adults.

Hopefully, you will read the enclosed letter to our Speaker and realize that, in eliminating all these nonsensical giveaways, you are about to destroy Public Television, which does a job no commercial television or cable system can afford.... And you are about to do it just when information, education and culture are needed most in this frustrated country of ours.

Mr. Gingrich said he too supports Public Television – that he contributes $2,000 a year.... But, Sue, how many folks do you know in Charlotte or in North Carolina who can afford $2,000 a year? The average public contribution is about fifty-five dollars a year after multiple appeals and auctions. The begging, it seems, is endless – just to stay alive. Sue, we cannot – we must not let Public Television go dark....

In 1997, the Appalachian State University station that Crutchfield had helped launch, WASU-FM, was named Station of the Year by the National Association of College Broadcasters.

Chapter Thirty-Nine
Little Pee Wee...Gone

"**D**EAR CHARLIE AND PEE WEE," wrote Rev. Billy Graham on May 8, 1996:

I could not help but think of you all during these past two weeks. We spent almost a week in Washington, and saw so many mutual friends.

The President [Bill Clinton] invited me over to the White House for more than an hour's conversation, then he came to the dinner that was given in our honor...after the Congressional Gold Medal ceremony in the Rotunda....

This week I have been in New York and have spent an hour with the anchor of each network. Most of these segments will be shown this week or next....

Charlie, so much of what has happened I owe to you. It was your call to me here in New York that helped start us on television in 1957. I told that to several interviewers....

I will look forward to seeing you in Charlotte in September when we come for the Crusade....

With many wonderful memories and a heart full of gratitude for your friendship, I am

Cordially yours,
Billy

Graham's warm letter must have been particularly welcome in the Crutchfield home that spring, although Pee Wee never shared her husband's admiration for the evangelist. Both Crutchfields were facing serious health problems. Pee Wee had been treated for breast cancer twice in the previous decade, and now, in her mid-80s, it returned, this time in her bones.

During her final illness, Crutchfield cared for her, did the cooking, became a good nurse. But after a fall at home left her with a broken hip, she was hospitalized for surgery in the spring of 1997. To provide the nursing care she needed during her recovery, Crutchfield moved her to the hospital wing at Southminster, a retirement home in South Charlotte where some of their friends were living.

He made a cassette tape of some favorite recordings she had selected, an eclectic collection that included "Til Then" by the Mills Brothers, "His Eye Is On The Sparrow," "Tiny Bubbles," "Yellow Bird," "Amazing Grace," "Together," "Are You Lonesome Tonight?" and others. He played it often for her at Southminster.

On Leslie's recommendation, he also hired a skillful and very personable nurse. Family members, including Pee Wee's sister Lewellyn from Tryon, her sister Lucille from Rockingham, and her half-sister, Elizabeth Johns, from Florida, visited her at Southminster, as did a number of old friends. They came to offer encouragement but surely realized they were probably saying goodbye.

She died early on an August morning, while her first grandson, Bo – Charles V. Tompkins III – with whom she always had a special relationship, was keeping watch for the night. Later that day, in his small date book, Crutchfield wrote, "Little Peewee...gone."

Both Crutchfields had already decided that they wanted to be cremated, and they wanted their ashes scattered on Grandfather Mountain. Pee Wee had also planned her memorial service in detail, well in advance, writing the program herself, including some of her own poetry. Doug Mayes had taped some readings at her request. With Leslie's help, she had taped the music she wanted played at the service

– not the usual hymns, but passages from British composer Gustav Holst's orchestral suite, *The Planets*. Grandson Aiken was assigned to play the tapes.

There were to be no eulogies, no minister. All of it reflected her lively curiosity about the possibility of an afterlife and about other mysteries of the universe. She had hoped the service would provide a time of quiet meditation for everyone in attendance.

For all the careful planning, however, no one had decided how long the service, or any of its parts, was supposed to last. As friends and family sat facing an empty pulpit in the Harry & Bryant funeral chapel, Aiken played the same taped music over and over. For all her grief, Leslie found herself struggling not to laugh. Somewhere, Pee Wee must have chuckled.

After sensing for some time that the congregation was impatiently waiting for something else to happen, Dick stood and delivered a spontaneous eulogy for his mother.

Crutchfield sat silently through the service. His only comment had been on the way to the chapel, when he said that it was "one ride I hoped I'd never have to take."

During a subsequent visit to Charlotte, Dick thought he observed a spirituality he had never seen before in his father. Confronting the reality of his wife's death and the prospect of his own, Crutchfield seemed to take at most a fading comfort in his extraordinary secular achievements.

He had never spoken much about his religious beliefs or other spiritual matters. While his children were growing up he had taken the family to services at Myers Park Presbyterian Church. After they left home he rarely if ever attended, although he continued to support the church financially. Some years later, when Leslie began attending Myers Park Baptist Church, she occasionally persuaded her parents to go with her. The minister there, the Rev. R. Eugene Owens, was politically and theologically liberal to the point of being controversial, but Crutchfield, as a communicator himself, admired his preaching. He also appreciated the eloquence and power of preachers such as his old friend Billy Graham and the late James A. Jones of Myers Park Presbyterian. Since his earliest days in radio, he had enjoyed old-fashioned gospel songs and singers.

He told Dick that after Pee Wee's death he had called Graham at his home in Montreat to seek some comfort and reassurance. He said Dr. Graham responded with a question: "Cholly, do you accept Jesus Christ as your Savior?" Years later, Dick could not recall his father saying how he had answered.

Dick's religious beliefs, like his mother's, had drifted a considerable distance from the teachings of Protestant Christianity. In searching over the years for some kind of transcendental identity, he had studied and embraced Native American spiritual practices. So when he and Leslie and their father carried Pee Wee's ashes to Grandfather Mountain, he proposed that they participate in a ritual there that he would lead, "to do our own ceremony for her."

He saw his father's acceptance of that idea as another indication that grief might have awakened in him some dormant spiritual dimension. That was what Dick hoped for, and perhaps it was true. Or maybe in his sorrow Charles Crutchfield simply wanted his family together – wherever, whatever. In either case, he voiced no objection to Dick's proposal for a ceremony at Grandfather Mountain.

CHAPTER FORTY
Grandfather Mountain

T WAS A SPECIAL PLACE for three generations of the Crutchfield family. Charles and Pee Wee and their children had enjoyed summer vacations in Banner Elk and Blowing Rock and Linville, all within sight of the 5,946-foot mountain, named for the huge outcropping of rock that resembled a profile of a bearded giant in permanent slumber on its western slopes. Crutchfield was a long-time friend of Hugh Morton, who owned the mountain and in the last quarter of the 20th century had developed it into a spectacular and environmentally exemplary tourist attraction.

Long before that development, Dick spent a cold night on the side of the mountain when he was a child accompanying his father and some friends on a bear hunt. Leslie's sons spent weeks of their boy-hood summers near the foot of the mountain, at Camp Yonanoka, founded by their grandfather, Charles V. Tompkins, and Hugh Morton's father, Julian Morton.

Dick was also aware that the Cherokees, who had roamed and hunted in those ancient forests centuries ago, considered the mountain sacred. He felt some sort of power there, and he sometimes mused that the rocky profile for whom the mountain was named was "that of an ancestral Indian chief lamenting the fate of his people."

And so, on a late summer day, Dick, Leslie, and their father motored through the foothills and up the Blue Ridge escarpment into the cooler air of the mountains. They parked just off the spectacularly suspended Blue Ridge Parkway viaduct, which partly girds the waist of Grandfather Mountain. Dick led them to a secluded spot defined by the root system of a giant hemlock. This is his recollection of what happened next:

"It was quite intimate and simple: a lit candle among the roots of that ancient tree, prayers of gratitude to Mom, and Divine Presence and blessings for the journey to rejoin her loved ones and ancestors. I felt it was very powerful and appropriate; I saw it in the reverence of Dad's whole demeanor, especially in his face. He was weeping quietly, lost in his thoughts...."

The second phase, which Dick undertook by himself, came the following day, after a night in a motel near Linville. Leslie and her father went to the Visitor Center and Nature Museum on the mountain to visit with Hugh Morton while Dick took the rugged Profile Trail to Calloway Peak, the highest of Grandfather's peaks at 5,964 feet, carrying his mother's ashes, to "do my own kind of prayer work...." It was a trail Leslie's son Aiken had helped build years before as part of a team led by Hugh Morton's son Jimmy. At the top Dick found "a cliff directly overlooking the spot we had chosen off the Parkway for our ceremony the day before. There I did my prayers and ceremony for Mom's spirit and released her ashes into the wind."

He also noted the time. When he rejoined his father and sister and told them what time he had released the ashes, Crutchfield pointed out – "in astonishment," Dick recalled – that at that same moment he and Leslie had been looking at a model of Calloway Peak on display in the Nature Museum. None of them believed it was a coincidence.

Before Dick left to climb the mountain with his mother's ashes that day, he told his father that he would do the same for him – and at exactly the same place. Crutchfield seemed pleased at the prospect.

That year Hugh Morton announced that Grandfather Mountain had donated seven conservation easement tracts of 146 acres each to the North Carolina Nature Conservancy in honor of his parents and grandparents, his son Hugh Morton, Jr., and several distinguished North Carolinians, including Billy and Ruth Bell Graham, Charles and Petie Kuralt, and Charles and Jacquelin Crutchfield. The easements prohibited construction of any buildings or roads or other development, except for hiking trails.

The Crutchfield tract stretched from the Wilson Creek Bridge on the Blue Ridge Parkway to the top of Calloway Peak.

Chapter Forty-One
Signing Off

HIS BELOVED PEE WEE was gone. So were his mother, his brother, his two sisters, and his best friends. And his father had never really been there. Now there were only Dick and Leslie.

Pee Wee had told Dick that she was afraid his father would not survive more than a year after she died. Perhaps that prediction reflected her concern not only for his failing physical health, but also for the emotional pain of losing her. It turned out to be prophetic.

He was heartbroken, literally as well as metaphorically, and never really recovered from her death. He was short of breath, had a blocked artery, and a defective heart valve and took nitroglycerin pills for chest pain. He moved into an apartment at Southminster in January and spent a lot of time there reading, looking through old scrapbooks, watching television, and playing the tape he had made for Pee Wee. Leslie took him to Saluda in hopes of cheering him up, but he didn't enjoy being there without Pee Wee.

Despite his grief, he never lost his sense of humor or his ability to enjoy some of his favorite activities, particularly those he shared with his children. He enjoyed going to movies, and on one occasion Leslie took him to see *Nixon*, Hollywood's version of his famous friend's downfall. They also went out to dinner, and one of his favorite restaurants was the Original Pancake House, in the SouthPark area, where they often split an omelet. Conversation was sometimes difficult, however, when he deliberately "forgot" to wear his hated hearing aid.

He was outspokenly appalled at much of what he saw on television, but he enjoyed watching televised ball games and the news. During newscasts he would switch back and forth among the local channels, comparing and critiquing. Pee Wee had disliked politics and most politicians, sometimes calling them "greedy bastards." Now when Crutchfield and Leslie or Dick saw politicians on television, they would mutter, "Greedy bastards," and laugh.

That year was a particularly meaningful time for Dick. He and his father had never in any sense been estranged, but Crutchfield's political views, as they swerved far to the right in the 1960s and 70s, created some space between them that Dick had found difficult to bridge. Crutchfield had supported his son's pursuits, including those that must have struck him as somewhat esoteric. But it's hard to imagine that there wasn't at least a trace of conscientiously concealed disappointment at Dick's lack of interest in broadcasting or any other kind of business career, and at his disinclination to pursue the American Dream as Crutchfield's generation had envisioned it.

Now, during visits to Charlotte, Dick spent time with his father that was precious to both of them. They took long drives with Dick at the wheel, observing the city's extraordinary growth, stopping at the Charlotte Country Club for lunch, near the house where Dick and Leslie had grown up, and sometimes just talking.

At first Dick found that "it seemed that his whole world, his purpose in life, his joy in living – everything – had been totally swept away." When Dick tried to offer words of encouragement, his father simply looked at him and said, "Dick, you don't understand."

But there were also mutual expressions of affection and glimpses of the old, sometimes sardonic Crutchfield wit, directed at himself and at his son. Dick says he felt "closer to him in those moments together than I had ever felt in my life." And he became "more aware of things about him that surprised and delighted me," such as

Crutchfield's easy, witty banter with old friends in the men's lounge at the Charlotte Country Club.

As the talk became easier, Crutchfield expressed his clear-eyed disappointment at what he saw as a loss of integrity at the broadcasting stations he once headed and in the American news media generally. He began to reminisce about the joys of his life with Pee Wee and their friends, and the pain of losing other loved ones and old friends such as Dr. Faison and Dr. Sanger.

During one of their drives around the city he commented that for an "out-of-towner" Dick seemed to know a lot of short cuts. Dick said, "Well, Paw, I'm not as dumb as I look." Crutchfield quickly replied, "Oh, I'm not so sure about that."

Leslie and Dick had set up a small office for him in his apartment at Southminster. One day, looking at the many awards hanging on the walls there, Dick joked, "Wow, Dad, you must have been one hell of a big shot." His father responded: "Well, I'm a big shit now."

As his sense of humor resurfaced, he also seemed to be able to express his emotions more easily and openly. On two occasions – both when they were alone in an elevator – he looked at his son and said, "Dick, I love you."

Even before Pee Wee died, Crutchfield was working with an attorney to organize his personal and financial affairs for the benefit of those who would have to deal with them after his death, and to set up generous inheritances for his heirs. To Dick, that was another indication that "what concerned him more than anything in life was the welfare of his family."

Leslie, a writer and poet, put her feelings into words in a letter to him that February, about six months after her mother's death.

Dear Paw:

I've been thinking about you all a.m. and about how very very important you are to me – how important you've always been, all my life – and how very very much I love you. I don't say it enough, especially since you've gotten older and especially since Mother died. But I hope you do know it and feel it.

You've not only been a rock, there for us all our lives, a stable certainty always there, but a warm and very loving support I can always count on. Always. Not to mention the years of hard, consistent work as a "provider" and the great care taken to assure Dick, Ma and me of security in the present and into the future.... And not to mention what comes across loud and clear as your genuine desire for Dick's and my happiness and fulfillment, no matter what that involves or what different roads we take from your own. That is real love, Paw, to truly want the other person's happiness and well-being no matter how it differs from your own ways of being and doing. And I am so grateful to you for that. I can't tell you how much it means to me that you want me to enjoy Saluda, to write, to travel, to do things that bring me joy whether those things would do the same for you or not, and whether or not you "understand" such desires.

What I also fail to tell you – and I can write these things better than I can say them, somewhat tongue-tied when it comes to verbalizing – is how very proud I am of you, Paw. Not just your career...but your success as a human being. It shows in the unadulterated respect shown you both by your friends and the people who've worked with you....

...I hope I can learn to love as well as you do. I hope I can live life as well as you have. And I hope that we can enjoy the time that you have left on this earth, that there are some years of quiet and deep pleasures for you. Pleasures in pretty days and favorite music and good books and familiar faces and good food and planting pretty flowers and watching the birds on your new patio in the summer! And pleasure in a few days in Saluda....

I cannot imagine life without you, Paw. An impossible thought.

All my love,
Lillie!

In August of 1998 Crutchfield was admitted to Carolinas Medical Center, where the best his doctors could offer him was a dilemma: he could have multiple bypass and heart valve replacement surgery, with a 50-50 chance of survival, or he could decline surgery and have just a short time left to live. As so often in his life, he decided not to wait passively for whatever might happen. He chose surgery.

Dick was in Arizona, visiting his daughter, Lilian, who was beginning graduate school. Before the surgery, Leslie made frantic calls to Dick's friend Herb Kincey, Jr., a Charlottean now living in Santa Fe. She knew Dick planned to stop for a visit with Kincey on the way back from Tempe. As a result, Dick had a chance to talk by phone with his father, who wanted to say goodbye in case he didn't make it through the surgery. Dick expressed his regret at not being there, but Crutchfield said it was more important for Dick to be with his daughter.

"I was gratified to have that chance to hear his voice, perhaps for the last time," Dick recalls, "and to tell him how much I loved him and how grateful I was for all he had done, for his just being who he was."

On the morning of the operation, the *Charlotte Observer* carried a story announcing the retirement of the head of First Union National Bank, Ed Crutchfield – no relation to Charles. Leslie showed her father the headline, which read: "Crutchfield Steps Down." He laughed.

"I didn't know I'd be in the headlines," he said. "I would step aside for the right deal."

He read the article and expressed his admiration for Ed Crutchfield.

As the nurse approached to inject him in the usual spot with a pre-anesthesia sedative, Crutchfield looked at her and said, in that deep, tweed-textured voice, "You just wanna see my fanny."

After the surgery he lay in a coma for several weeks. Leslie's telephone rang constantly as people called to ask how he was doing. She simply told them, "About the same."

Dick returned from the West, and he and Leslie went to the hospital with the tape of favorite songs Crutchfield had made for Pee Wee. With them was Becky Holmes, the Southminster chaplain who had become one of Crutchfield's favorite friends during his time there. They were somewhat surprised when no one objected as they took the tape player into the Cardiovascular Intensive Care unit. Leslie and Dick played the tape into their father's ear, singing along with the music. He opened his eyes briefly, for the last time.

Crutchfield had said he wanted Gene Owens to conduct his funeral, so it was held at Myers Park Baptist Church. Owens gave a brief eulogy, and the church's retired music director, James Berry, sang "How Great Thou Art" in his booming baritone. Also present were the surviving members of the Briarhoppers, now legendary and still performing from time to time. They sang a gospel song. Later, as Dick Crutchfield concluded his eulogy, he turned to Briarhopper Whitey Grant and asked, "Do y'all know what time hit is?" Grant replied, "Hit's Briarhopper time," cuing the band into its theme song, a farewell serenade to their old friend Charlie Briarhopper:

> *Wait 'til the sun shines, Nellie, when those clouds go drifting by.*
> *We will be happy, Nellie, don't you sigh.*
> *Down lovers' lane we'll wander, sweethearts you and I.*
> *Wait 'til the sun shines, Nellie, by and by.*

As he had promised a year earlier, Dick, accompanied this time by his son, John, again made the climb up the Profile Trail on Grandfather Mountain to Calloway Peak. There, from a wind-blown cliff more than a mile in the air, he broadcast the ashes of Charles Crutchfield.

ACKNOWLEDGEMENTS

Profound thanks to Leslie Crutchfield Tompkins and Richard Crutchfield for initially commissioning this biography of their father and choosing me to write it.

They and I are grateful to Cyndee Patterson and Pat Martin of the Lynnwood Foundation for recognizing the value of this project as part of the preservation of Charlotte's history, and for helping obtain financial support for the research, writing, and publication.

We also express appreciation to all those whose contributions, large and small, made this book possible.

We especially want to recognize the generous support of Heath Alexander, Mary Lou and Jim Babb, the George Baxter Foundation, Carol and Ike Belk, Mr. and Mrs. Howard C. Bissell, Tom Cookerly, John and Judy Crosland, the Crothers Family Trust, the Dickson Foundation, Mr. and Mrs. Henry J. Faison, Greater Media Charlotte/WBT, Luther H. Hodges, Jr., the John F. Ladley family, the family of Dosty and Ed O'Herron, Rose and Bailey Patrick, J.M. Bryan Taylor, and Jane Dickson Williamson.

And a special thank-you to the Dowd Foundation, Doug Mayes, Raleigh and Katy Shoemaker, and to Charles V. Tompkins (on behalf of Bo, Aiken, and David).

Jerry Shinn
Beech Mountain, NC
June 2016

BIBLIOGRAPHY

"A Grand Trip: The 1936 Visit of FDR to the Smokies," *Great Smoky Mountain Colloquy*, Volume 12, Number 2, The University of Tennessee Libraries, Fall 2011.

Altman, Nancy J., *The Battle for Social Security*, John Wiley & Sons, Inc., 2005.

Claiborne, Jack, *The Charlotte Observer: Its Time and Place, 1869-1986*, University of North Carolina Press, 1986.

Cline, Ned, *Adding Value: The Joseph M. Bryan Story*, Down Home Press, 2001.

Daniel, Pete, *Lost Revolutions: The South in the 1950s*, University of North Carolina Press, 2000.

Davis, Anita Price, ed, *North Carolina During the Great Depression*, McFarland, 2003.

Edwards, Bob, *Edward R. Murrow and the Birth of Broadcast Journalism*, John Wiley & Sons, 2004.

Graham, Billy, *Just As I Am: The Autobiography of Billy Graham*, HarperCollins, 2007.

Leuchtenburg, William E.,*The White House Looks South*, LSU Press, 2005.

Persico, Joseph E., *Edward R. Murrow: An American Original*, Mcgraw-Hill, 1988.

"Peruna and the Bracers," *Colliers Weekly*, October 28, 1905.

Rogers, John William, *The Lusty Texans of Dallas*, Dutton, 1960.

Warlick, Tom and Lucy Warlick, *The WBT Briarhoppers*, McFarland, 2007.

Spartanburg High School yearbooks, 1928 and 1929, Spartanburg High School, Spartanburg, S.C.

City Directories, late 1920s – early 1930s, Spartanburg County Public Library, Spartanburg, S.C.

Crutchfield Family Archives, the Charles Harvey Crutchfield Papers, 1942-2000, Collection #04022, the Southern Historical

Collection at Louis Round Wilson Library, the University of
North Carolina at Chapel Hill.

INTERNET SOURCES:

www.americanradiohistory.com

Billboard Magazine archives: www.billboard.com.

www.btmemories.com/

www.Converse.edu

"Decisions of the National Labor Relations Board."
  www.nlrb.gov/cases-decisions.

Federation of Historical Bottle Collectors, www.fohbc.org.

www.presidency.ucsb.edu

www.Sciway.net.

www.stlmedia.net

www.StudySC.org.

Sullivan, Jack, "The Peruna Story: Strumming That Old Catarrh."
  www.yumpu.com/en/document/view/53381200/the-peruna-
  story-strumming-that-old-catarrh.

"The Tom McMurray Collection." www.reelradio.com.

www.wofford.edu

"U.S. Supreme Court, Labor Board v. Electrical Workers, 346 US
  164 (1953)." www.Justia.com.

INTERVIEWS

From 2008 through 2012, I conducted one or more personal interviews with:

Babb, James M. , former Jefferson-Pilot Broadcasting executive

Conrad, Barbara, former administrative assistant, Jefferson
Productions

Crutchfield, Richard Dale, son of Charles Crutchfield

Inman, Robert, former WBTV news anchor.

Mayes, Doug, former WBTV news anchor.

McMillan, J. Alex, former Republican congressman, former head of
  Harris-Teeter supermarkets and friend of Charles and Peewee

Crutchfield.

Tarleton, Cullie, former Jefferson-Pilot Broadcasting executive.

Thomas, John, former chancellor, Appalachian State University.

Thompson, H.A., former WBT announcer.

Thompson, Jan, former producer, Jefferson Productions.

Tompkins, Leslie Crutchfield, daughter of Charles Crutchfield.

ABOUT THE AUTHOR

Jerry Shinn grew up in South Carolina, graduated with Honors in Creative Writing from the University of North Carolina at Chapel Hill, and is a former associate editor, editorial page editor, and award-winning columnist for the *Charlotte Observer.* He now lives and writes fiction, poetry, history, biography, commentary, and music in the North Carolina mountains.